D1496402

The Enigma of Colonialism

The Enigma of Colonialism

British Policy in West Africa

Anne Phillips

Reader in Politics & Government
City of London Polytechnic

James Currey
LONDON

Indiana University Press
BLOOMINGTON AND INDIANAPOLIS

James Currey Ltd
54b Thornhill Square, Islington, London N1 1BE

Indiana University Press
10th and Morton Streets
Bloomington, Indiana 47404

British Library Cataloguing in Publication Data
Phillips, Anne
The enigma of colonialism: British policy in West Africa
1. West Africa. Colonisation by Great Britain, history
I. Title
966

ISBN Cased 0-85255-025-1 (cased)
ISBN Paper 0-85255-026-X (paper)

Library of Congress Cataloging in Publication Data
Phillips, Anne.
The enigma of colonialism: an interpretation of British policy in West Africa /
by Anne Phillips.   p.   cm.
Bibliography: p.
ISBN 0-253-34409-3
1. Great Britain——Colonies——Africa, West.   2. Africa, West——Politics
and government——1884-1960.   3. Africa, West——Colonial influence.
I. Title.
JV1027.P5   1989
325'.341'0966——dc19   88-13617

Typeset in 10/11 pt Baskerville by Colset Pte Ltd, Singapore
Printed in Great Britain
for Villiers Publications London N6

Contents

v

Acknowledgements

With less exaggeration than usual, I can say that this book owes its existence to the help and encouragement of my thesis supervisor, Geoffrey Kay. His own study of colonialism in Ghana first inspired me to think of issues of colonialism and development, and if working with him sometimes took me down what seemed like side-tracks, he continually stretched me to greater theoretical breadth and precision. He also taught me the value of short sentences. I am very much in his debt.

Like many books that are based on theses, this one has been with me for far too long, and those who have aided me en route have become too numerous to mention. But I would like to thank the Social Science Research Council, which financed the research for a year, and City of London Polytechnic, which allowed me some relief from teaching in order to write it up. Stephen Feuchtwang made careful and detailed comments on early drafts; and Colin Leys and John Lonsdale suggested a number of ways in which the arguments could be developed. I only regret that I have not been able to follow them all through.

1
The Makeshift Settlement

As the first of the African colonies gained their independence, appraisals of the colonial record divided into two schools: apologetics or condemnation. The 'imperial balance sheet'[1] was added up: an accounting employed on the one hand to demonstrate the benefits colonialism had brought its subjects, and on the other to establish the exploitation it had practised upon them. The units of calculation were hardly commensurable (mileage of roads down one columm, deaths under forced labour down the other) and there seemed little meeting space between the two sides. Critics of colonialism documented its brutality, while those more sympathetic to its achievements proffered a contrast of before and after, stressing the poverty and uncertainties of pre-colonial life (e.g. Gann and Duignan, 1968). From the latter perspective, colonialism's 'failures' were only those revealed by subsequent history. With hindsight it became clear that more could have been done to develop social services, promote political participation, or establish the groundwork for industrial growth, but criticisms based on post-war criteria could be easily dismissed as beside the point. Where failures were too evident for evasion, a mild critique of incompetence was substituted for the more devastating attacks of the opposing school. Colonialism was too *ad hoc* and even 'absentminded' to be able to get it all right. 'Had the British been able to foresee how quickly they would devolve power to the indigenous people after World War II,' Gann and Duignan meekly acknowledged, 'and had they not, as it were, decolonised so absentmindedly, they might have equipped their charges in a more adequate fashion for future independence.' (Gann and Duignan, 1968:375).

The balance sheet approach to colonialism has by no means died out, and the still widely read work of D. K. Fieldhouse[2] has kept calculations of colonial 'profit' alive. Rejecting what he calls the 'myth of economic exploitation' – the dangerous and to his mind all too prevalent belief that modern empires 'were great machines deliberately constructed by Europe to exploit dependent peoples by extracting economic and fiscal profit from them' (Fieldhouse, 1982:380) – he has tried to show how poor were the profits colonialism rendered, and how much greater the returns from the non-colonized world. His evidence falls short of establishing his case, for a venture may fail and yet be exploitative, and the fact

1

that returns from Africa were so relatively poor does not prove the casual nature of capitalist concerns. But that said, Fieldhouse and other critics of the radical school do have a point. They raise a question that we cannot ignore: if colonialism was indeed a product of capitalist forces – as most well-thinking radicals will be likely to presume – then why were the interests of capital so ill-served?

It is the history of Africa that is the most enigmatic, for this last wild adventure of colonial ambition yielded the poorest returns. After eighty years of European rule, European capital had made little headway. Trading companies had of course continued their expansion, but direct investment was low and concentrated in a few mining enclaves. Only the gold and diamond mines in South Africa had attracted significant private capital. Beyond this the bulk of direct investment was public. Total investment in the British colonies was estimated in 1936 as £941m.: of this, £523m. was invested in the union of South Africa; and of the total investment, approximately 48 per cent came from government funds[3]. Lord Hailey drew on these figures in 1938 to make his appeal for a new development initiative, but by 1956 he was still painting a gloomy picture. The initiatives undertaken by the Colonial Development Corporation[4], set up partly in response to Hailey's earlier pleas, were proving far from successful: by 1955, only one of the African enterprises financed by the Corporation was making a net trading profit (Hailey, 1956:1344). Last ditch attempts to promote development had come too late, and when the colonial experiment was formally concluded, Africa was all too obviously marginalized in the world economy.

Africa emerged from colonial rule with few of the pre-conditions for sustained capital accumulation. Most obviously and significantly, it lacked what had been the *differentia specifica* of capitalist development elsewhere: free wage labour. Capitalism does not normally effect exploitation by dragging down living standards – a strategy which is limited by nature – but by increasing the productive powers of capital. With control of the labour process, capital can harness the productive forces to the task of accumulation. It can break those natural barriers which constrain mercantile capital, and impose limits to the extraction of profit. By raising the productivity of labour, capital can reduce labour costs without destroying subsistence, and embark on the process of continual expansion which has characterized its most dynamic periods. But to achieve this, capital needs wage labour: workers who are, in Marx's ironic term, 'freed' from the ownership of means of production, freed from control over the production process, freed to sell their labour-power as a commodity.

Yet Africa emerged from colonialism without this pre-condition. Indeed, Goran Hyden has suggested in his provocative account of Africa's dilemmas, that it is the one continent where peasant production was actually *created* in the last one hundred years. 'Colonialism did not erase the pre-capitalist modes of production. It did destroy the pre-colonial ones but it generated a new pre-capitalist mode based on independent peasant production.' (Hyden, 1980:42). Only a small minority of the population works for wages, and fewer still for capitalist firms. The economic upheavals of the last twenty years have largely passed the continent by. No African nation appears in the list of 'newly industrialising countries', and only South Africa has a manufacturing sector which accounts for more than 20 per cent of gross domestic product (GDP). (Hoogvelt, 1982:25). As far as capital is concerned, Africa is rarely a focus of attention and while multi-national corporations pour into the export-led economies of South East Asia, only oil-rich Nigeria has inspired a few entrepreneurial dreams. African countries predominate in all the lists of low-income and most underdeveloped countries. Think of Africa and you think of famine, apartheid, wars, refugees. If colonialism was a project of capitalist expansion, then in Africa it signally failed in its task.

Colonialism did effect the transformation of former subsistence farmers into producers of export crops, establishing the dominance of commodity production, but outside the areas of white settlement it did not do much more. Through most of the continent, pre-colonial property relations survived – at least to the extent of providing the majority of Africans with access to land. In contrast to, say the Philippines, where the ownership of land was concentrated in a few hands, and nearly 50 per cent of those working in agriculture were landless labourers, producers in Africa were not separated from their means of production, and the capitalist wage relation did not become prevalent. The forms of exploitation practised in colonial Africa were more akin to those which characterized early capitalist development in Europe: the 'robbery' of mercantile capital which buys cheap to sell dear; and where wage labour did exist, the extraction of what Marx has called an absolute surplus value from workers paid a bare subsistence. In the political economy of colonialism, capitalist relations proper were a rare exception.

This paradox of colonialism was at its most evident in the British territories, where officials often luxuriated in what seemed anti-capitalist bias, glorying in their self-proclaimed role as guardians of a pre-capitalist order. As Hetherington, among others, has argued, they practised a form of paternalism based on what they believed were the dangers of the modern economy for African communities.

> Sometimes the emphasis was on the administrative policy of indirect rule, which was supposed to prevent too rapid change; sometimes it was on the necessity for a restraint on commercial and industrial activity so that teachers and missionaries could undertake the transformation of African society before the individual lost contact with the economic and social security of tribal life. (Hetherington, 1978:71)

Whichever it was, British colonial practice seemed to pride itself on retarding rather than hastening change, drawing on the values of feudalism rather than those of capitalism.

3

It was this that led Heussler (1963) to focus on the patterns of recruitment to the British colonial service, suggesting that it was these that
produced the unmistakeable 'type'. Officials were drawn disproportion-
ately, he argues, from the younger sons of the lesser landed aristocracy,
men who found few openings for themselves in twentieth century Britain,
and were ill at ease with the values of the contemporary capitalist world.
Sir Ralph Furse, who controlled recruitment to the Colonial Service in
the inter-war years, was 'unswervingly aristocratic' in his predilections
(Heussler, 1963:69), giving his preference to applicants who were
'organisation eccentrics'. Heussler describes the typical favoured
candidate:

> . . . modern industrialisation and urbanisation were anathema to
> him, as were the *nouveaux* who epitomised these trends. He cared little
> for money as such; he preferred the country to the city, and was
> usually happy in an exclusively male society. (Heussler, 1963:104)

The description is apt, as examination of official thinking in British West
Africa will show, but the explanation is unsatisfactory. However *ad hoc*
colonial policies appear, they cannot be reduced to the accident of one
man's dominance in official recruitment. The apparently anti-capitalist
bias of colonial policies demands further explanation.

The case of British West Africa, where white settlement was discouraged by climatic conditions, is of particular importance here. As colonies
that told model stories of 'African development', with their economic
expansion based very largely on African-owned farms, these most clearly
exemplified the 'autocratic paternalism' of colonial rule. British colonialism in West Africa was celebrated by its practitioners and admirers
for enlightened encouragement of peasant production and avoidance of
the evils that attended wage labour. In his influential testament to *The
Economic Revolution in British West Africa*, first published in 1926, Allan
McPhee praised these policies as incomparably superior to the excesses
that had been revealed in the Belgian Congo (McPhee, 1971). Resistance
to European plantation estates, restriction of capital to a merchant role,
discouragement of private property in land: all these were central planks
in the West African policy as it had emerged by the inter-war years. The
phenomenal rise of the cocoa industry in the Gold Coast, entirely on the
basis of African initiative[5], and apparently within traditional relations of
peasant production, was cited as proof of the policy's worth, and successive governors affirmed West Africa as the antithesis to the discredited
'capitalistic policy'. Far from imposing capitalist relations, these colonial
states seemed concerned to protect Africans from the potentially brutal
assaults of European firms, and the debates which dominated the 1920s
centred around the problems of preserving West Africa from what was
seen as the destructive tide of modern individualism. In a language that
recurred in much of the inter-war writing, McPhee trusted that 'the spirit
of individualism' which had (by implication so unfortunately) triumphed

in England, would not become dominant in West Africa. He hoped that 'the survival of the communal spirit among the natives' would be strong enough to counteract 'the Anglicised and individualistic tendencies of the Coastal natives', and looked forward to a 'new species of regional development . . . confirming the truth of the old saying "Ex Africa semper aliquid novi" ' (McPhee, 1971:311).

Clearly in this conception, the task of colonialism was not to separate producers from the means of production, nor transform peasants into wage workers. On the contrary, the priority was to ensure that Africans were protected from that privatization of land which had characterized the development of capitalism in Britain. The colonial governments, McPhee urged, should prohibit free sale and mortgaging of land, since otherwise 'the land system of British West Africa will slide down the slippery slope into landlordism and native expropriation, which is the very antithesis of the present "West African" policy of development' (McPhee, 1971:308). Landlordism, it seemed, was a dirty word. The preferred ideal was that of a peasant community, happily producing commodities for sale abroad. Capital could enter in a merchant capacity, and its presence would be tolerated where mining had to be done. But other than that, its role should be minimal. In British West Africa at least, it seems that colonialism deliberately withdrew from the project of capitalist expansion.

How do we begin to make sense of this? One way would be to take colonialism at its own estimate, accepting at face value its self-proclaimed duty to civilize and protect. But this hardly stands up to closer scrutiny, for only the most superficial account would regard colonialism as simply protective or benign. The level of coercion documented by Suret-Canale in his study of French colonialism (Suret-Canale, 1971) was reproduced in much the same way in the British colonies, while the systematic and sustained compromise that British rule made with slavery is enough to dispel any illusions of good intent. As will emerge in the course of this book, the first governors of the West African colonies were prepared to contemplate wide-ranging schemes of social disruption, including measures for the expropriation of African land, and for the employment of indentured labour on a scale that would have mirrored the much more obviously exploitative developments in British Malaya. Governors not only contemplated but connived with slavery, postponing until well into the twentieth century the final liberation of slaves. Britain had taken an early stand against slave trading but, despite all its claims to a 'civilising mission', did not take a stand against slavery itself. The freedom of the slave population was to be sacrificed to the interests of Britain's slave-owning allies. If British West Africa was able to offer itself by the 1920s as the model of colonial development, this was only by judicious rewriting of the past.

The enigma then remains: neither benign nor thoroughly exploiting, neither servant of capital nor agent of good. It is a combination with which conventional history has no problem, for it would take for granted that colonial rule was an *ad hoc* mixture with policies that varied from governor to governor, and accident accounting for many of the events. But for those – like myself – who see the scramble for Africa as reflecting a crisis in capitalist development, it is not possible to leave matters there.

Early critics of colonialism in Africa talked of the forced creation of a proletariat (e.g. Woddis, 1960), but this carried little conviction. If it had some pertinence in the areas of white settlement, it was hardly applicable elsewhere. Forced to acknowledge this, Marxist critics of colonial rule came to rest their case on the very backwardness of the exploitation that had been imposed. Thus Suret-Canale, in the most impressive of the early critiques, argued:

> The very limited funds provided by capitalist investment were applied not to progress in production or in technical fields, but essentially to the extraction of high profits with no modification of pre-colonial techniques – in other words, principally by intensifying the work demanded of the population (Suret-Canale, 1971:294).

But then colonialism's crime, in this view, was that it failed to impose normal capitalist production; that instead of modifying pre-colonial techniques, it relied on the brutalities of forced labour, lower wages, and a longer working day. Defenders of colonialism could so easily turn this on its head, as when Gann and Duignan responded to Marxist critics by noting that 'the real trouble with many colonies was not the extent of enterprise but its relative absence; there were usually too few capitalists, rather than too many' (Gann and Duignan, 1968:375). That colonialism was brutish was not hard to establish. But how to go that one stage further, and prove that it had worked to capital's advantage?

Relief was soon in sight, for the emergence of underdevelopment theory in the late 1960s provided a powerful framework for making sense of the colonial experience. Beginning with the work of Paul Baran (1957) and continuing through Andre Gunder Frank's analyses of Latin America (1969a; 1969b) and Samir Amin's analyses of Africa (1973; 1975; 1976), what can be broadly categorized as underdevelopment theory argued that it was typical of capitalism that it prevented – 'blocked' – capitalist development. Capital accumulation, it was argued, operates through dividing the world into two parts: that which enjoys 'normal' capitalist development and that which suffers 'underdevelopment'. Countries in the former group extract a surplus from the latter sometimes through what is little more than robbery or, more commonly today, through investment or the inequalities of the terms of trade. The developed countries build on this surplus to confirm and extend their world domination. The underdeveloped countries not only lose resources, but what is potentially even more damaging, they take on a political and economic structure that sustains and extends their stagnation. Ruled over by what Frank so evocatively called a 'lumpenbourgeoisie', these countries cannot look to their ruling groups for economic salvation, for national development is not the project of a 'lumpen' or 'comprador' bourgeoisie, which makes its living in the interstices of multinational capital, and has no interest in radical change.

Crucial to the arguments of underdevelopment theory has been the notion that capital asserts its dominance through a variety of relations of production. Within this framework, capitalism is no longer defined as the extraction of relative surplus value from wage labour, but rather by its division of the world into two: monopoly and satellite, centre and periphery, developed and underdeveloped. Capitalism exists wherever a region is integrated into the world market and wherever producers serve the needs of this market. The precise relations of exploitation – whether serf labour, petty commodity production, wage labour, maybe even slave labour – are of secondary significance.

It was this theoretical sloppiness that called forth Ernesto Laclau's now classic critique (Laclau, 1971), where he suggested that Andre Gunder Frank was operating with a non-Marxist conception, treating capitalism as if it were a mode of exchange rather than of production. But in response to and in refinement of the original theories, a number of writers have then turned this into a conscious position, arguing that the mechanisms of so-called 'primitive accumulation' are as much a part of modern capitalism as the employment of wage labour, and even, in stronger versions, its most effective method of exploitation. Immanuel Wallerstein, for example, has argued that a world system 'is a single division of labour comprising multiple cultural systems, multiple political entities and even different modes of surplus appropriation' (Wallerstein, 1980:5), and that a capitalist world system is one in which production is production for sale. Taking the argument a stage further and drawing on the writings of French anthropologists, Samir Amin has suggested that the very persistence of pre-capitalist modes of production is what makes it possible for capital to 'super-exploit' workers in the periphery. 'Backwardness', in this argument, becomes a source of capitalism's profits (Amin, 1976). In richer countries, for example, employers have had to pay male workers a wage that at least partially covers the costs of supporting a wife and child. In peripheral countries they can get by with paying a bare subsistence, while the wives and children have to make their living independently from the land. The cheap labour thus made available in the peripheral countries keeps down the prices of exported goods, allowing a 'hidden transfer' from peripheral to core countries. Capitalism, in other words, thrives on what may appear 'traditional' or pre-capitalist forms and if colonialism failed to eliminate these, this is precisely what we should expect.

As long as this paradigm dominated discussion, the enigma of colonialism could escape attention. The blocking of capitalist development, the maintenance and defence of pre-capitalist forms, the glorification of a petty-commodity producing peasantry: all these followed neatly and inevitably from underdevelopment theory. Colonialism is a product of capitalism and capitalism blocks development.

The starting point of underdevelopment theory is surely correct, and in the broad sweep of its arguments it has the ring of intuitive truth. The plight of today's ex-colonies, as Gunder Frank has so persuasively argued, does not stem from some 'original sin' of *un*development, but owes much of its character (Frank would say all) to the particular way in which these countries were incorporated into the international division of labour. That this history must be part of the explanation is now almost universally recognized, as is the absurdity of any simplistic 'stages of growth' that calls on such countries to reproduce the phases of development passed through by their erstwhile colonial masters. But once we move beyond the general to the more particular, the details prove seriously wanting.

Since the halcyon days of the early 1970s, underdevelopment theory has lost its paradigmatic appeal, and its arguments have been challenged along a number of lines. For analysts of contemporary third world states, the language of puppet regimes or comprador bourgeoisie throws too little light on the complexity of class relations in underdeveloped countries, while the assumption that local capital plays a necessarily dependent role in accumulation does not seem to fit the reality today[6]. The broad contrast between the developed and the underdeveloped world is too neat and derives from an ideal-type of 'normal', independent, development, which neither fits the history of all the advanced capitalist countries, nor offers a useful yardstick for measuring 'distortions' elsewhere (Phillips, 1977; Gülalp, 1986). Of course underdeveloped countries do not follow an ideal path of development, but what does this tell us of the forces at work? Recent marked variations in the experience of the underdeveloped countries – the phenomena indicated in the new categorization of Newly Industrialising Countries – call out for much greater differentiation and precision (Smith, 1980).

For our understanding of colonialism the crucial weakness in underdevelopment theory is its assumption that capital is both rational and omnipotent. Born as it was out of the successes of post-war capitalism, when the advanced countries at least seemed to have discovered the key to crisis-free accumulation, and when the conflicts between capital and labour seemed temporarily moderated by decades of continuous growth, underdevelopment theory accepted the new consensus of a capitalism without contradictions. What capitalism – and by extension colonialism – had brought into existence must be what capitalism needed and desired. The more classical image of a system torn by contradictions, unable to fulfil even its own limited objectives, doomed to promote the very forces that would eventually destroy it, dissolved in what for socialists was a post-war gloom, and capitalism was presumed to be only too successful in its dangerous pursuits. Underdevelopment was what capitalism had produced; underdevelopment must be what capitalism wanted.

As we have seen, this led to the notion that pre-capitalist forms of exploitation were as much a source of capital's profits as the extraction of relative surplus value that classical Marxism had identified as capital's main concern. The intense poverty that unquestionably exists in the ex-colonies was then equated with high rates of exploitation – which do not. This is not to deny that both international and local capital reap the rewards of cheap labour in the underdeveloped world: clearly the wave of new investment in South East Asia has been drawn by the attractions of low wages. But it is to say that capital needs wage labour, and that if whole areas of the once colonized world are still unavailable for capitalist production, this presents a problem for capital's expansion.

In the plethora of Marxist writing on development and underdevelopment, few started from this crucial premise, two major exceptions being the work of Geoffrey Kay (1972; 1975) and that of Pierre-Philippe Rey (1971; 1973). Both these writers see capitalism as essentially an expansionary force, and one that seeks to impose its own relations of production. What we call underdevelopment marks for the present a failure in this project. As Kay has noted in his often quoted paradox, 'radical critics of orthodox development theory were so keen to prove the ideological point that underdevelopment was the product of capitalist exploitation, that they let the crucial issue pass them by: capital created underdevelopment not because it exploited the underdeveloped world, but because it did not exploit it enough' (1975:x). Kay's explanation of this shortfall derives partly from his analysis of merchant capital, which predominated for too long in the colonized world, relying on pre-capitalist mechanisms of unequal exchange. The argument is supplemented, in his brief but provocative account of colonialism in Ghana, by an assessment of the limits to colonial power. The frailty of the colonial state, he suggests, was such that it could not contain an African capitalist class. As the expansion of the cocoa industry began to generate this dreaded phenomenon, colonialism had to inhibit its own processes of growth.

The argument Rey pursues is very different in form, though he too takes it for granted that a failure to develop and extend capitalist relations demands investigation and that it cannot be explained away as the inevitable and predictable result of world accumulation. 'Let us stop reproaching capitalism with the one crime which it has not committed, which it could not think of committing; constrained as it is by its own laws of constantly expanding the scale of its reproduction'[7]. Far from acting as a block to capitalist development, he argues, colonialism took on the task of transforming recalcitrant conditions. If the transition to capitalist relations of production is nonetheless incomplete, this testifies to the resistance of pre-colonial modes. The argument draws heavily on Marx's analysis of the transition from feudalism to capitalism. The feudal mode of production in Europe generated from within itself the forces that led to capitalist production. Pre-colonial Africa by contrast contained no such internal momentum. Taking as his case study the experience of colonialism in the French Congo, Rey then argues that violence was necessary to effect the transition. The task of colonialism was to provide the disruption that would shake previous foundations, to force the separation of producers from their land and inculcate the 'habits' of wage labour. The brutalities of railway construction, the years of forced labour, the technically irrational wastage of human labour and life in the building of the Congo railway, were a crucial part of this process. Within this framework, 'underdevelopment' marks the strength of pre-capitalist modes and the way they have resisted novel relations[8].

My argument begins, with both of these writers, from the presumption that a failure of capitalism requires explanation. Where I part company with Rey is on the relationship between capital and the colonial state, for in one important respect at least his analysis merely mirrors underdevelopment theory. For underdevelopment theorists, the colonial (and later post-colonial) state intervenes as an agent of capital to obstruct the development of indigenous capitalism; for Rey it intervenes (however unsuccessfully) to promote the development of capitalist relations. In both cases the colonial state is presented as a simple agent of capital, and capital as a logic which dictates determinate forms of either development or underdevelopment.

Thus at a time when Marxism had largely retreated from a crude identity of state and capital in its analysis of the advanced countries (e.g. Poulantzas, 1969; Miliband, 1970; Holloway and Picciotto, 1978), discussions of colonialism accepted a version of the state as the mouthpiece of capital. The intricacies of modern state theory bypassed the analysts of colonialism. The colonial state was imposed externally at the instigation of European capitalists and was relieved of the burdens of universal franchise; on such tenuous grounds, it appears, critics of colonialism have presumed a state which could serve unconditionally the interests of capital. Yet as Lonsdale and Berman (1979) have argued in their analysis of Kenya, 'the state cannot be the obedient servant of capital', a claim which is as true of the colonial state as of its progenitor in Europe.

The constraints on the colonial state were greater than those which operate in Europe, precisely because of the violence it required to carry through any transformation. In Britain, the compulsion to labour was constructed over centuries. One by one, alternative means of subsistence were stripped away and the necessity of wage labour imposed. Subsistence came to depend on the consumption of commodities, and money became the only medium through which needs could be met. Once this situation became routine, and only then, could the state enjoy its liberalism. With needs defined through commodities, and wages the only access, the compulsion to labour appeared as a natural necessity.

The force which had created, and continued to impose, 'free' labour, was generalized throughout society and became virtually invisible.

In Africa, this generalized force which guarantees the wage relation was absent. Needs were still expressed in terms of use-values, and dependence on a money income was limited. Relatively free access to land ensured subsistence to most Africans and, for those producing cash crops, provided some money earnings. As Rey correctly emphasizes, wage labour could be imposed only through direct coercion. Yet the state which inherited this task was incomplete and undeveloped: a political power which was in many ways a mere facsimile of a state. Colonial rule could be sustained only through a complex of shifting alliances with local rulers, and colonial officials were acutely aware of the limitations of their control. Colonialism was necessarily makeshift. Its history was one of adjustment to conditions it could not dictate, and the abruptness of decolonization gave open expression to a lack of control which had existed all along.

It is against this background that the formation of colonial policies must be understood. The anti-capitalism which apparently characterized so much of colonial thinking arose out of the constraints of local conditions. It was determined neither by the demands of capital accumulation nor by the peculiarities of colonial recruitment. Rather, it was forged out of the experience of colonial administration, and emerged as an uneasy resolution to the often conflicting requirements of colonial rule.

In particular, the political weakness of the colonial state limited its capacity for direct coercion, and this soured its relations with private capital. The state was forced into an alliance with local chiefs as the only reliable guarantors of labour, which in turn dictated the terms on which colonialism operated. The recurrent problems of land and labour revolved around this alliance with chiefs. Free access to land precluded the formation of a landless proletariat, and was ensured by relations of communal land tenure which installed the chiefs as agents of political order. The coercive powers of these chiefs provided the colonial state with the means to recruit labour, but to sustain these powers the right to alienate land had to be curtailed. There was no way out of this circle. The proletarianization which could in principle have broken through it was well beyond the capacity of the colonial states.

The importance of local constraints in determining the course of official thinking is confirmed by the discontinuity in colonial policies. The history of British West Africa divides, I argue, into two phases. The first, from effective colonization in the 1890s to the outbreak of the First World War, was one of experimentation in which the colonizers pursued projects for importing private property and wage labour wholesale into Africa. At this point, the anti-capitalism described by Heussler was rarely evident. The British arrived in West Africa confident that they could write history. They viewed their new estates as a *tabula rasa* on which entirely novel relations of production could be inscribed. They expressed impatience with the backwardness of local conditions, and viewed communal property relations as a constraint on development. They anticipated a transformation of ex-slaves into wage labourers, and when such dreams proved a chimera they toyed with the alternative of importing wage labourers from other colonies. At this stage it was accepted that the colonial administrations should serve private capital, and the future development of the colonies was assumed to rest on attracting further private investment.

The recalcitrance of local conditions soon forced a retreat to what I call the West African Policy. This was most clearly articulated in the deliberations of the West African Lands Committee (set up in 1912), and affirmed the peasant road of development. By this time, private land tenure was regarded as a problem rather than a solution, and private capital as a disturbance except when it restricted itself to merchant activities. The report of the West African Lands Committee never achieved the official stamp of approval but its basic principles informed colonial practice in subsequent years. History was rewritten to provide an apparent continuity with earlier policies, but this new consensus was a recognition of previous defeats rather than a continuation of original proposals. Capital did find a niche for itself in these newly constrained surroundings. Merchant firms continued to dominate in West Africa as they had before the advent of colonial rule, and industrial capital largely mimicked these firms by leaving production in the hands of African peasants. At certain points, capital sought to push beyond these limits, but in the crucial case of Lever Brothers (discussed in Chapter 5), was thwarted by the state.

In this second phase, between the two World Wars, the colonial states confronted the inadequacies of their new policy which began to fall apart from the day of its formulation. The model of West Africa never fully corresponded to the reality, and colonialism became a series of *ad hoc* adjustments to the changes which threatened political order. The favouring of peasant production deprived both capital and the state of control over colonial production, and efforts to force peasants to act as their masters desired were generally unsuccessful. The independence which peasants retained may have been partly illusory since what they produced, and when, was determined by the market. But they continued to control their own labour process and resisted proposals for 'improved' techniques. Colonial officials (and after them African politicians) were convinced that the peasants were wrong: they set up commissions on 'quality control' to grapple with the task of introducing improved methods of production. But to enforce such improvements, they had at their disposal only market prices and administrative decrees. They could not enter directly into production and dictate the changes they desired. These disadvantages of peasant production were supposed, in the colonial vision, to be balanced by the political stability of a peasant order. But here too the model barely approximated to real conditions. The development of commodity production refused to remain within the confines of an idealized peasantry. African farmers accumulated land, employed wage labour, got themselves into debt, and generally refused to remain model peasants. The colonial states were attempting to freeze the development of commodity production at that utopian point which allowed them to maintain control. They were forced to contain the process as it threatened to get out of hand, and much of the inter-war policy deliberations were concerned with this problem of re-establishing the ideal equilibrium. As a consequence, they were unable to promote even their compromise solution of a peasant road. The Chief Census Officer of the Gold Coast admitted in 1931, 'it is probable that the nation is advancing faster than may seem good to the Government, who actually has had occasion to act as a brake rather than as an accelerating force' (Cardinall, 1931:75).

This second phase then was one of adjustment, compromise and ultimately defeat, as the impossibility of the colonial balancing act became clear. By the time of the Second World War the failure of colonialism was apparent, as the forces it had unleashed threatened to destroy the fragile political order on which it relied. The pace of accumulation was outstripping the capacities of the state, and the colonizers abandoned their territories when they could no longer paper over the cracks. Decolonization was to this extent a recognition of the failures of colonialism rather than a response to the powers of nationalism. The independence movements which took over in Africa did not inherit a stable polity, but one which was already coming apart at the seams. The resultant chaos, partially described in the literature on underdevelopment, was only to be expected.

Colonialism, in this analysis, was essentially a makeshift settlement. And to this extent its character has been more readily perceived by orthodox historians, with their insistence on the *ad hoc* nature of colonial rule, than by radical critics who have too easily assumed a logic of capital behind the manoeuvres of local officials. Policy was formulated against a backdrop of recalcitrant conditions and was as a result marked by discontinuities and inconsistencies. I argue, nevertheless, that there *was* a policy, articulated in Colonial Office writings, in statements by governors, and ultimately in a public version (such as McPhee's book) of what the West African colonies represented in comparison with colonial policy elsewhere. But within this policy there were disagreements, and in colonial practice it was impossible to find a consistent expression of the supposed objectives of colonial rule. The variations and inconsistencies do not undermine the claim that there was a West African Policy. Rather, they indicate the makeshift nature of the colonial consensus, which could not provide solutions to every problem that arose. Tensions and conflicts existed throughout the formation of colonial policy, and indeed it is only possible to explain the rapid shift in the 1940s by reference to these. The West African Policy was a consensus built on shifting sands. It was an attempt to hold together in harmony a number of conflicting processes, a complex of objectives which were often denied in colonial practice, frequently challenged by administrators, and ultimately incompatible. But the incompatibility does not detract from the persistence with which the policy was pursued.

This book is based on examination of Colonial Office correspondence, supplemented by published material such as Legislative Council Debates, Departmental Reports, Blue books, and Sessional Papers. It focusses on changing policies with regard to land and labour issues, as and when they were considered of sufficient moment to demand consultation by Governors and Colonial Office. It is not a complete study of the effects of colonial policy. Since governors were notoriously ill-informed of developments within their colonies, it can be assumed that the actual consequences of colonialism, those changes which from a distance will appear of greatest historical importance, may not have surfaced directly in this correspondence. In terms of an overall analysis of colonialism, these unreported developments are crucial. But for an analysis of the strategies pursued by the colonial states, and the dilemmas confronted in this process, what matters are the terms of reference provided by the governors themselves.

I concentrate on the experience of the Gold Coast and Nigeria which between them accounted for the overwhelming proportion of the British West African trade. The economically marginal colonies of the Gambia and Sierra Leone are discussed only at those points where their experience was significant to the formation and tensions of the West African Policy in general: i.e. in the first twenty years when the principles of land and labour policy were being forged, and in the case study of Lever and the palm oil industry, when Sierra Leone became one of the sites for Lever's projected developments. Beyond these, the analysis of the West African Policy in the inter-war years, as it pursued its troubled course through a territory it could not control, is based on the tensions which arose in the two major West African colonies.

The selectivity inevitably limits the conclusions which can be drawn. The book deals primarily with land and labour issues, and not with the entire range of concerns that come under the rubric of 'development'. It focusses on parts of British West Africa, and tries to derive from these an analysis of British West Africa in general. How far the conclusions can indeed be generalized, whether they have anything to contribute beyond the analysis of British colonies in Africa, and whether even within the British territories they have any relevance for those areas which drew substantial numbers of European settlers, is an issue to which I shall return in the final chapter. But since the underlying argument is that colonial policies necessarily developed in response to a complexity of local constraints, we should expect variations on a common theme.

NOTES

1 A term used in Gann and Duignan, 1968:chapter 22, and in Suret-Canale, 1971, Part 2: chapter I.3

2 A recent introduction to the politics of the Third World refers to Fieldhouse's work as still the 'best general history of colonialism'. Clapham, 1985, p. 188.

3 U.S. Department of State Bulletin, 31 August 1953, quoted in Hailey, 1956:1332. Hailey's vast *African Survey* was favourably received at the Colonial Office, and his criticisms were given considerable weight in the formulation of the 1940 Colonial Development and Welfare Act. See Pearce, 1978, and Bowden, 1980.

4 The Colonial Development Corporation was set up in 1948 and financed initially by Government funds, but with the expectation that it would ultimately attract substantial private capital. It was charged with responsibility for financing projects which were unattractive to private investors, but which might be expected to achieve self-sufficiency within a few years.

5 McPhee credited the colonial governments with the inspiration for this development but as others (e.g. Green and Hymer, 1966) have argued, the rise of the cocoa industry was very much an African affair.

6 See particularly the debates on Kenyan capitalism: Leys, 1975; 1978; 1980; Swainson, 1977; 1980; Henley, 1980; Kaplinsky, 1980; Langdon, 1981; Beckman, 1980.

7 Rey, 1973, p. 16. For discussions of Rey's work, little of which is available in English translation, see Bradby, 1975, Foster-Carter, 1978, and Brewer, 1980.

2
Pre-colonial West Africa

As has been indicated, West Africa came to be regarded as the home of peasant production, and by the twentieth century the 'myth of the amorphous peasantry' (Hill, 1968) was born. This characterization soon established itself as orthodoxy, and West Africa was presented as a world of homogeneous communities, made up of a mass of small farmers engaged in a combination of subsistence farming and production for export[1]. Central to the colonial version of this mythology was the favouring of communal land tenure over private, and family labour over waged work. Production of export crops for the modern world could build on traditional African relations of production. One of my arguments is that a commitment to peasant production arose in the course of colonial rule. It was not dominant in earlier colonial thinking, which by contrast assumed the development of both wage labour and private property in land as normal elements in the expansion of colonial trade. The commodity-producing peasantry was largely a product of colonialism. Neither the idealized version which informed colonial policies, nor the more complex reality which troubled local administrators, existed at the time of colonization. Commodity production certainly pre-dated colonialism, but the relations under which it operated were varied and relied more extensively on slave labour than the first officials liked to admit. The aim of this chapter is to sketch out some of these variations.

Africa in the nineteenth century had already experienced several centuries of trade with the outside world. West Africa in particular had supplied gold for European expansion from the eleventh to the seventeenth centuries, and had later been a source of slaves for the plantation economies of the West Indies and the Americas. Internal and external trade were well developed. Local markets, largely under the control of women traders, existed throughout most of West Africa. Long distance trade between West and North Africa dated from at least 1000 B C. By the Middle Ages, a flourishing trans-Saharan trade had been established, with gold, cotton goods and slaves from the south being exchanged for cowries, salt, and weapons from the north. Trade with Europe began in the eleventh century and though small in volume was crucial in content, since West Africa became a major source of gold. By the sixteenth century the Gold Coast was providing the bulk of the world's gold supply, and competition for it resulted by the end of the seventeenth century in the establishment of a number of trading outposts along the coastline. But it was the creation of the sugar plantations in the West Indies which transformed West African trade. From the seventeenth century onwards, slaves replaced gold as the major export, and Portuguese and Dutch traders, representatives of the 'old' world economy, gave way to the French and British. Millions of Africans were tracked down, captured and exported over the next two centuries, to provide the labour for plantation economies across the Atlantic.

The increased demand for slaves stimulated slave-raiding and slave-dealing, and while African slavery far pre-dated the Atlantic trade (Goody, 1980), the new conditions undoubtedly intensified the reliance on slave labour. Slave wars became a profitable option and, under the influence of the new markets, military aristocracies rose to power. The creation of a complex infrastructure for the procurement of slaves simultaneously increased the numbers available for local use, and as Rodney (1966) has argued, provoked the employment of slaves in local production[2]. The slave ships set off at lengthy intervals, periods between capture and export were often prolonged and inevitably the mass labour force accumulated for export was set to work in the interim within West Africa. The Atlantic trade did far more than increase the volume of trade between Africa and the rest of the world: it generated new political structures in the more centralized states and increased the reliance on slaves in domestic production.

In the kingdoms and states of pre-colonial West Africa, slave labour was widely used in agriculture, mining, and war. In the Ashanti empire which, by the early nineteenth century, claimed formal control over an area of 125,000–150,000 square miles and jurisdiction over a population of 3–5 million people (Hymer, 1970), slaves played an important role within the domestic economy. Some spheres, such as gold-mining, depended entirely on slave labour since free born Africans refused to work in them (Wilks, 1975). Slaves made up the core of the standing army. They were used in the manufacture of armaments (mainly bullets) and were a major source of labour for clearing uncultivated land and setting up plantations. Estimates of the slave population of West Africa are notoriously unreliable since early European travellers rarely distinguished between slaves and low status Africans, and probably exaggerated the extent of slavery to justify colonial intervention[3]. Nevertheless, the recurring estimate that slaves made up one-quarter to one-half of the total population, gives some indication of the numbers involved (Miers and Kopytoff, 1977:60–61).

Arguments over the extent of slavery continue to be clouded by the suggestion that West African slavery was a peculiarly 'benign' version, which allowed the slaves considerable freedom and the possibility of redemption. 'What gives African "slavery" its particular stamp in contrast to many other slave systems', wrote Miers and Kopytoff, 'is the existence of (the) "slavery"-to-kinship continuum"[4]. According to this view, slaves were merely the most marginalized in societies with many gradations of kinship and quasi-kinship, and were ultimately likely to be integrated. The argument derives from what was indeed a peculiarity of African slavery – the limitations conventionally imposed on the rights of masters to re-sell their slaves. In West African slave societies, a slave captured in the course of a military campaign or purchased at a slave market, was simply a commodity to be bought or sold at will. But a slave born in servitude could not normally be separated from his/her family except as punishment for serious acts of disobedience. In addition, slaves had the right to purchase their freedom, and favoured slaves would be granted land which they were free to work on the two days a week when their labour was not required. The picture was further complicated by the intermediate relationship of 'pawning'. Indebtedness could lead a free African to pawn himself (or more frequently, his girl children) into a relationship that was often akin to prostitution, and agree to work as a slave for a number of years or until the debt was cancelled. Much has been made of the parallel between this form of 'voluntary servitude' and non-slave forms of patron-client relationship. A recent study of Sierra Leone defends this as a form of dependence voluntarily sought 'in order to escape the dangerous exposure that not infrequently resulted in involuntary servitude' (Abraham, 1978:20). The argument is self-defeating, since it has to acknowledge the extent of slavery proper in order to explain the so-called voluntary servitude. Moreover, the defence of West African slavery on the grounds that it was no more oppressive than the normal relations between chiefs and commoners can be turned on its head, and employed to illustrate the degree of coercion embodied in 'normal' non-slave relationships.

The form of domestic slavery which features in such defences was in addition only one of the many variants of slavery found in pre-colonial West Africa. Domestic slaves did work alongside free born Africans and lived in similar conditions; they could reasonably hope that their descendants would be assimilated into the community as free members even though these descendants were excluded from becoming chief and cultural prejudices against them survived their formal liberation. But where clear distinctions were made between the work of slaves and that of free Africans, even this incomplete assimilation did not occur. Where slaves were made to work part of the week on their master's land, and the rest of the week on a personal plot which provided means of subsistence, the extraction of labour rent continued from generation to generation. The only relaxation was that the proportion of time demanded for the master's land could be reduced over the years, with the possibility that proceeds from the personal plot might be enough for redemption. In the third form of slavery, the slave villages or 'plantations' where slaves were completely segregated from free Africans, and where they were required to deliver a rent in kind or money to the owner of the village, prospects for redemption or assimilation were virtually non-existent.

In the nineteenth century slave production was massively intensified, despite the abolition of the slave trade and the rise of the alternative 'legitimate commerce' in palm products. As Klein (1971:28) has argued, 'legitimate commerce did not replace the slave trade. Instead it contributed to the last brutal phase and led to the extension of European control over the continent'. The abolition of the slave trade remained largely a formality until the abolition of slavery itself in America – a process that did not begin till 1863. Denmark declared slave trading illegal in 1802 and Britain followed suit in 1807, even taking on responsibility for enforcing its laws on all merchants on the West Coast, with an anti-slavery patrol to police the coastline. But despite this, and the remarkable growth in the alternative trade in vegetable oils – British imports from West Africa rose from 1,000 tons in 1810 to 10,000 tons in 1830 and over 40,000 tons by 1855 (Hopkins, 1973:128) – the traffic in slaves continued, and even increased throughout the period. Moreover, where the Atlantic trade was seriously threatened, the tendency within West Africa was to redeploy slaves into domestic production in Africa.

In the slave empire of Dahomey, the kings simply used slaves who would previously have been exported to produce the new palm products – 'military aristocrats were converted into planters, and slave merchandise into producers' (Meillassoux, 1971:59). In the Ashanti empire, pressures towards redeployment of slaves were intensified by the political dangers of a surplus of slaves. In empires organized around military campaigns, which could generate up to 20,000 captives in a single expedition, the potential loss of the American market threatened disastrous consequences. As Wilks (1975) has shown, there was much concern in the years 1810–20 that the accumulation of slaves inside the empire might end with the slaves outnumbering their rulers; even before this happened, an alliance might emerge between the growing numbers of slaves and the poorest of the free Ashanti. Two solutions were possible, and in Ashanti both were adopted. The supply of slaves could be brought under control, primarily by a restriction of military activity, and it is significant both that a decree was passed freeing all Muslim slaves in 1808, and that the influence of the 'war party' began to decline from this period onwards. Or, secondly, the slaves could be dispersed and isolated from potential allies among the poorest Ashanti: they could be sent off to slave villages, settled on previously uncultivated land, and segregated from free Africans. Thus the abolition of slave trading by the European powers set in motion pressures towards an intensification of slavery as a mode of production in Africa. Slaves were increasingly used, not just as additional members of a household, but in specifically slave enterprises which had much in common with the plantation developments of the West Indies.

The development of slave villages was particularly marked in the area which subsequently became Northern Nigeria. Here the Hausa rulers who had dominated the area for centuries were dislodged in a series of holy wars which led to the formation of the Sokoto Caliphate, the largest state in pre-colonial West Africa, covering approximately 250,000 square miles (Adeleye, 1971). An Islamic revivalist movement was launched in 1804 by the Fulani pastoralists who had settled the area from the sixteenth century. The war was supported by Muslim and non-Muslim Hausa disaffected with their corrupt rulers, and over a period of thirty years an Islamic empire was forged. This was organized into a number of emirates owing allegiance to the Caliph at Sokoto. Numerous slave villages were set up in the emirates in the course of the nineteenth century. In these villages agricultural production was carried on almost entirely by slave labour, and a proportion of the products was duly remitted to the owners of the village. The extent of this development is hard to estimate, but Mason (1973) has shown that 1,611 such villages were created in the Bida Emirate alone in the last half of the nineteenth century, and has suggested that as much as half the population of the Emirate could have been working on these slave farms[5]. Again the evidence points to the nineteenth century as a period of intensification of slavery, rather than of its decline.

Against such evidence, the notion of an amorphous peasantry seems absurd, and it may appear extraordinary that later commentators could describe West Africa as 'democratic communities consisting of multitudes of small farmers or peasant proprietors', or claim that the 'temporal lord scarcely exists on the West Coast, and there is no conception of a landlord in the European sense' (Jones, 1936:51). The societies which the British colonized in West Africa contained two major empires: the Ashanti empire which covered the central region of what was to become the Gold Coast, and the Sokoto Caliphate which extended over the vast area of Northern Nigeria. In the former, a class of wealthy financiers had emerged – the *asikafo* – who controlled large estates, owned substantial wealth in the form of gold dust, and were in a position to make loans to the state. Their capacity to accumulate was constrained by the state and in the early nineteenth century the kings of Ashanti imposed extraordinarily high death duties to limit the inheritance of wealth. But such laws could be evaded. The *asikafo* were prominent, first in the financing of wars, and later in running the Company of State Traders, which was set up in the nineteenth century with a monopoly over long distance trade. Trade chiefs were appointed with exclusive licences and responsibility for recruiting the carriers, largely from the slave and female population. They received a commission on the profits, which went to the state treasury. The agents of this company accumulated significant fortunes (Wilks, 1975). In the Sokoto Caliphate (otherwise known as the Fulani empire), the power of the state was considerable, as the following comment indicates:

> The Caliphate government, through its local village heads and other officials, distributed land to freemen, but only to those who had

effectively become citizens and who paid taxes. Outside these places, farmers were subject to enslavement, and annual expeditions organised at various levels of government, including emirates and their numerous dependencies, cleared the countryside of independent peasants and effectively limited access to land. Land was not usually marked, but was tightly controlled. (Lovejoy, 1973:349)

In the Ashanti empire the nineteenth century did ultimately witness a decline in slave production, and at the same time a weakening in the power of the state itself. By 1874, the Ashanti had suffered serious military defeat at the hands of the British, and the Gold Coast government felt able to enforce the abolition of slavery within the hinterland areas of the Gold Coast Protectorate. In the Fulani emirates, however, slave production was intensified. Even in the southern Yoruba states some of the important chiefs and rulers set up palm oil estates worked by slaves (Hopkins, 1973:143). In the inland parts of what was to become Sierra Leone, slavery remained an important source of labour power (Abraham, 1978). Moreover, the development of legitimate commerce, which before colonization centred on the great Niger Delta, relied extensively on slave labour for transport. Trade was controlled by trading 'houses', whose chiefs mediated between European merchants and markets in the interior (Dike, 1956), and these houses used slaves to transport goods up and down the Niger.

It has been argued (Hopkins, 1973) that the rise of legitimate commerce nevertheless marked an important shift, and began the transition to the peasant production which was viewed as West Africa's defining characteristic by the twentieth century. In the last twenty years of the nineteenth century, vegetable oils and kernels made up over 70 per cent of the value of exports from the Gold Coast, over 80 per cent from Lagos, and over 90 per cent from the Niger Delta (Hopkins, 1973:141). And while Hopkins admits that some of the production, as well as much of the transport, relied on slave labour, he argues that most of the new exports came from the multiplicity of small farmers. His argument is that the early centuries of overseas trade were relatively insignificant for West Africa, whose real economic history began with the development of palm oil production. The slave trade, he suggests, barely touched the surface of African societies, while by contrast legitimate commerce finally drew the mass of small farmers into trading relations with Europe.

> The capital and labour requirements of slave raiding and trading had encouraged the rise of a relatively small group of large entrepreneurs, many of whom became the rulers or senior officials of great states in the Western Sudan and in the forest. Producing and selling palm oil and groundnuts, on the other hand, were occupations in which there were few barriers to entry. Legitimate commerce therefore enabled small-scale farmers and traders to play an important part in the overseas exchange economy for the first time. (Hopkins, 1973:125–6)

Moreover, he argues, the imports from the earlier trade were limited to the restricted market of wealthy Africans: state necessities such as guns, or luxury commodities for the ruling élites. By contrast, the imports exchanged for the nineteenth century palm products – cheap textiles, iron goods and alcohol – sought out a potentially mass market of ordinary Africans. 'Modern economic history' thus began here. It was not until the overseas trade embraced this mass of small farmers that the transformation of the West African economies got under way.

The argument is important, and there can be no doubt that the implications of mass commodity production are radically different from those of trade in gold, ivory and slaves. But in terms of an understanding of colonial policies, Hopkins's analysis is unhelpful, since it reads into the nineteenth century developments which were not to become apparent until later years. Significantly, the model for discussions of peasant production – the Gold Coast cocoa industry – established itself only *after* colonization. The cocoa farmers of Akwapim began their westward migration to the empty forest lands of Akim in the 1890s (Hill, 1963), and cocoa production in Ashanti developed some twenty years later. At the time of colonization the only significant 'peasant' sector was in palm oil production and, as has been shown, much of this still relied on large estates and slave labour. The vision of British West Africa as a world of small peasants became possible in the twentieth century, but was not yet determined in the years of colonial conquest.

West Africa in the 1890s still offered scope for contrasting notions of development. It contained its centralized states and empires with their history of slave production and their evidence of social differentiation, but at the same time it contained the basis for a future peasantry. The discrepancy between the two views of West Africa stems partly from the peculiarity of African modes of production which, as recent French anthropology has emphasized[6], seemed to permit a coexistence of subsistence farmers and centralized states, with the latter only barely impinging on the former. As Coquery-Vidrovitch (1976:105) has argued, the 'African despot exploited less his own subjects than the neighbouring tribes'. Where slave labour was important to an economy, it drew on captives from slave wars rather than the indigenous population. Where military conscription was built into the structure of a state, it was usually the slaves or their descendants who were called up for service. The subsistence communities who lived under the formal rule of such states retained considerable autonomy, particularly since the power and wealth of their rulers was not derived from ownership of the land.

As Hymer (1970:34) has argued in relation to pre-colonial Ghana, 'such leisure classes as there were depended upon gold-mining and long-distance trade rather than land' and this limited their impact on subsistence farmers. It is this characteristic of land tenure in pre-colonial West Africa which has sustained images of a classless society, against all the apparently conflicting evidence of social differentiation and centralized states. To the extent that valid generalizations can be made, a common pattern was settlement by lineage groups who asserted their claims to land by migration and cultivation (Ward Price, 1933; Meek, 1968; Elias, 1951). The disposition of this land normally rested with chiefs or elders who were in a position to determine the allocation of unused land to strangers entering the community. In addition they were responsible for redistribution, within the lineage, of land which fell into disuse when families migrated or died out. Generally, two principles operated: (1) anyone seeking access to land had to ask permission of those who claimed jurisdiction over it, and was normally granted this permission provided that jurisdiction was acknowledged through a (usually token) gift; (2) anyone who already had land could expect to retain it for ever, but had no right to alienate it. In other words, a system of usufruct existed, but not freehold ownership. Variations developed according to firstly, the nature of political authority within the group, some of which had chiefs, but not all; secondly, the extent to which they came under some wider political authority, which might insist on consultation over disposition of the land; and thirdly, the development of a money economy, which affected the nature of the 'gifts' paid and transformed them into a kind of ground rent.

Colonial officials came to describe this system as 'communal land tenure'. Their description conjures up a false vision of primitive communism, and encouraged a picture of West Africa as an area untouched by the social divisions which attend the accumulation of wealth. What truth was there in this? It was indeed the case that (free born) Africans had easy access to land. Throughout most of West Africa, large tracts of uncultivated land were available, and strangers were generally welcomed to a community since their presence and allegiance increased the prestige of chiefs. Furthermore, the natural abundance of land was not artificially constrained by the emergence of a landlord class. Since land could not be alienated as private property there was no possibility of the polarization into a landlord class on the one side and a landless proletariat on the other. It would be wrong, however, to conclude that pre-colonial Africa was a congenial 'state of nature' such as that which Locke (1690) envisaged before the introduction of money – a rural idyll where no-one infringed on the rights of another, and differences between individuals arose exclusively from how hard each worked. Quite apart from the qualifications of slavery and centralized states, this communal land tenure permitted relations of coercion between chiefs and commoners.

Even in those parts of West Africa correctly regarded as more homogeneous, such as parts of Eastern Nigeria, power structures existed which gave chiefs and elders extensive control over women and younger men (e.g. Ottenberg, 1971). Though distinctions in wealth were minimal, it was the elders who controlled the movement of women and the access of men to marriage, and who dictated contributions to the communal labour of weeding common land, clearing bush, and maintaining paths.

For the young men who performed this labour, such relations were generally acceptable, since time would ensure that they too became elders. But with the advent of colonialism, such mechanisms of control over communal labour were to provide an important source of labour power for the colonial states.

The argument of this chapter is that while pre-colonial West Africa contained large numbers of subsistence farmers who, by virtue of their usufruct rights in land, could potentially become the peasant proprietors described in twentieth century accounts, the West African peasantry was not yet established at the time of colonization. The Gold Coast cocoa farmers had not yet made their mark, and the development of palm oil exports, largely from the Niger Delta, was by no means wholly dependent on the work of small scale farmers. Slavery remained an important part of the economies in the north of Sierra Leone and Nigeria, and while these areas were to be relatively marginal in the subsequent development of colonial trade, in the 1880s and 1890s the future scenario was unknown. It is only with hindsight that West Africa appears as a world of peasants. When the new governors arrived to take up their duties – often from prior service in colonies which relied on indentured labour – they did not begin from this assumption.

The formation of colonial policies began, to this extent, in a vacuum. West Africa was by no means a *tabula rasa*, and centuries of trade had laid the foundations for a further development of African commodity production. But in the late nineteenth century the trajectory of West African development was ill-defined, a claim which is confirmed by Hopkin's argument that colonial rule was imposed in a period of crisis in legitimate commerce. Prices for palm oil peaked in the 1850s, and fell over the next twenty-five years by nearly 50 per cent (Hopkins, 1973:133). The volume of oil exports stagnated and it seemed that only active colonial intervention could rescue the West African trade. The administrators who took on this task began with little sense of the specificity of British West Africa, and were by no means wedded to the limitations of peasant production. Their conception of what was possible in these colonies ranged more widely and, as will become clear, it was only out of the experience of the first twenty years that the peasant road became an attractive alternative.

NOTES

1   The official treatment of the Gold Coast cocoa farmers as mainly smallholders with farms of two to three acres is the clearest example of this. Until Hill's pioneering work, the role of migrant farmers, who bought up several farms and employed wage labour, was largely overlooked in studies of the cocoa industry (Hill, 1963: Appendix 1.1).

2 Rodney argued a stronger case than this, that the Atlantic trade created slavery in Africa, but subsequent research (e.g. Goody, 1980) undermines this claim.

3 This was the argument put forward by Fage (1969) as part of his attempt to minimize the impact of the slave trade on the development of slavery inside Africa.

4 Miers and Kopytoff, 1977:24. For a discussion of this view, see Klein, 1978; Cooper, 1979; Watson, 1980.

5 For further details on the slave villages of the Sokoto Caliphate, see Lovejoy, 1973; Hogendorm, 1977.

6 See especially the articles by Coquery-Vidrovitch, Meillassoux, Dupre and Rey, collected in Seddon (ed.), 1978.

3

'Developing the Estates': Slavery and Forced Labour

We are landlords of a great estate; it is the duty of the landlord to develop his estate. (Joseph Chamberlain to Birmingham Jewellers and Silversmiths Annual Banquet, 1 April 1895)

Until 1885, British colonial possessions in West Africa were restricted to the small coastal colonies of the Gambia, Sierra Leone, the Gold Coast and Lagos, and even this limited presence was criticized earlier by a Parliamentary Committee which recommended withdrawal. The subsequent protectorates were established from this time onwards through a combination of treaties with African chiefs and wars of conquest. The extension of the Gambia to a strip of land 200 miles up the river began in 1891, the Sierra Leone Protectorate was declared in 1896, Ashanti was finally occupied in 1895 and declared 'open to British trade'[1] the following year, at which point the various treaties with chiefs in the Northern Territories also became effective. The vast colony of Nigeria was the last to be established and the territory occupied by the Royal Niger Company was not taken over by the Colonial Office until 1900, when it was joined with the existing Niger Coast Protectorate in Northern and Southern Nigeria. The continuing wars of occupation delayed the establishment of effective colonial administration until 1906 (Crowder, 1962:189). All four colonies remained administratively divided into the Colony proper and Protectorates. Nigeria was in addition divided into a Southern and Northern Nigeria Protectorate, and before amalgamation in 1914 these retained separate governors. The Gold Coast was similarly sub-divided into the Ashanti Protectorate and the Northern Territories. Though from 1914 onwards each colony came under the jurisdiction of a single governor, the internal divisions remained important since administrative decrees varied from one part of the colony to another.

In the earlier period the small coastal administrations were reluctant to assume an active role. Even in the Gold Coast where legends of Ashanti gold inspired a minor 'gold boom' from 1878–82, the colonial government was not prepared to intervene to aid the new mining companies (Dumett, 1966: chapter 2; Silver, 1981: chapter 2), and most of these early mining companies disappeared into oblivion. The major change in official attitudes coincided with the appointment of Joseph Chamberlain as Secretary of State for the Colonies in 1895. Chamberlain was a committed imperialist, and more radical than his contemporaries in insisting on the role of public investment in 'developing the colonial estates'. His vision of the desired relation between Britain and the colonies was not in itself unusual. The colonies were to serve as sources of raw materials for British industry, and simultaneously as markets for its products. Where he differed was in his sense of the urgency of the task; with the rise of German competition, it became necessary to create new markets as well as consolidate old ones. Private capital was to be encouraged to invest, with government-financed railway schemes as the main attraction. State investment in railways could serve a dual purpose: provide outlets for British capital goods, and inducements to future colonial investors. In his insistence on the role of state railways, Chamberlain pursued a strategy which went beyond the immediate self-interest of private firms. He resisted private pressures for railway contracts and continued, in the face of some criticism, to insist that only the state could adequately undertake such major investment[2]. The potential fruits of such development were, in his view, too important to countenance possibly ineffective and under-capitalized private ventures.

The visions evoked by Chamberlain were on a grand scale, and presupposed colonial states powerful enough to effect radical change. The colonies were to be opened up to capital. Hopes centred especially on the Gold Coast mines, where Chamberlain now predicted a 'gigantic industry springing up'[3], and where a new railway was promised to link the Tarkwa gold area with the port of Sekondi. Plantation developments were also projected, as they had been before the arrival of Chamberlain. A *Report on Economic Agriculture on the Gold Coast* in 1889 took it for granted that future development would combine the 'petite culture' of Africans with the establishment of large European-owned estates, and indeed the report called for the training of Africans as managers of such estates, since the dangers of the West Coast climate would discourage lengthy residence by Europeans[4]. Confidence was high but, as the exaggerated expectations from Gold Coast gold indicate, knowledge was limited. Proposals were both naive and sweeping, as when a memorandum of 1897 on *British Possessions in West Africa* described the Hausas as 'quite the best native material', and recommended a railway network to encourage their migration: 'if we could gradually substitute the Hausa for the low-type Coast Native, there would be a great future for our West African Colonies'[5]. Similar delusions were to surface later in plans to import the Orient, and substitute hard-working Indians and Chinese for the unpromising Africans.

Railways, mines and plantations alike depended for their success on the availability of workers, and in the first twenty years of administration the British confronted the problems of labour supply and the difficulties

27

of creating 'free' labour. In Britain, the compulsion to work was constructed over centuries but, with relatively few exceptions, Africans would 'work' only when forced to. In a world where most producers were guaranteed access to land, and hence to subsistence, direct compulsion was required to produce wage labourers on a sufficient scale. As was soon to become apparent, the problem of development was not confined to the construction of railways. More fundamentally, it rested on the difficulties of creating a labour force for public and private employment.

The colonial governments first faced this problem when they sought out the mass of unskilled labour necessary to complete the conquest of West Africa and carry out the initial programmes of road and railway construction. Without trains or motor transport, the numbers of porters alone were immense: it took 1,000 to transport a regiment of soldiers from one part of West Africa to another[6]. The limitations of the labour market were quickly demonstrated and, in the first decades of administration, colonial officials cast around for any solution. They toyed with the idea that ex-slaves could become the future reserve army of labour. In the interim they experimented with purchasing slaves for government work. They looked to the few coastal towns (particularly Freetown and Lagos), where some rudimentary labour market existed, as recruitment centres for all four West African colonies. When this proved impossible they turned their gaze to the Orient, and speculated on the prospects for mass importation of Indian or Chinese labour. All these alternatives were unsatisfactory, and the colonial governments came to depend on the chiefs as their main recruiting agents, a dependence which provided a link with the emerging policies on land (see Chapter 4). Since the chiefs derived their powers from their role in the allocation of communally held land, the demands of labour supply reinforced a commitment to communal land tenure. By the time of the First World War, a new pattern had emerged. The chiefs could serve as guarantors of the political order, recruiters of unskilled labour, and simultaneously protectors of the peasantry from the ravages of private property.

The story which was to lead to this resolution began with the problem of slavery. As has been shown, master-slave relations existed on a significant scale in pre-colonial Africa, and these relations persisted under colonialism though their extent is poorly documented. The Colonial Office maintained a discreet silence on the subject. As one official remarked, 'it is not an issue on which it is advisable to say much'[7]. British rule was supposed to imply the abolition of slavery, and governors who wrote to London for advice were often reprimanded for bringing such matters to the attention of colonial officials. Despatches referring to slavery could provide easy ammunition to the anti-slavery societies[8].

But despite the distortions and confusions imposed by the policy of 'judicious silence'[9], it is clear that at the time of colonization slavery persisted in agricultural production in the north of Nigeria and Sierra Leone, and continued to exist within the Northern Territories of the Gold

Coast[10]. Colonial administrators feared a premature abolition of slavery. In particular, the slave villages established in the emirates of Northern Nigeria were regarded as fundamental to agricultural production. In 1900, the Resident of Bida described the plight of the master whose slaves had deserted him:

> His farms lie idle for want of hands to till them, his house falls down for lack of hands to care for it; his wives or at any rate concubines have gone with their, i.e. his (sic) children, he is left destitute and as the farm slaves have been careful on going to take all the grain and crops that are their master's property he has not even food to support the remnant that remain with him.

He went on to predict devastation for the future:

> If slavery – the native labour system – be abolished, with what are we to replace it? It will take years – generations – to teach the pagans who form the slave population the meaning of hired labour, and if the existing labour system is broken down *before* there is a new one to replace it nothing but ruin and famine can result.[11]

In this comment, there was no hint of the future vision of a peasant agriculture. The resident assumed that the choice was between slavery or free labour, and he doubted the ease of the transition from one to the other. Given this, he argued, slavery must be condoned.

The problem was most acute in Northern Nigeria where the scale of slavery is indicated by an estimate in 1908 that emancipation with compensation at the going rate would cost the colonial treasury several million pounds[12]. In Southern Nigeria the problem was what to do with the canoe slaves, since the colonial government feared the disruption of trade if these were to claim their freedom. In Sierra Leone, ironically the colony established as a haven for freed slaves from Britain[13], agriculture in the Protectorate was similarly dependent on slavery and as late as 1925 it was estimated that slaves still constituted one-seventh of the population[14].

The colonial governments accepted and utilized slavery, not only to preserve existing agriculture and trade but also to recruit labour for government work. The principled opposition to slavery which supposedly characterized British intervention in Africa was evident only in the efforts to eliminate slave raids. Early legislation was designed to bring an end to slave raiding and dealing, but without premature disruption to slavery itself. This practice had been initiated by the Royal Niger Company, which in 1897 proclaimed the abolition of the 'legal status of slavery' within the Niger Territories it controlled, a cryptic formulation which was meant to establish slaves and freemen as legal equals, without necessarily dismantling slave relations. The absurdity was seized upon by the slaves, who deserted en masse[15]. The colonial governments tried to hold the situation in a series of similar *ad hoc* measures, all characterized by the same obscurity. In 1900 the Colonial Office drew up a proclamation for Nigeria, which remained silent over the existence of slavery *per se* but firmly asserted slave raiding and dealing as punishable offences. Similar legislation had been adopted without difficulty in the Gold Coast and was accepted in the Slave Dealing Proclamation (1901) for Southern Nigeria. Lugard considered even this too radical for the North and introduced his own variant, the Slavery Proclamation (1901), which merely outlawed slave raids. No-one doubted the importance of eliminating these raids, which kept the regions of Northern Nigeria in a constant state of war and devastation, and interfered with agriculture. But on this issue too, discretion was advisable. A memorandum distributed to officers in the North in 1901 warned against 'needless' harassment of caravans in the search for recently captured slaves[16].

Given the vigilance of the anti-slavery societies, it was impossible to pass legislation which explicitly admitted that slavery was being maintained, and this created endless scope for confusion. The first difficulty for colonial governors was what to with runaway slaves. They could turn a blind eye to slavery without too much fear of scandal, but how were they to respond to co-operative chiefs who requested assistance in the recapture of deserters? The problem was first presented to the Colonial Office by the Governor of Sierra Leone in 1894, producing this exasperated comment:

> This is one of these awkward questions for the Government at home which no-one but a weak Governor like Sir F. Fleming would think of bringing before us. I would be almost inclined especially as Sir F. Fleming has come away, to preserve a judicious silence and return no answer to this despatch.[17]

On this occasion a cryptic despatch was sent to Sierra Leone, approving the Governor's conduct in refusing assistance. A similar despatch from the Governor of Lagos in 1897 led to a more lengthy answer. Governor McCallum proposed that any runaways who made it to Lagos should be accorded government protection, but that runaways inside the Protectorate should be returned, so as to 'counteract the social disorder which any continuance of such absconding would bring about'[18]. In terms which were echoed by the later Resident of Bida, he argued:

> any sudden interference with domestic slavery is to be deprecated . . . (it) should not be annulled until we have a much closer hold over the country than we have at present and until we can by our own influence and example show gradually how free labour can be substituted for serf labour without loss to the masters and without dislocation of industries, trade and agricultural enterprise.[19]

Here, as in other instances, the assumption was that free wage contracts would eventually replace slavery. The issue was not how to transform these slaves into self-sufficient peasants, but how to regularize the master-slave relationship and give it the modern form of wage labour. The Colonial Office shared this concern, and the minutes on the despatch consisted of a lengthy discussion of the problems of creating a free labour market in Nigeria. On the specific proposal for assisting the return of runaways in the Protectorate, the Colonial Office was more circumspect, particularly as McCallum was preparing to commit himself in writing in a circular to African rulers. As always on the topic of slavery, nothing should be put on paper:

> Whether the policy be right or wrong, such a letter would be most injudicious. Copies of it would certainly reach this country, and it would be difficult to defend the Governor's conduct. Colonel McCallum should be instructed on no account to write any such letter and as far as possible to avoid committing himself in writing to any general statement of policy on slavery.[20]

The 1901 Proclamations hardly dissipated these problems. The Northern Nigeria Proclamation in particular was a classic example of colonial evasion, which sought to eliminate future sources of slaves by abolishing slave raids and declaring the freedom of all born after the Proclamation, but at the same time keeping existing slaves firmly within their bondage. The slaves were more simple-minded and decided they were free. As the Acting Governor complained in 1901, colonial officials who sought to return the resulting runaways were now in the position of breaking their own law, which made action to return runaways a punishable offence[21]. The 'anarchy' precipitated by the Proclamation and aided by some over-fervent administrators, who shared the slaves' interpretation of the legislation, was described by the Resident of Nupe Province:

> . . . the farm slaves of the Sarikin Paieko were apparently told by Major O'Neill that they were free. They immediately considered that they were also free to appropriate their master's property, seized the farms on which they were employed, took their master's produce and sold it to the whiteman and up till now have prevented their master from sending other men to work his farms or from collecting his property. Two messengers sent by me to Paieko to induce the tributary towns to their allegiance are at present held up in Paieko by these slave bandits who are lying in wait on the Paieko-Argeye road to catch and kill them. Such is the natural result of the indiscriminate freeing of slave low class pagans before they have been educated to know the meaning and duties of freedom.[22]

Despite Colonial Office pressure, Lugard declined to modify the legislation to resolve this 'anomaly'. He preferred the more discreet process of sending memoranda to his political officers to guide their efforts to 'discourage the assertion of freedom'[23]. The colonizers were well aware of the complexities of the situation, as the 1902 memorandum on farm slaves indicates:

> 'Plantation slaves', usually called 'farm slaves' in Nigeria are not in all cases (or even generally) household slaves. Their status I think more generally approximates to that of serfs attached to the soil than of

slaves, that is to say they are inalienable from the land, cannot be sold, and have certain rights as regards produce, the houses they live in, or the hours or days they are allowed to work for themselves. It is important that these farm servants or serfs should not leave their traditional employment in agriculture, and be induced to flock into the big cities as 'free' vagrants without means of subsistence. Residents will therefore do their best to discourage wholesale assertion of 'freedom' by such persons, explaining to them the difference between their status as serfs, and the status of a real slave. On the other hand where possible, and by gradual means it will be the object of the policy in the Protectorate to induce masters to enter into a form of labour contract which will grant greater freedom to the individual.[24]

There were plenty of mechanisms at hand for 'discouraging' runaway slaves. If slaves had no access to land, and were denied government assistance in finding jobs, they could be treated as vagrants and returned to the only work they knew, i.e. to their old masters. The solution to the canoe-slaves problem represented the height of such techniques. The Southern Nigeria House Rule Ordinance (1901), together with the Masters and Servants Proclamation (1903), managed to reinforce 'slavery' without explicitly using the term. The slaves were treated as 'members of a Native House', and the head of the house was confirmed in powers very like those of slave masters. No member of a house could take up alternative employment without the permission of the head, who in turn could insist that a proportion of the wages be paid to the house. A system of twelve-year apprenticeship was introduced, and was explicitly discussed in Colonial Office documents as the alternative to slave raids in recruiting labour[25]. Anti-slavery societies remained unconvinced, and continued to raise scandals when a colonial government intervened to return runaway 'slaves' to these houses[26].

Legislation for the preservation of slavery, both implicit and explicit, was protracted over many years. The Native House Rule Ordinance was not repealed until 1914, and in Sierra Leone slavery was not abolished until 1927. As late as 1925, when a new ordinance was being proposed for Sierra Leone, Governor Slater argued against legislation to prevent detention of slaves against their will:

. . . in theory at least it makes such immediate emancipation possible, and if a large number of slaves forthwith elected to claim their freedom on learning that their masters could no longer detain them against their will, the Chiefs and other slave owners might well become gravely distracted, and that at a time when we wish them to concentrate all their energies and goodwill on the furtherance of a vigorous programme of agricultural development.[27]

The 1926 Ordinance still compromised with slavery, but was enough to produce the anticipated desertions, and the government was faced again with the dilemma of whether to enforce the return of runaways [28]. At this point it gave up, and finally passed the Legal Status of Slavery (Abolition) Ordinance. But as the Southern Nigeria legislation established, abolition of slavery *per se* did not entail dissolving the coercive powers of chiefs or former slave owners. If anything, formal abolition was based on the retention of such powers. In Sierra Leone legislation survived which gave chiefs the right to control the movements of their people, and even to demand payment (2/- to 4/- per head) from anyone wishing to leave their jurisdiction[29].

These examples clarify the degree to which slavery was condoned in colonial West Africa. More important to the argument was the employment of these relations to provide workers for the state. Slave labour was widely used for porterage, railway construction and military conquest, and the government was even prepared to purchase slaves when necessary. In the 1890s, for example, the Governor of Lagos pursued a number of schemes for utilizing slave labour, one of which was simply to buy slaves. He asked the Colonial Office to approve the payment of bounty to slave masters who could provide much needed military recruits, and asked further, if he could 'redeem' slaves in local slave markets[30]. The proposal was always referred to as 'redemption' or 'ransoming' of slaves. The idea was to buy slaves at the going rate of £2 per head, deduct the purchase price from their wages, and release them after their time was served. The scheme was open to misinterpretation: anti-slavery 'fanatics' might read it as an acknowledgement of the right of masters to sell their slaves. But such criticism, it was hoped, could be deflected when the ultimate result was a freed slave. The Colonial Office had no objections, and Governor McCallum went ahead with his plans. A later request for the payment of £1 bounty to masters of Yoruba slaves recruited for military service was, however, refused. On this occasion, officials in London feared that recruits purchased in such a way might make poor soldiers: 'If the Yorubas are so likely to desert, it is not worth while to offer a bounty of £1 to get them'[31].

One of the difficulties with slaves was that they were unreliable. It was thought that they had an easy life in their slavery, and were not yet educated to the values of hard work. Thus McCallum was pessimistic about the longterm benefits of employing ex-slaves. Another of his schemes involved the recruitment of slaves for work on the railway extension to Ibadan and in this plan, part of their wages would be given to their masters and the rest set aside to pay for their 'redemption'. But:

> I had not been many weeks in the Colony before I saw that any such expectation was futile. Yorubas held in slavery enjoy any amount of freedom, and from all I can ascertain they would not, in most instances, take their redemption even if offered to them. They have time to themselves to work in gardens of their own; they are well taken care of by their masters and the whole institution (now that dealing in slaves has been abolished) is of a patriarchal character.[32]

The statement is hard to reconcile with the simultaneous fears that slaves would desert their masters, and testifies more to the unpleasantness of government work than to the joys of 'patriarchy'. Nevertheless, this unfavourable assessment of slaves was echoed many times over. There would be no easy transition from slave to free labour. Liberated slaves were more likely to migrate to the cities and swell the ranks of urban malcontents than to present themselves in orderly fashion for work[33].

The only places where ex-slaves did become available for waged work were in Freetown and Lagos, and though this offered a temporary respite to the problems of labour recruitment, it was not to be a permanent solution. Slaves escaping their servitude in Sierra Leone and Nigeria flooded to these coastal towns, and Freetown in particular became a potential labour reserve for all of West Africa. This dismayed the chiefs who saw a mass exodus of their labourers to the coast[34], and caused consternation to the Sierra Leone Government which found itself with stagnant production in the Protectorate and a swollen city in Freetown[35]. Mass urban employment, of the kind which was to become common throughout West Africa after the Second World War, developed at the beginning of the twentieth century in Sierra Leone. This reserve army was a source of labour for many parts of the colonies but, as soon became clear, it too was fraught with difficulties.

The Colonial Office first recognized the emergence of this labour reserve in 1897, when the Governor reported on the scale of emigration for work in the Belgian Congo, Fernando Po, São Tomé and elsewhere. No less than 4,415 workers had been recruited for employment outside British West Africa in the preceding two years[36]. Recruitment for the Congo had already been a cause for concern. The Congo Free State had been taking workers from Sierra Leone, Lagos and the Gold Coast since the 1880s, and reports of ill-treatment had regularly reached colonial governors. As it became clear that workers hired for the Congo Railway were being commandeered into military service for the state, the Colonial Office intervened to halt recruitment by the Congo Free State[37]. Recruitment for private capital on the railway was allowed to continue, and it was not until 1897 that recruitment for service outside the British colonies was halted.

Demands were constantly made from other parts of British West Africa for Sierra Leone workers, and especially from the Gold Coast, where the government was unable to raise enough labour for railway work. A major confrontation soon developed between the Governors of Sierra Leone and the Gold Coast over this recruitment. In 1901 King-Harman, Governor of Sierra Leone, refused the Gold Coast request for permission to recruit 400 carriers, arguing that the export of labour was leading to serious decline in agriculture:

> In the Colony, I meet men of property who have formerly employed and are anxious to employ 100–200 men, daily, on their farms and plantations and who can now obtain but a dozen or two, and it is pitiful to travel, as I have done, through miles of fertile land

uncultivated for want of a population. In the Protectorate, the unanimous and ever present complaint is the desertion of the 'boys' [i.e. slaves] and the absence of labour. The natural wealth of the Protectorate is to a large extent not harvested and undeveloped, and the trade of the Colony is thereby seriously interfered with. We want at least double the population we have and I would not willingly spare a single man.[38]

Nathan, Governor of the Gold Coast, responded by raising his demand to 1,000 and produced a lengthy rebuttal of the arguments against recruitment:

> The labour of a Mendi or Timani will produce a bigger profit if he leaves the Sierra Leone Protectorate for regular work than if he remains in it to cultivate the soil, and further that profit goes to himself instead of being partly devoted to support in idleness a chief and his dependants. Naturally of course the chief prefers the man to remain in his country to contribute to his support but it is questionable how far the Government is justified in advantaging the chiefs at the expense of their people. The Governor of Sierra Leone uses as an argument against labour going from the Colony that the payment of the house tax there is 'largely dependent on the gathering of the palm kernels and the rice crops, and that this has been interfered with by the deportation voluntary though it may be of the youth and strength of the country'. This is quite possible but if the youth and strength return to the country with money with which to buy imported goods and so voluntarily pay customs duties, the receipts from these dues are increased, probably – by reason of the much larger sums of money earned – to an extent that compares very favourably to the amount of the tax that would have been unwillingly paid by the same people had they remained in the Protectorate. I do not attribute much weight to the further argument that men return to the Protectorate with a taste for drink and a distaste for agricultural labour. The possession of money enables them to satisfy whims which in time become wants that only fresh labour can supply. It is by the creation of wants in the natives of West Africa that a gradually growing inclination to work will be produced – not by keeping them to a labour which while it provides them with rice and palmwine gives no margin for luxuries.[39]

Nathan's arguments failed to convince the Colonial Office, which pointed out that as Acting Governor of Sierra Leone in 1899, he had produced cogent arguments himself against such recruitment[40]. The fact that Nathan as Acting Governor of Sierra Leone vehemently opposed the drain of labour from Sierra Leone, while Nathan as Governor of the Gold Coast found numerous reasons to favour it, indicates how far the outlook of officials was determined by their immediate situation. The problems created by the absence of a free labour market were sufficiently intractable for consistency to fall victim to expedience.

The immediate issue was whether the four British colonies could be treated as a single unit for the purposes of labour supply. If this was accepted, then some form of labour market did exist. The coastal towns drew Africans from the interior, particularly in Sierra Leone where oppressive slavery inland coexisted with the relative freedom and independence of British West Africa's most Europeanized town. If the unemployed Africans who congregated in Freetown could be treated as a labour reserve for all four colonies, then it would be possible to deal with recruitment through a relatively free labour market. Even then it would not be 'free labour': Africans would be indentured for a minimum of one year's employment, employed as single men, and expected to work thousands of miles from the place of their engagement. But they would be voluntarily employed, not compulsorily recruited.

The uneven development of the four colonies meant however that open recruitment would sacrifice the development of one colony to that of another. The colony of the Gambia was so tiny that it need not be considered here. Sierra Leone and the Gold Coast, however, presented a sharp contrast. From the early twentieth century, the Gold Coast became the centre of the most rapid West African development. The cocoa industry provided opportunities for large numbers of Africans, both as farmers and as porters. Gold-mining established itself as a labour-intensive industry requiring many thousands of labourers. The expansion of the colony's trade enabled the government to embark on more extensive programmes of road and railway construction, which further increased the demand for labour. Sierra Leone, with its stagnant agriculture and urban unemployment, seemed an obvious source for Gold Coast labour requirements. Successive governors of Sierra Leone were less taken with this project, and rejected the only possible defence: that it would solve the growing problem of unemployment. As Sierra Leone governors saw it, their task was to discourage migration to Freetown, to persuade, and if necessary force, Africans to return to the Protectorate, and to restore a possibility for cash crop production. Their fear was that if Freetown became an employment centre for the rest of West Africa, the movement to the coast, and depopulation of the interior, would only accelerate.

In 1901 one of the Gold Coast mining companies proposed to the Colonial Office the formation of a private Labour Bureau to co-ordinate labour recruitment throughout British West Africa. This provided an occasion for all West African governors to give their opinions on the question of recruitment between colonies and, incidentally, on the place of private recruiting agencies. The response from Northern Nigeria was unenthusiastic: the North was short of workers, and already relied on recruits from Lagos and the South[41]. The response from Southern Nigeria was more promising. The Acting High Commissioner considered that workers were potentially available, if only they could be persuaded out of their 'apathy' and taught 'the many benefits which can be obtained by the result of work'[42]. He expressed none of the later fears of proletarianization, but did question whether a private Labour Bureau could do the job. In a foretaste of future practices, he supported the commissioning of chiefs as labour recruiters, as more appropriate for West African conditions.

The Governors of Lagos and Sierra Leone were opposed to the scheme. MacGregor, Governor of Lagos, echoed Southern Nigerian doubts about private agencies:

> Doubtless in a very few months such a company would be in conflict with the ruling chiefs, and disastrous war would be inevitable. The recruiting of labourers in every country in a condition similar to this must be in the hands of the Government, and can never be controlled as the bureau proposes, by the employer. The employer himself requires as much attention as the labourer; and the Government of each country is the only power that can attend to both efficiently.[43]

Quite apart from this reservation, MacGregor claimed there was no surplus labour to be mobilized by a labour bureau, or by any other body. Lagos already sent workers to the Gold Coast railways, into military service in the Gold Coast, and into Southern and Northern Nigeria. No margin remained for private concerns. The Governor of Sierra Leone repeated the by now traditional arguments against the use of Sierra Leone as a labour reserve:

> I cannot too strongly insist on the indisputable fact that the population of Sierra Leone Colony and Protectorate is unequal to actual agricultural requirements, and that to induce the deportation of labour would be to inflict a very grievous injury on the community.[44]

Since Lagos and Sierra Leone were the only anticipated recruiting grounds, their opposition was decisive. Their comments were passed on to the Governor of the Gold Coast, who bowed to the inevitable and in 1904 rejected the labour bureau scheme[45]. The Colonial Office was not prepared to force Lagos and Sierra Leone to capitulate to the mining companies. Since each colony was to be financially self-sufficient, the Colonial Office could not countenance a drain of labour from some colonies to others, lest it threaten 'autochthony'.

The options were already closing in. Recruitment between the colonies was rejected as a means of easing the labour supply. Slavery was under stress, and could not be relied upon to produce 'reliable' workers. As the labour crisis deepened, another strategy was proposed: importing a labour force from India or China. The most consistent advocates of such schemes were, significantly, governors from the Gold Coast. They were the ones to face the most immediate shortages, and their interest in indentured labour was reinforced by their prior experience in colonies which relied on such labour. William Maxwell, Governor of the Gold Coast from 1895–7, came from the Malay States and pursued this solution to particularly obsessive lengths. Despatches on such diverse topics as direct taxation and the conditions of life for Europeans were concluded with a plea for indentured labour from the East[46]. He campaigned – unsuccessfully – for a subsidized monthly steamship service between West Africa and the East as the best guarantee of large scale immigration[47]. The ideology underlying such proposals was explicitly racist. Different races were characterized by different degrees of industriousness. West Africans were lazy and indolent, while Indians and Chinese were honest and hard-working. 'No real progress will be made in the development of the resources of this Colony', he argued, 'until a more energetic race than that which now inhabits it is at work here'[48]. In similar tones, the Acting Governor of the Gambia complained, 'I am afraid we will never get the full value out of land in West Africa until a people more intelligent, industrious and ambitious, is imported, such as the Indian coolie or Chinese'[49]. Since wage labour was assumed to be natural, the only explanation for African reluctance must be an intrinsic inferiority of the race. Another race should be substituted for the first inhabitants so as to ensure progress.

In 1895, Maxwell asked the Colonial Office to approve an import of 800 indentured labourers from the Straits Settlement for work on the Gold Coast railway, and even went so far as to propose the encouragement of Chinese capitalists to take up gold-mining in the colony. The rationale for the latter scheme was explained by Antrobus of the Colonial Office:

> It appears to be impracticable to import Chinese labourers on a large scale, and therefore Sir William Maxwell has put forward this scheme for getting some Chinese capitalists in the hope that it would lead to the immigration of Chinese labourers. If that should be the case, the country would probably be developed much more rapidly than it would be by English capitalists with native labour, and the English capitalists would probably be able to employ Chinamen or get more work out of the natives than they do at present.[50]

The proposal for large scale importing of indentured labour was backed by the Crown Agents, who were daunted by the difficulties of raising unskilled labour for forthcoming railway work. Labour supplies in the colony were pitiful and, as they saw it, the choice was between recruitment of workers in Liberia or indentured labour, preferably from India[51]. The Governor of the Straits Settlement was more pessimistic. In the absence of scheduled ships between his colony and the Gold Coast, transport costs would be high. Workers would have to be sent in specially chartered ships, and as it was unlikely they could be recruited in batches of more than 200, they would have to be sent over in half-empty ships, or else kept in Singapore until enough had accumulated for a full ship. Either way, the costs would be prohibitive[52].

As it happened, only the second suggestion, for attracting Chinese capitalists, was put into practice, and in 1896 fifteen miners were brought over for an initial experiment. Two developed illness on the journey and had to be sent back. The rest suffered badly from malaria and returned to Kuala Lumpur with no intention of repeating the experience. The total cost to the government was £2,710 18s 3d[53]. Proposals for indentured labour were resurrected in 1901 at the time of conflicts between Sierra Leone and the Gold Coast over labour recruitment. Both governors turned to the possibility of coolie labour as the way out. The Governor of Sierra Leone thought it would be 'a godsend to West Africa'[54], and the Governor of the Gold Coast advocated the import of 800 Tamil labourers from Ceylon as an alternative to recruitment in Sierra Leone[55]. The mining companies exerted similar pressure. In July 1901 a deputation from these companies met Chamberlain to discuss the chances of bringing in Chinese workers, but failed to convince the Colonial Office of the viability of their proposals[56]. Even the Crown Agents were by now less optimistic[57], and by 1904 the Governor of the Gold Coast was adamant that he would not 'under any circumstances recommend the introduction of Chinese labourers into West Africa'[58].

The problems with the scheme were overwhelming, and only an acute labour shortage could have provoked support for such unlikely solutions. There were four serious objections to the proposals: first, the cost of transport would be exceptionally high when there was no regular service; second, available evidence suggested that Chinese and Indian workers would be just as susceptible to the dangers of the West African climate as Europeans; third, the Government of India was no longer prepared to countenance mass emigration of indentured workers; and fourth, there was concern, based on experiences in other colonies, that racial tensions would develop between imported and indigenous workers[59]. Beyond Maxwell's ill-fated experiment, the only use made of workers from the East was in a few areas of skilled work. Nigeria occasionally employed Indians as printworkers, clerks and engine drivers, but found their demands over pay and conditions excessive, and was glad to replace them with West Africans[60]. Mass employment of indentured labour from India or China was never a serious possibility, and the number of occasions on which it was proposed is evidence of the urgency of labour supply problems rather than the viability of the proposal itself[61]. In these early years, the colonizers were prepared to try anything, and bizarre visions of importing the Orient seemed as promising as any other. This option too was closed by the Colonial Office and colonial governments were forced to seek solutions within their own colonies.

What this meant was acceptance of direct compulsion and reliance on the coercive powers of the chiefs. Alongside their more dramatic solutions, the colonial governments were always attracted to what came to be described as the 'West African custom'[62]. Thus, rejecting the schemes for employing redeemed slaves on the Illogun-Ibadan railway, McCallum concluded an agreement with the Bale of Ibadan for provision of 1,000 workers to undertake the earthwork and provide the sleepers and ballast[63]. McCallum was well aware that these 'workers' were in fact domestic slaves, but the details of recruitment could safely be left to the chiefs themselves. Local chiefs were employed as 'assistant Engineers' at 5/- a day to supervise the work[64]. The practice of paying chiefs for their services as recruiting agents was established in the 1890s, and in Lagos alone £4,000 was set aside in 1897 for payments of monthly stipends to co-operative chiefs[65]. Sir Frederic Hodgson, Governor of the Gold Coast from 1897–1900, summarized the broad terms of this form of labour recruitment. In his evidence to a 1909 Parliamentary Committee on the employment of Indian indentured labourers in the colonies, he said:

> You see in Africa it is very different. You go to a chief and you say, 'Chief. I want so many labourers'; he says, 'All right, you shall have them; how many do you want?'; you tell him and they come to you and they are bound to work. The chief talks to them if they do not work.[66]

With the chiefs accepting a double role as recruiters and enforcers of labour discipline, the advantages were obvious, and this procedure was widely used in the recruitment of unskilled labour.

The requirements for skilled labour were relatively minor, and could normally be met. Creoles from Sierra Leone were available for clerical work. Kru workers from Liberia could be taken on for shipping and dock work. Beyond this, each colonial government built up a small nucleus of permanent workers for the railways and Public Works Department (PWD). Although these workers proved a problem in being the first to organize effective strikes (Hughes and Cohen, 1978), there was never any difficulty over recruitment to such jobs.

It was in the mobilization of unskilled labour that the colonial states faced their real problems, and here they turned to the chiefs. The construction of roads was divided into two categories: the majority of roads were designated as either 'Native' or 'political' roads, and these were constructed and maintained by unpaid compulsory labour through what amounted to a system of labour-taxation[67]. All able-bodied males between fifteen and fifty (in Southern Nigeria this applied also to women between fifteen and forty) were liable to a maximum of twenty-four days' labour each year[68]. Failure to comply could lead to a fine of £1 or one month's imprisonment – an equation which indicates the low value set on labour. Sierra Leone was unusual in having no legislation to this effect, and the Gambia in having no time limit on the number of days which could be demanded. But the system as practised was standard through British West Africa. Recruitment was organized by chiefs and headmen, who received payment for satisfactory completion of the work, the going rate in 1907 being 10/- per mile[69]. The system allowed chiefs enormous discretion, which occasionally generated comment. In 1927, for example, the Secretary for Native Affairs in the Eastern Provinces of Nigeria noted:

> It did not surprise me to see Ibibios cultivating a farm in front of a road overseer's house, and it is quite obvious that such a system gives an unscrupulous overseer endless opportunities for blackmail. Now wherever I have been along these roads all the labour I have seen has

belonged to the farming or producing class. The semi-educated youth may do his share but if so he was singularly inconspicuous among the gangs I saw.[70]

The system produced cheap roads. Roads constructed by the PWD cost £812 per mile if made of gravel, £1,232 if coated in tarmac, and £87 per mile to maintain. A report on Ashanti in 1926 revealed that the political roads, which did not have a tarmac surface, cost £100 per mile to construct, and nothing to the state for maintenance[71]. As might be expected, the majority of roads in West Africa were 'political' roads.

The way the system worked was shrouded in as much mystery as the relations of slavery. It is clear that it depended on a tight control by chiefs over their people, but it was never suggested that this control was anything other than a respectable feature of pre-colonial society. Colonial officials did not seek to deny the 'element of compulsion', but felt the use of force was sufficiently explained in references to the inadequacy of voluntary mechanisms. If Africans did not choose to work, then of course they must be compelled to. Thus a memorandum prepared by the Chief commissioner of the Northern Territories explained:

> For essential public works and for carriers, labour is found on a compulsory system by instructions to chiefs to supply a quota . . . The need for money is not sufficient to make the people come forward purely (sic) voluntarily.

The system was perfectly innocuous since

> . . . on the whole Chiefs have fair control of their people and orders given to Chiefs for supplying carriers, labour, grass, timber etc. are promptly carried out without trouble . . . Civilisation has not yet reached the stage among the rural community to breed a desire for independence from tribal authority. A tendency in this direction is becoming noticeable in towns.[72]

In this way, the system of labour recruitment was presented as a product of African 'desire' to remain under their chiefs, rather than as a subjection to powerful figures who controlled their access to land and privilege.

Despite constant denials, the main difference between this form of labour and that employed by the PWD was that work for the latter was paid. Recruitment methods were similar – through chiefs and headmen – and the labour was largely compulsory. Labour for porters was almost always forced. Chiefs were expected to find the requisite numbers to transport colonial officials through their territory, though the work itself was paid. Recruitment for road and railway work by the PWD was 'voluntary, except for essential public works'[73]. The workers were paid, but 'the labourers are found by the Chiefs of a division being asked to supply a proportion of their able-bodied population'[74]. The methods of recruitment were virtually identical for the unpaid form of labour-taxation and for the supposedly voluntary paid work for the PWD.

Uneven development in British West Africa meant that a labour market did exist in some areas, such that government departments could sometimes meet their needs without force. The clearest evidence of compulsory recruitment comes from the inland areas, where commodity production and the money economy had not established themselves to the same extent – most notably Northern Nigeria and the Northern Territories of the Gold Coast. In some areas, labour requirements could be fulfilled by migrants from the less developed French colonies, seeking means to pay their taxes, or simply escaping the labour obligations imposed by their own governments. But what gave the colonial states the flexibility to carry out work in areas and at periods when such labour was not forthcoming, were the numerous administrative mechanisms at their disposal. The inmates of prisons, for example, were called upon to increase the meagre labour supply for the PWD. Long-term prisoners were employed not only on the tailoring work which is standard throughout most prison systems, but on many extra-mural construction projects. To give just one example: in 1919, the prisoners in the Southern Provinces of Nigeria contributed 719,044 days labour for the PWD[75]. When the combination of free and prison labour was still inadequate, the chiefs were called on as labour recruiters. Here the differences with the recruitment methods for political roads were minimal.

The Gold Coast Government responded to its shortage of labour for the Sekondi-Kumasi railway by introducing in 1901 a system of payment to chiefs for the workers they 'recruited'. The Government paid 4/- per head for each worker recruited for six months, and a further 4/- for anyone persuaded to continue beyond this period[76]. Such recruitment methods encouraged chiefs to coerce their people into employment, and could not be universally practised because of potential scandal. In an incident documented by Mason (1978), the Nigerian Government was forced to set up an official enquiry into the use of forced labour on the Baro-Kano railway after allegations of semi-slave conditions. The enquiry admitted the use of non-market compulsion, but was at pains to discount rumours that chiefs and headmen expropriated part of the wages of the workers they recruited. The report denied complaints of brutality, but did not conceal the absence of a free labour market:

> It is true that labour supplied through the Political Staff are not volunteers in the sense of their being recruited in an open labour market, for such a market exists only on a very limited scale. Nor can the labour supplied through the Political Staff be described as voluntary in the sense of native labour being recruited by recruiting agents moving about the country and offering inducements and persuasion to individuals to enter into contract to work. Such a system is not possible until the country has emerged from the patriarchal stage, nor is it possible while we continue to rule the country through native rulers, as such a system would have a tendency to undermine and damage the prestige of the native administration and organisation.[77]

As late as 1928, Nigerian officials admitted the extensive reliance on forced labour:

> We are endeavouring to secure free labour wherever possible or volun-
> tary labour recruited by contractors; but in the present state of devel-
> opment of the country the only efficient contractors are the native
> administrations and the chiefs.[78]

Where these methods were employed to secure workers for the state, they could be defended as the West African form of taxation. The colonial states were not developed enough to impose modern forms of taxation, and colonial officials turned this weakness into a defence. Transport was being developed in the interests of the community, and if the community declined to finance it through taxes, it must pay in labour services. The Gold Coast after all was to remain free of direct taxation after the disastrous attempt to impose a poll tax in the 1860s, and significantly the Sierra Leone Government, which had managed to introduce a hut tax despite violent opposition, was the only colony not to legislate for compulsory labour[79]. Taxation and labour services were continually counter-
posed; when in 1918, direct taxation was introduced in Abeokuta Prov-
ince in Nigeria without any reduction in labour demands, it provoked what the Commission of Enquiry felt to be a justified resentment, leading to mass rebellion[80]. This defence of forced labour as the alternative to taxes could be sustained only for the political roads, but it served as a cover for 'political' labour on other government projects.

The colonial states thus constructed an alternative to free labour. As long as they could rely on chiefs to recruit labour and impose discipline, labour shortages could be met. The failure to create a working class could even be turned into an achievement, as later officials warned of the dangers of proletarianization and presented the alternative labour system as a happy symbiosis of the old and the new. But the methods evolved for meeting the government's problem had also to serve for private capital. Private companies turned to the state for assistance in their search for workers and put the state under pressures which it rarely faces in advanced capitalism. The colonial governments acceded to these pressures, but often with reluctance and a nervous apprehension of public scandal. Coercion of Africans for the building of roads could be defended as a form of taxation, but coercion on behalf of private capital was more contentious. The state was caught between two unpleasant alternatives: either it put its resources at the disposal of these companies and sinned against the prescriptions of liberal democracy, or it left the companies to their own devices and threatened the fragile political order of the colonies. Neither alternative was welcome, and the hardening of attitudes to private foreign capital must be understood in this light.

Despite expectations, plantation developments were minimal, and though a few were set up near Accra and Lagos (Hopkins, 1973:211) the main debate over plantations was to come later as Lever pursued his projects for the palm oil industry (see Chapter 5). In the earlier years of the twentieth century, it was mainly the Gold Coast mining companies that demanded African labour, and it was in its relations with these companies that the government had to face the consequences of the limited labour market. In 1897 the Ashanti Goldfields Corporation was formed, and in 1901–2 the second 'gold boom' took place, with an estimated 400 companies floated to develop the supposedly endless gold reserves (Silver, 1981:49). European mining operations coincided, however, with the rise of the cocoa industry which made extensive demands for labour for both farm work and porterage, and simultaneously encouraged government investment in railways. In this competitive labour market, the mining companies usually lost out, since even those Africans prepared to work for wages usually avoided the dangers of mine labour. For a number of reasons, the Ashanti Goldfields Corporation was usually able to meet its labour needs[81], but the other mining companies faced a chronic labour shortage throughout the first thirty years of the century. As has been mentioned, they appealed in 1901 for a private labour bureau to assist recruitment, and later supported proposals for importing Chinese labourers, but neither of these schemes came to anything. Subsequent negotiations pointed up one of the problem areas in official labour policy: the state had to choose between allowing the companies to solve their problems in their own way, which could interfere with the emerging pattern of co-operation between government and chiefs, or it had to assume responsibility for the labour needs of the companies. Faced with this choice, the state usually opted for the latter, but relations with the companies were increasingly fraught.

As it became clear that they could rely neither on recruitment from Sierra Leone, nor on indentured labour, the mining companies turned to South Africa for inspiration. They proposed the introduction of pass laws to enforce labour discipline on recalcitrant Africans (Mason, 1978; Silver, 1981: chapter 3). They wanted a system of labour registration in which workers would have to submit their certificates to the employers for the duration of their contract. Any worker who absconded could then be readily identified. Governor Nathan was prepared to condone this scheme and introduced a Concessions Labour Bill (1903) which embodied these proposals, but the succeeding Governor was antagonistic and insisted that recruitment remain under the control of the state[82]. He proposed that the Transport Department take on the job, using village headmen to find the workers. As a concession to the companies, the Department would draw up a written contract recording a description of the worker, so as to aid apprehension of deserters[83]. The issue was whether companies should be permitted to regulate their own labour, or forced to submit to government regulation. Capital objected to the new scheme, claiming the fees for workers were prohibitive. More importantly, as Silver suggests, they resisted the loss of their disciplinary powers consequent on government payment of wages. The Transport

Department scheme was thus short-lived, and constantly undermined by the companies' own private recruiters who continued to compete with the official schemes, offering higher wages. 'Its atrophy', Silver argues (p. 59), 'was therefore the consequence of the struggle between the mines' management and the colonial government, over the extent to which the companies were to be allowed a free hand with respect to the problems of labour control'.

Labour shortages continued. In 1906 the government began the practice of recruitment of forced labour from the Northern Territories which, with occasional suspension, continued for the next twenty years (Thomas, 1973; Silver, 1981). The companies pressed for greater autonomy in the field, and in 1909 proposed a Labour Bureau in which the state would have minority representation. The plan again was for pass laws to prevent desertions, and mining compounds to imprison workers at their place of employment. As with their first attempts, they met with some sympathy from colonial officials, but Governor Rodger returned to the colony determined to resist and was able to persuade the Colonial Office that the proposal was unacceptable[84]. The conflict between government and companies reached its height when Mr Giles Hunt, representative in the Gold Coast of the Mine Managers' Association, declared that 'the Association is not prepared to admit that the recruiting of labour must be subject to Government regulations'[85]. At this point, the company directors felt things had gone too far and hastened to conciliate the Governor by dropping Hunt and appointing a replacement[86]. Government recruitment for the mines continued[87].

Governor Rodger was echoing the doubts expressed earlier on the proposal for a private Labour Bureau to organize recruitment throughout West Africa. As in the earlier case, the fear was that a private body, lacking the experience of government officers, would find itself 'in conflict with the ruling chiefs' and undermine the existing arrangements for labour recruitment. In a world where labour depended on force, capital could not be trusted to act freely. Conflicts were developing over the growing independence of the mining companies, particularly in the mining villages which they had set up in 1903. These never developed into the closed compounds of South Africa, but they did remain primarily under the control of the companies, and the government was unable to assert itself as the sovereign power. The compounds became like private empires, and were a by-word throughout West Africa. Thus in 1912 the Governor of Northern Nigeria acted on the experience of the Gold Coast Government to make it clear that mining companies in Nigeria would have no authority over the camps. A Colonial Office official commented at the time that in the Gold Coast 'there are "mining villages" in which the Government has practically no control, and where a Government doctor is only allowed to walk around on being invited to do so, and cannot insist on any sanitary requirements being complied with, or call for any statistics'[88].

Conditions in these villages came to a head in 1923, when the death rates of workers reached proportions alarming even to the colonial state. Deaths among underground workers at the Taquah and Abosso Consolidated mines reached 64.7 per 1,000 without counting deaths from accidents, and, as a Colonial Office official remarked, even in the Transvaal death rates were only 11.2 per 1,000[89]. At this point government involvement in recruitment from the Northern Territories was halted, and the companies stumbled on until famine in the 1920s and then the world depression of the 1930s finally solved the problems of labour supply.

The crucial point in relations between capital and the state was not the use of force as such, but the extent to which the state could exercise sovereignty. The use of direct force was of course embarrassing. As its extent became clear, it became more difficult to defend, and Guggisberg, Governor of the Gold Coast, explained that he had not realized that Political Officers specified the actual *number* of workers to the chiefs they employed as recruiters[90]. But, as a Colonial Office official cavalierly remarked in 1924,

> . . . in dealing with the primitive races of tropical Africa it is difficult to say where persuasion ends and compulsion begins – especially when it is remembered that most, if not all, of them are living under a patriarchal system which places great power in the hands of the Chief.[91]

Faced with a choice between government recruitment for private enterprise, and private control over recruitment, the colonial states always preferred the former. The official position was that companies could not be trusted. Their relative ignorance of local customs could provoke serious confrontation. Better by far to entrust the problem to officers with good local contacts, and some understanding of local constraints. Yet government involvement in mass recruitment was also fraught with difficulties, as the scandal of mortality rates in the Gold Coast mines revealed. The government could hardly afford to be cast in the role of recruiting Northern Territories' workers 'to be sent down to their deaths'[92]. Liberal democracy in Britain and African opposition in the colonies would not stand for it.

There was no way out of this dilemma. Every alternative to a free labour market carried its own difficulties: slavery could operate only in secret, ex-slaves were perceived as poor workers, recruitment from less developed colonies undermined the principles of financial self-sufficiency, and indentured labour from the East was a hopeless dream. The incapacity of the state to establish a free labour market inevitably led it into deteriorating relations with capital operating in the colonies. In this situation, the government developed a more critical approach to the mining companies. Increasingly, the Gold Coast Government expressed opposition to the disruptive activities of the companies, and the rise of the cocoa industry provided it with a rationale for disparagement of gold mining.

> The period of ambiguity in the relationship of the colonial state with the mining companies had lasted until about 1909, during which time gold production was increasing dramatically, both in absolute terms, and as a proportion of total export revenue. However, by 1909 the trend in cocoa production had made clear the export potential of the crop, and by 1910 cocoa had assumed its position as the Colony's primary source of export revenue. Not coincidentally it was in the 1909–10 period that the government came out strongly in opposition to the interests of the mining companies. (Silver, 1981:66)

This distancing from the mining companies became even more explicit in later years. Guggisberg in particular took up a 'somewhat controversial' position in his report on the mines in 1926:

> Much as I recognise the value of mines to this country, there is no question whatever but that, first and foremost, this is an agricultural country and its future development depends on the maintenance of our agricultural exports. There is no doubt that mining companies increase to an appreciable extent the spending power of the people, but on the other hand they bring in their train certain very undesirable factors. It is my considered opinion that, if the whole of the mining operations disappeared from the Gold Coast tomorrow, it would be for the good of the people and would not affect the revenue of the country.
>
> Unfortunately however, the Gold Coast is peculiarly rich in minerals and Government would be undertaking an impossible task to oppose their development. All that we can do is to give them such facilities in communications as are possible and to safeguard the people against the evil effects of the mining operations.[93]

High on Guggisberg's list of the 'evil effects' was the creation of a class of wage labourers, now seen as less civilized than their peasant brothers:

> . . . the inhabitants of the mining villages form a cosmopolitan crowd of hired labourers, whose moral development compares very unfavourably with that of the rest of the country.[94]

This problem was extensively discussed in the inter-war years (especially in Orde-Browne, 1933 and Merle Davis (ed), 1933) – how to deal with the destructive effects of the new class on the social and political fabric of the colonies? Workers from the Northern Territories could at least be shipped back to their homes on the completion of their twelve-month contract[95]. But the remainder of mine workers were recruited on a daily basis from the inhabitants of the villages and surrounding areas. These workers were irregularly employed, and they necessarily supplemented their wages by income from other quarters – petty trade, some subsistence farming and, as Silver (1981) has shown, theft of gold ore.

Their irregular employment would hardly induce the values of thrift and hard work which formed the basis of Guggisberg's conception of 'moral development'.

By the 1920s it was commonly suspected that the colonial states were antagonistic to private foreign capital. They had not allowed the mining companies all they wanted, they were seen as reluctant to condone further sales of land to European companies, they were criticised for their policy of state railways and for their insistence on a state monopoly in the coal fields in Nigeria. In 1923 the Secretary of State appointed a committee to investigate these suspicions 'that private enterprise is not welcome to the administrators of the territories concerned'[96], and critics were able to give full rein to their dissatisfaction:

> What is there to encourage British enterprise in West Africa? The Government have (sic) seized on anything that they consider profitable. They take the railways. They immediately take all the sites in a town. They also seize the harbours and you have instances of coal. What is there left? It is a policy of a kind of State owned country. There is nothing left for private enterprise.[97]

Such complaints were extreme, but similar doubts were widely expressed and were to some extent justified. When it came to questions of labour control, the colonial states clearly preferred public over private initiatives, and what resistence there was to private investment had its roots in this. As the Committee reported:

> . . . its political staff is in a far better position to handle indigenous labour than the contractor, who necessarily enters as a competitor against other employers, including the State itself.[98]

It concluded that the existing emphasis on state construction and management was the most appropriate to the circumstances. The argument was not new. As early as 1901, Chamberlain defended his policy of state railway construction on the basis that government could better co-ordinate labour supplies. 'If the line to Coomassie is to be finished within a reasonable time', he argued, 'it is necessary, owing to the scarcity of labour, to decline to take up, or allow anyone else to take up, any scheme involving the employment of many labourers until the line has been finished to Coomassie.'[99]

The same argument was applied to the coal fields at Enugu in Nigeria, where state mines operated from 1915. The London, Liverpool and Manchester Chambers of Commerce joined forces with other representatives of private capital to question this state monopoly, and again the defence was that the state could best ensure labour supplies. In his address to the Nigerian Legislative Council in 1923, Clifford argued:

> All the labour employed in the Government colliery is voluntary, but a good deal of consultation with the local chiefs and detailed arrangement and organisation on the part of the Political Officers had been needed before the stream of supply has been made to flow as evenly

and as regularly as it flows today. For recruitment of its labour, a private company, of course, would have to rely upon its own resources without looking to Government for any extraneous aid; and its advent to the coal field could hardly fail to increase the cost of labour and therewith the cost of the coal at the pit's mouth.[100]

Even with the formal reference to the labour as 'voluntary', there could hardly be a clearer statement of the continuing dependence on the co-operation of chiefs to guarantee labour. The government feared that the entry of private capital into these coal fields would either produce a free labour market and force up wages, or place the government under pressure to recruit labour for capital. The Governor's address to the Legislative Council in the following year was devoted to the place of private capital in Nigeria. He insisted that private firms could never recruit the workers necessary for railway work, and made it clear that the state would not help them out:

> . . . an undertaking by Government to provide and maintain a labour force for use by a private firm, appears to me to be open to the gravest objections; but it is none the less quite certain that, lacking such an agreement, no firm of contractors could obtain the labour it would require to carry out the work which is at present being done by the Department.[101]

He went on to reaffirm his opposition to private investment in the coal-fields. If private collieries set up in competition with the government colliery, labour supplies would soon be inadequate:

> Government would have no alternative but to exert its influence and authority to secure for the Government Colliery the labour necessary to prevent its operations, which are a matter of vital importance to the whole of Nigeria, from being brought to a standstill.[102]

This inevitable favouring of the Government Colliery would, he predicted, produce an 'acute sense of grievance' among the directors of the private mines.

Resistence to private recruitment of labour was fuelled by the fear that it would push up wage rates. The colonial governments had early discovered that manipulation of master-slave relations, and subsequent reliance on chiefs, ensured labour at low wages, and they suspected that private capital would disturb the labour market. Hopkins (1966) has shown how much the problem of wage levels preoccupied Governor McCallum in Lagos. Wages in the city, at over 1/- a day, were considered exorbitant compared with those paid in the interior in the late nineteenth century. As Hopkins has demonstrated, McCallum's concern was to establish a low wage economy in Lagos. His problem was not how to find workers, but how to reduce the costs. The alliance with chiefs provided a means to lower the price. But private companies, without access to these chiefs, might have to pay more and force up overall wage levels.

Government opposition to private capital centred on the question of labour, and arose from the absence of a completed labour market in the colonies. The fundamental fact was that no free labour market existed, and the state was incapable of establishing one. It feared the development of such a market as a threat to the political order which, by the twentieth century, centred around alliances with local chiefs. Economically, it was anxious that such a market would force wages up and make its own wage bill too high in relation to its capacity to raise revenue. Even without these fears, it was unable to pursue the task of creating a working class, a task which had taken many centuries in Britain and which required a more centralized state power than that enjoyed by the colonial governments. The consequence was, however, that the government had to exercise a direct, specific force to guarantee labour, and this presented it with a series of difficulties. Firstly, it was inconsistent with the practices of liberal democracy which provided the ultimate reference point, and thus was the grounds for scandal. Secondly, it led to impatience on the side of private capital, which wished to recruit for itself but which in so doing would challenge the sovereignty of the state.

The problems with forced labour, whether for public or private employment, were never considered sufficiently overwhelming to dictate state withdrawal from the use of coercion. In the absence of free labour, the colonial governments believed they had no alternative and, as has been demonstrated, they were usually able to rationalize the use of force through reference to the backwardness of the African mentality. But as Ormsby Gore stated in 1926:

> . . . the trouble with compulsion in any form is that it is only successful in the long run if it is carried out consistently and completely. It is no use imagining that you can continue a voluntary system with a small amount of coercion. Any such scheme breaks down at the point where you are not prepared to go further with compulsion.[103]

The colonial states were not sufficiently secure in their control to be able to countenance the degree of coercion required for full-scale 'development of the estates', and in this context, gradually withdrew from their earlier commitment to private foreign capital.

Trapped between the impossibility of a working class on the one hand, and the many difficulties of forced labour on the other, the colonizers came up with the magical solution of a thriving peasantry. Needless to say, when faced with this thriving peasantry, they looked on it with horror, since it failed to conform to their misty ideal. But in principle at least, the 'policy' of peasant agriculture provided a way through their difficulties. It combined the advantages of expanding commodity exports with submission to traditional authority, and seemed to relieve the colonial governments from their insoluble problems with private capital.

The formulation of this West African Policy took place in discussions of land policy. Though the ultimate difficulty lay in the absence of free labour, the problem appeared to the colonial administrators in the guise of a land question. In their discussion of colonial progress, the first administrators unconsciously adopted a vulgar Marxist paradigm: they believed the development of the productive forces was being held back by existing property relations, and they turned to land policy as the key to future expansion.

NOTES

1 The Governor, Sir William Maxwell, made this announcement in 1896 to the Cape Coast Chamber of Commerce, and copies of this speech were subsequently distributed to the London, Liverpool, Manchester and Glasgow Chambers with an appeal to them to extend their activities. C. O. to Chambers of Commerce, 25 April 1896, *Further Correspondence Relative to Affairs in Ashanti*, African West 504, 1896.

2 By the turn of the century, the number of requests from interested construction firms was such that the C.O. sent a statement of Chamberlain's position on railway construction to the Crown Agents, in the hope that they would then explain to these companies the very limited prospects for private contracts. See C.O. to Crown Agents, 25 June 1901, *Further Correspondence Relating to Concessions and Railways Gold Coast 1901*, African West 652, 1902.

3 Notes on the meeting of Gold Coast traders held at the C.O. 28 March 1899, *Gold Coast: Further Correspondence (December 1898-December 1900) Relating to Land Concessions and Regulations*, African West 578, 1900.

4 *Report on Economic Agriculture on the Gold Coast*, 1889 in Metcalfe, 1964:434–7.

5 *Memorandum on the British Possessions in West Africa*, African West 534, 1897:28.

6 Governor to Secretary of State, 8 October 1897, CO 147/119.

7 C.O. minutes on Governor to Secretary of State, 20 December 1897, CO 147/121.

8 The two main groups at this time were the Anti-Slavery Society and the Aborigines Protection Society, which merged in 1909 to form the Anti-Slavery and Aborigines Protection Society.

9 C.O. minutes on Governor to Secretary of State, 17 January 1894, CO 267/407.

10 For details on slavery in the Northern Territories, see Acting Governor to Secretary of State, 19 January 1910, CO 96/493.

11 Enclosure 1 in Acting High Commissioner to Secretary of State, 7 November 1901, CO 446/17.

12 High Commissioner to Secretary of State, 16 November 1908, CO 446/76. The estimate was based on the assumption that full redemption price would be paid. The current price for slaves was £10–£40.

13 The first settlement was set up in 1787, when the Sierra Leone Company – a philanthropic venture, including William Wilberforce among its directors – arranged for the passage of 411 former slaves from England (and sixty European prostitutes). The necessity for some such enterprise had been created by a court judgement in 1772 that all slaves living in England were to

be considered free. The number in England at this period is estimated at around 15,000. See Buell, 1965:859.

14 Governor to Secretary of State, 12 March 1925, CO 267/607. Three years later it was estimated that 117,000 of the inhabitants of the Protectorate were still slaves. File 9041, CO 267/625.

15 Acting High Commissioner to Secretary of State, 7 November 1901, CO 446/17. An estimated 30,000 slaves had escaped from the Bida Emirate as a result of the 1897 declaration.

16 Enclosure III, in High Commissioner to Secretary of State, 21 August 1903, CO 446/36. This letter was a lengthy discussion of the issue of domestic slavery and contained copies of revealing memoranda sent by Lugard to his Political Officers, advising them on appropriate action for dealing with slavery.

17 C.O. minutes on Governor to Secretary of State, 17 January 1894, CO 267/407.

18 Governor to Secretary of State, 20 December 1897, CO 147/121.

19 ibid.

20 C.O. minutes on above.

21 Acting Commissioner to Secretary of State, 7 November 1901, CO 446/17.

22 Enclosure II in above.

23 High Commissioner to Secretary of State, 21 August 1903, CO 446/36. Lugard deprecated the Acting High Commissioner's anxieties, and it is hard to tell how far the disagreement arose out of the rivalry between the two men and how far from a principled disagreement over slavery. But certainly Lugard's despatch reads as an attempt to present his views on slavery as unique in contemporary debates, without apparently coming to any conclusions which differed from his rivals.

24 Enclosure III, in CO 446/36.

25 C.O. Memorandum on Slavery in Northern and Southern Nigeria, 6 August 1904, Acting Governor to Secretary of State, 15 October 1910, CO 520/95.

26 One example from 1906 arose as a result of Government intervention to return two runaway slaves whose escape had been effected 25 years previously; it was subsequently agreed that old cases should not be pursued. British and Foreign Anti-Slavery Society to C.O., 10 October 1906, CO 520/40, and 4 February 1906, CO 520/54. In 1910 another scandal developed when the District Commissioner agreed to carry out corporal punishment on a runaway slave. Acting Governor to Secretary of State, 15 October 1910, CO 520/95.

27 Governor to Secretary of State, 12 March 1925, CO 267/607.

28 The Ordinance declared all born after the legislation as free, all existing slaves as free on the death of their masters, and, crucially, stated that the courts would not in future deal with any claims for the return of runaways. Slavery was therefore maintained as an interim measure, but the mechanisms by which it could be enforced were withdrawn, and not surprisingly the ordinance quickly became meaningless.

29 File 9041, CO 267/625.

30 Governor to Secretary of State, 26 July 1897, CO 147/115. The Chief Medical Officer considered 'there would be no difficulty in obtaining recruits if the Government set about it in earnest, as Hausa slaves (were) not

much valued in the interior on account of their propensity to run away.'
31 C.O. minutes on Governor to Secretary of State, 15 December 1897, CO
147/121. This comment was prompted by the events of the preceding
months, when Yoruba carriers, recruited to transport the Second West
Indian Regiment, had fled on hearing rumours that they might be press-
ganged into fighting. Governor to Secretary of State, 28 October 1897, CO
147/119.
32 Governor to Secretary of State, 16 August 1897, CO 147/116.
33 See for example Acting Governor to Secretary of State, 3 August 1898, CO
147/134. The occupation of the interior had led to mass escapes of slaves: 'it
has created a class of loafers who being able to get sufficient to live on from
the natural resources of the country will not work now that strong compulsion is absent. This is the outcome of slaves in large numbers obtaining their
freedom and time alone can mend it.'
34 In 1897, the Timani chiefs from the Protectorate petitioned the Governor to
halt the exodus of labourers from their territory. Enclosure in Acting Governor to Secretary of State, 16 June 1899, CO 267/447. As the Governor was
to comment in 1901, these Africans were 'in search of more remunerative
labour than they can obtain from the Chiefs whose retainers (sic) they are'.
Governor to Secretary of State, 24 July 1901, CO 267/458.
35 The Government shared the fears of Lionel Hart, a recruiting agent
operating in Freetown: 'hundreds of them may be seen daily walking the
streets with no work to do' and they were becoming 'a standing menace to
the security of property in Freetown'. Enclosure I in CO 267/447.
36 Numbers recruited from 1894–96:

1894	273	Congo
1895	101	São Tomé
	178	Fernando Po
	177	Axim
	17	Grand Bussu
	1,774	Congo
Total	2,247	
1896	237	Fernando Po
	1,158	Congo
	500	Panama
Total	1,895	

What finally brought the situation to the attention of the C.O. was the
discovery that the Governor had permitted recruitment of 500 workers for
the Panama Company which was already becoming a byword for its ill-
treatment of labourers. The C.O. had assumed that all recruitment had
ended in 1890 when an embargo on recruitment for the Congo Free State
was introduced. Governor to Secretary of State, 7 April 1897, CO 267/432.
37 The correspondence on the ill-treatment of workers in the Congo was published in *Correspondence Respecting the Engagement of Labourers in the West African
Colonies for Service in the Congo Free State and their Alleged Ill-treatment*, African
West 432, 1893, and *Further Correspondence Respecting Engagement of Labourers in*

West African Colonies for Service in the Congo Free State and their Alleged Ill-treatment, African West 473, 1896.

38 Governor to Secretary of State, 13 July 1901, CO 267/458.

39 Governor to Secretary of State, 19 October 1901, CO 96/383.

40 At that stage Nathan argued that recruitment for Ghana was 'most undesirable': 'I do not believe that there is a superabundance of labour in the Colony itself at the present time and I have no doubt that the future development of the Protectorate depends on no encouragement being offered to able-bodied men to leave it and come into the Colony either for shipment to other places or to replace men that have been shipped'. Acting Governor to Secretary of State, 16 June 1899, CO 267/447.

41 Acting High Commissioner to Secretary of State, 13 September 1901, CO 446/16.

42 Acting High Commissioner to Secretary of State, 12 August 1901, CO 520/8.

43 Governor to Secretary of State, 1 August 1901, CO 147/156.

44 Governor to Secretary of State, 24 July 1901, CO 267/458.

45 Governor to Secretary of State, 6 February 1904, CO 96/416. At this point the Governor was confidently asserting that the mines had overcome their earlier problems in recruitment, and could do without either workers from Sierra Leone or indentured labourers from China. That this confidence was misplaced was to become clear by 1906, when recruitment problems arose again.

46 Governor to Secretary of State, 8 January 1897: 'It is impossible, with merely negro agency, to create the roads railways and buildings which we require and to turn to advantage our mines and forests as it would have been to effect, with the aid of the Malay alone, the change which has already been worked in the Protected Malay States during the last twenty years.'

Governor to Secretary of State, 16 January 1897: 'It has been declared to me that it is absolutely necessary for the West Coast trader to live at his place of business, because be cannot trust negro watchmen to keep his goods in safety. To this I can only reply that it is quite possible to import honest watchmen from India.' Both in CO 96/288.

47 Governor to Secretary of State, 8 January 1897, CO 96/288.

48 ibid.

49 Acting Governor to Secretary of State, 8 August 1901, CO 87/164.

50 C.O. minutes on Governor to Secretary of State, 7 January 1897, CO 96/288.

51 Crown Agents to C.O., 4 September 1895, CO 96/262: 'The construction of railways about to be undertaken on the West Coast of Africa will necessitate a large introduction of labour, which must almost of necessity be obtained in India.'

52 Governor to Secretary of State, 7 August 1895, CO 273/205.

53 Enclosure I, in Governor to Secretary of State, 6 February 1904, CO 96/416.

54 Governor to Secretary of State, 24 July 1901, CO 267/458.

55 Governor to Secretary of State, 19 October 1901, CO 96/383.

56 C.O. minutes on Lord Harris to Secretary of State, 30 June 1901, CO 96/392.

57 Crown Agents to C.O., 28 December 1901, CO 96/386. The Crown Agents

were, however, pressing for recruitment from Sierra Leone as their preferred alternative.

58 Governor to Secretary of State, 6 February 1904, CO 96/416.

59 Thus for example, the comment from Ommanny of the C.O.: 'I do not like the idea of introducing the labour of an alien race into West Africa if it can be avoided.' Minutes on Governor to Secretary of State, 19 October 1901, CO 96/383.

60 For example, Indians were employed as guards by the Transport Department in Northern Nigeria, and caused a great deal of trouble. On the completion of their four-year service in 1909, reports were submitted on them: one of them had 'all the dangerous characteristics of a sullen Mohammedan – lazy, insubordinate and defiant', and was considered an agitator and troublemaker. Enclosure in Acting Governor to Secretary of State, 18 November 1909, CO 446/85.

61 The question of indentured labour was pursued again in the evidence of the Gold Coast Secretary for Mines to the Parliamentary Committee on emigration; this was of course at a time of labour shortage for the mines. *Report of the Committee on Emigration from India to the Crown Colonies and Protectorates: Part II: Minutes of Evidence*, Cd. 5193, London 1910:44–7.

62 Term used by Governor McCallum to Secretary of State, 16 August 1897, CO 147/116.

63 ibid.

64 Enclosure II, in Governor to Secretary of State, 12 October 1897, CO 147/119.

65 Governor to Secretary of State, 25 July 1897, CO 147/115. The Governor wrote recommending a monthly stipend of £3 to the Bale of Ejinrin Market, 'as very favourable arrangements have been made for obtaining carriers to Jebu Ode and Ibadan through this man'.

According to the Governor of Sierra Leone in 1908, the practice of paying stipends on this basis was not normal in his colony, but he asked permission to pay an annual £40 to the Paramount Chief at Moyambu: 'There is a larger proportion of natives available for employment as carriers in his chiefdom than elsewhere in the Protectorate; these conditions have naturally made it customary to recruit carriers from the chiefdom whenever a large number of carriers or labourers is required; on all such occasions Chief Lamboi is regarded as responsible for arranging that the required number of carriers or labourers is available.' Governor to Secretary of State, 16 April 1908, CO 267/503.

66 *Report of the Committee on Emigration from India to the Crown Colonies and Protectorates Part II; Minutes of Evidence*, Cd. 5193, London 1910:131.

67 When the American scholar R. L. Buell carried out his study of labour policies in Africa in the 1920s, he was very critical of this system, not so much because of the principle of labour taxation, but because there were no institutions beyond the local chiefs to enforce it and to ensure its fair application. What Buell failed to recognize was that the colonial governments could only operate this system through the chiefs, and had to accept the scope for corruption which it offered to chiefs and headmen as the bribe for ensuring that the labour was made available. See Buell, 1965:659; 716; 828.

68 *Compulsory Native Labour*, Parliamentary paper 20, vol. LXX, 1908.

69 This was the payment offered in Northern Nigeria. *Compulsory Native Labour*, op. cit.

70 Quoted in Buell, 1965:716.

71 Memorandum by Chief Commissioner of Ashanti for visit of Ormsby-Gore in 1926, CO 96/662.

72 Memorandum by Chief Commissioner of Northern Territories for visit of Ormsby-Gore in 1926, CO 96/663.

73 ibid., p. 9.

74 ibid.

75 Annual Report of the Nigerian Prisons Department, 1919.

76 Governor to Secretary of State, 21 January 1901, CO 96/394.

77 Report on Enquiry, enclosed in Acting Governor to Secretary of State, 4 November 1909, CO 446/85.

78 Quoted in Buell, 1965:659n. The full quote is as follows: 'Were the Government to rely solely on such labour as can be recruited individually at current labour rates, it would be impossible to build railways or to undertake any other public work of magnitude. We are endeavouring to secure free labour where possible or voluntary labour recruited by contractors; but in the present state of development of the country the only efficient contractors are the native administrations and the chiefs. It is through them that labour is recruited and the difference between them and private contractors is simply that, whereas the private contractor reckons to make a profit on his contract, the native administrations do not expect to receive any consideration from the government for recruiting their peoples for work. Labour is employed at the normal daily wage which applies to voluntary labour in the district in question.'

The difference between chiefs and private contractors was not of course just the question of costs, but that the chiefs had a leverage over the members of the lineage.

79 The Poll Tax had been imposed in 1852 on the areas of the Gold Coast under British administration, and was finally repealed in 1866 after extensive refusal to pay. No further attempts at direct taxation were made in the Gold Coast. Yet when the 1896 Hut Tax Ordinance for the Sierra Leone Protectorate provoked the 1898 Hut Tax War in which 1,000 lost their lives, the colonial government insisted on enforcing the legislation.

80 *Report of Commission of Enquiry into the Disturbances in the Egba Division of Abeokuta Province*, enclosed in Acting Governor to Secretary of State, 21 January 1919 CO 583/72. In this area there was a history of resistance to unpaid compulsory labour, and the introduction of direct taxation had been sold to the people as an alternative to such work. Yet the local Resident continued to make exactions of compulsory labour, writing to the Oshile in February 1918 as follows: 'If you are really serious, and understand the importance of this road, you will see that no less than 600 men work daily on this two mile portion, and that they all perform a full day's work. Two or three hours per diem is ludicrous, and I can quite understand the Director (of the Public Works programme) having lost his faith in Egba promises of labour when we are fully aware of the exceedingly bad progress of the embankment approaching Awba.'

81 Silver gives a number of explanations for this divergence between the companies: (1) Asante men preferred to work in the Ashanti mines, rather than

migrate further south to the Tarkwa mines, (2) when workers from the north migrated south for work, they were intercepted by the Ashanti Goldfields Corporation which thus had a geographical advantage, (3) the AGC provided better food, (4) and most importantly, the gold in the Ashanti mines, being visible gold veins, was an easier target for the theft of gold, and thus provided a useful supplement to the mine wages (Silver, 1981:53n).

82 Governor to Secretary of State, 15 March 1904, CO 96/417. The Governor accepted the mining companies' presentation of their reasons for pursuing this legislation – that they wished to end the practice in which workers left one mine for another before working for long enough to justify the advance the company had paid them. If this was indeed the only problem, then, as the Governor suggested, it could be dealt with by the mine managers reducing the size of the advances, and thereby the temptation.

83 Enclosure 17 in Governor to Secretary of State, 30 October 1909, CO 96/486. (Thomas, 1973) The incidence of desertion alone indicates the unwillingness of the new 'recruits'. The most dramatic was that in May 1909: 'Captain Warder originally left Gambaga with 500 labourers, but by the time he reached Tarquah the number had been reduced to 258. These labourers worked in a fairly satisfactory manner until the 27th June [they had arrived on 22 May], on which day 153 men left their work. On being notified of this desertion, I went to the Abbontiakoon Mine and having collected all the labourers, including those that had left the camp, had a talk with them. It was impossible to reason with them, as their only reply to anything said was that they wanted to go home. I finally got the headman to promise that they would remain at Abbontiakoon until the arrival of Colonial Watherston [the Chief Commissioner of the Northern Territories who was expected with another batch of recruits] who was due to arrive in Tarquah on the 1st of July. However the labourers next day began to desert and by the end of June there were only 27 of them left. These 27 men worked on until the 26th July when they also left the mine.' Report by Secretary for Mines, enclosed in Governor to Secretary of State, 5 January 1910, CO 96/493.

84 Governor to Secretary of State, 30 October 1909, CO 96/486.

85 Enclosure 5 in Governor to Secretary of State, 14 February 1910, CO 96/494.

86 C.O. minutes on meeting held at C.O., CO 96/494.

87 Between 1912 and 1920, the mines largely organized recruitment for themselves, and when in 1920 they began again to rely on the government, it was through their own choice. At this point the large-scale government recruitment for railway work interfered with their labour supplies, and the mining companies came to realize that it was only through making use of the government that they could hope to satisfy their demands. The story of this is fully documented in Thomas, 1973, and Silver, 1981.

88 C.O. minutes on Acting Governor to Secretary of State, 17 June 1912, CO 446/105.

89 Enclosure 1 in Governor to Secretary of State, 9 November 1923, CO 96/641.

	Nos. employed		Deaths per 1000			
	Surface	Face	Surface	Face (illness)	(accident)	Total %
Abbonitakoon Mines Ltd	637	917	10.99	17.45	1.09	15.44
Taquah & Aboss Consolidated	1165	1051	6.86	64.70	1.90	35.20
Prestea Block A Ltd	1284	752	8.56	22.60	1.33	14.24
Ashanti Gold-fields Corporation	1688	927	1.19	–	1.08	1.15

(The Secretary for Mines was dubious of the very favourable figures from Ashanti, though one clear difference was that the Ashanti mine did not rely on Northern Territories labour.)

90 Governor to Secretary of State, 19 January 1924, CO 96/644. He put this down to 'an excess of zeal on the part of Political Officers in their keen desire to help the mines'.
91 C.O. minutes on Governor to Secretary of State, 19 January 1924, CO 96/644.
92 The Chief of Navrongo complained to the District Commissioner in 1923 that his people were already accusing the chiefs of this. Quoted in Thomas, 1973:99.
93 Guggisberg's remarks on Memorandum by Secretary for Mines for visit of Ormsby-Gore, CO 96/662.
94 ibid.
95 The system of payment preferred by colonial administrators was that workers from the Northern Territories would receive only subsistence pay while at the mines, then two-thirds of the balance in a bulk sum on leaving the mine (so that they could purchase goods for their return) and the rest from the District Commissioner on their return. See Enclosure 3 in Governor to Secretary of State, 5 January 1910, CO 96/493.
96 *Private Enterprise in British Tropical Africa*. Cmd. 2016, London 1924.
97 J. H. Balty to Private Enterprise Committee, CO 966/1:240.
98 *Private Enterprise in British Tropical Africa*, Cmd. 2016, London 1924:9.
99 Secretary of State to Governor, 18 March 1901, *Further Correspondence Relating to Concessions and Railways*, African West 652, 1901.
100 Governor's Address to Nigerian Legislative Council, Lagos: Government Printer, 1923:116.
101 Governor's Address to Nigerian Legislative Council, Lagos: Government Printer, 1924:243.
102 ibid., p. 53.
103 *Report by the Honourable W. G. A. Ormsby-Gore on his visit to West Africa during the year 1926*, Cmd. 2744, London 1926:108.

4

'Developing the Estates':
Land Policies
in the First Twenty Years

The pattern of labour policies was reproduced in deliberations over land. Just as the first solutions to the labour problem presupposed the formation of a free labour market, so the first considerations of land policy assumed a speedy transition to private property in land. As always, land and labour were two sides of the same coin. A free labour market could never come into existence while communal land tenure guaranteed access to the land. Private property offered one mechanism for the dispossession of agricultural producers and their transformation into landless labourers available for employment. In the first decades of colonial rule, the dissolution of communal tenure was widely favoured, and officials pursued policies whose principles were totally contrary to those adopted in later years. The sale of land to private capital was promoted, individual ownership by Africans was encouraged and African tradition was derided as an obstacle to progress. None of what became the pillars of the inter-war West African Policy was sacrosanct.

In the course of the first twenty years, colonial administrators learnt their limitations and retreated to the dream of a thriving peasantry. Communal ownership was the cornerstone on which this dream was constructed. It was believed to prevent reckless alienation of land, discourage absentee landlordism, and halt the formation of a landless rabble. It secured the chiefs in their traditional authority, and thereby strengthened their role as recruiting agents for the colonial states. It was hoped that these chiefs could also serve as modernizing agents, and press their people to employ the more efficient techniques of production favoured by colonial officials. The reversal of earlier visions for land reform was an acceptance of the limits of colonial power. The creation of a free labour market was abandoned as a task deemed to be beyond the capacity of the colonial states.

The story of this retreat is a complicated one. New governors arrived in West Africa full of reforming zeal. The field was open to experimentation, and numerous schemes for change were pursued. But few of these ideas achieved the status of legislation, since the constraints which dictated colonial practice soon made themselves felt. The dreams which underlay these early experiments have thus been blurred by the inaction of the colonial states. The extraordinary degree to which colonial policies changed has been concealed by the relative continuity of the legislation. A study of colonial practice alone would confirm the myth so assiduously propagated in later years: that West Africa was dominated by peasants, and that colonial policy always sought to preserve this. It is only by considering the preambles to policy, the deliberations of what might have been possible, that the contrast with later years becomes apparent. In the dreams of projects that were never completed, we can mark the dramatic shift which the fragility of colonial control eventually imposed.

The 'problem' of land first appeared as a problem of guaranteeing rights for private capital. With rumours of gold, and prospects for rich rubber and timber developments, British firms soon began to push beyond the trading stations through which pre-colonial trade operated, and to purchase land for mining and, to a lesser extent, for agriculture. In the absence of private ownership, prospective investors found it hard to establish secure rights to the land. Individual Africans might be willing to sell the land they occupied, since the ready availability of agricultural land allowed them to move on. But when their rights were usufruct rights, they had no titles to transfer, and other members of the kinship group were likely to challenge the sale. Chiefs were frequently willing to dispose of the 'stool' land they held in trust for the community, and when so much of this was uncultivated, such transactions might seem straightforward. The land, however, was not 'their' land and, even if the community failed to raise objections, superior chiefs might claim jurisdiction over the territory and threaten intervention. The new 'owners' faced a potentially endless succession of claimants to their land, and anxious firms turned to the Colonial Office for protection[1].

One widely favoured solution in the early 1890s was for the state to appropriate the land and set itself up as landlord to the new investors. The state could then guarantee security of tenure to European firms while enjoying the additional advantage of a rent from their activities. The Governor of the Gold Coast suggested in 1889 that all land be declared Crown Land, with any existing rights recognized only for the lifetime of the holders[2]. A version of this was put forward in the Crown Lands Bill (1894) which would have vested all so-called waste lands (a flexible concept, which could embrace vast territories) in the state. In the Ashanti Protectorate, where administrators were dreaming up plans for extracting a war indemnity from Ashanti chiefs – the anticipated secret treasures not having materialized – appropriation of gold-bearing land was similarly discussed[3]. In the Gambia, the Governor proposed that the state take over all Colony land and all 'unoccupied' Protectorate land,

and then rent it to Africans or interested Europeans[4].

None of these proposals was carried through, though all were given serious consideration. In each case confidence failed at the last moment and the legislation was dropped or reached the statute books in such modified form as to rob it of significance. The colonial states were not in a position to challenge the clientèle of powerful chiefs on which they already relied, and the disadvantages of premature confrontation usually outweighed the benefits of land reform. In the Gold Coast an alliance of chiefs and lawyers was formed to resist such legislation (see Kimble, 1963) and, even without such direct opposition, colonial administrators hesitated before the task confronting them. The arguments against wholesale expropriation were often expressed in legal terms: the opinion was that appropriation could be defended only in cases of conquest. But the real weakness in such schemes was that they assumed a state more powerful than the colonial one. The government could not afford to arouse the hostility of the chiefs[5].

The terms of the argument were nevertheless markedly different from those of twenty years later. This weakness of the colonial state was not yet romanticized into a strength, and the argument that the model colonies should promote African production, on the basis of African tenure, was not yet prominent. Most importantly, the communal system of land holding, later celebrated as the mainstay of the African policy, was in these years perceived as an obstacle to progress. In the interests of both African and European production, individual land tenure should be imposed. In the Gold Coast Colony for example, the Chief Justice suggested a tax on land as the best way to undermine the 'present wretched system of land tenure'[6]:

> Such a law would operate as a gigantic partition suit, gradually working itself out with comparatively little friction. By this means land would soon be rested in definite persons. Families and tribes would agree to split up the land jointly or in common, and to pay for portions, and so land would soon become individually owned. Tracts of waste land would in many cases remain unpaid for, and would gradually fall into the hands of the Crown.[7]

The impatience with communal land tenure was characteristic of the period, and was echoed in the comments of Governor Maxwell in 1896:

> It will very likely be advisable to make native tenure more secure by declaring that any Native who obtains a Government certificate shall have personal proprietorship, and shall hold his land free from the operation of native laws or customs which often make lands practically inalienable by the recognition of the right of every member of a family to an individual share in the property.[8]

The main objection to communal land tenure was that it hindered state and capital in the 'development of the colonial estates'. It set too many difficulties in the path of anyone who needed land. Maxwell's frustration was vigorously expressed in his famous despatch to Lord Ripon in 1895:

> . . . the Colonial Government is in the ridiculous position of being unable to erect a building or log out a road on waste land, without having to go through a tedious legal process, concluding usually with payment to some individual or community, whom the prospect of gain has prompted to lay claim to the land. If it were decided, at some future time, to import Chinese or Indian coolies, for public works or as settlers (a scheme which has its advocates), I should, under the present condition of things, be unable to allot them land for buildings and cultivation without applying to some native authority for permission.[9]

It was this potential in communal land tenure to produce an 'owner' for any plot of land – even that which to colonial officials appeared derelict – which most incensed administrators. The related concern to establish private property within African agriculture was subordinate. Maxwell certainly thought it desirable that African cultivators should hold their land 'free from the operation of native laws or customs' and hence free from the conservative pressures of other members of the family, but this objective he was prepared to shelve. The Public Lands Bill which he presented to the Colonial Office in 1897 contained a clause allowing the Supreme Court to impose partition of family property at the request of some members of a family, a clause which would have encouraged the more 'progressive' African farmers, but he withdrew this at the committee stage, commenting that it was a matter which should be taken up at some later date:

> . . . that proper powers should be given to the Supreme Court, upon the application of a person or persons beneficially interested in what is here called 'family property', to order partition, I am quite convinced. But this is a matter requiring separate consideration, and it does not, perhaps, appropriately form part of a measure which has for its objectives the settlement of the broad principles of private and public rights in land.[10]

Maxwell undoubtedly favoured private property for the dual purpose of aiding sales to Europeans and of encouraging settled agriculture among Africans, and saw nothing to recommend communal tenure. But the immediate problem was to settle conditions for European appropriation of land.

Direct appropriation by the state was an attractive solution to this problem but was considered unnecessarily provocative. If the government could assert administrative authority over the land, and assume the power to regulate land sales and validate concessions, this would probably be adequate. This was the 'public lands' alternative, which was implemented without opposition in the Gambia with the Protectorate (Public Lands) Ordinance (1896) and the Public Lands Holding Ordinance (1897). Under this legislation, all land belonging to conquered or deposed rulers, and all land not yet owned by individuals, came under government control but not under its legal ownership. Occupants of the now 'public land' had to obtain a land certificate and pay annual rent to the government, a policy which was expected to encourage European investors and simultaneously promote individual holdings among Africans. The Colonial Office fully supported this second objective – 'the introduction of individual landholders will tend to strengthen the administration of the Protectorate'[11] – but in the face of some opposition, the requirement for compulsory registration was dropped. As with so many endeavours of these years, fears of African reaction moderated the original proposals and the subsequent legislation was less ambitious. It was hoped nevertheless that the new Ordinances would be strong enough to attract capital, and the Governor announced his intention of 'bringing to the notice of capitalists and the Public in Europe, the chances there are now in the Gambia of acquiring landed property and safely investing capital in what [he believed] would prove a lucrative investment'[12]. These hopes were not to be fulfilled, and few investors expressed an interest in the tiny Gambia. It was in the much more attractive Gold Coast that the real test of the public lands alternative took place.

Here the problem was less how to attract capital than how to regulate the rapidly developing market in land. There was a danger that the colony would become identified with purely speculative, even fraudulent capital, and that serious investors would be frightened away. Many companies were floated on the basis of an enticing prospectus detailing the land acquired in the colony. One case which caused alarm to the Governor in 1897 was that of the 'British India Rubber Exploration Company Ltd.' which advertised itself as owning 500 square miles at Appaboomah, rich in 450,000 rubber trees, with land titles duly registered at the Colonial Office. As Maxwell pointed out, there was no such district as Appaboomah, no land around Cape Coast was so well endowed with rubber trees, no one in the area had ever heard of the company, and no mechanism existed for registering land at the Colonial Office[13]. The company was subsequently liquidated. Such occurrences were by no means unusual. Throughout the late 1890s and early 1900s the Colonial Office was overwhelmed with correspondence on fraudulent claims[14].

The hope was that public lands legislation would provide the government with the means to control this land market, to weed out speculative concessions while strengthening productive ones. After an interim announcement that no concessions would be valid without the Governor's approval, the Public Lands Bill was drawn up in 1897[15]. As in the Gambian legislation, the basis on which land was declared 'public' was extensive. The claims of African chiefs to the land were irrelevant, as was actual occupation by Africans. Only land which could be clearly shown to have an individual owner was excluded from the definition. A Concessions Court would validate sales to Europeans and ensure that all relevant chiefs had agreed to the sale. It would also ensure that an adequate rent was paid, that the government received a 5 per cent royalty on minerals, rubber and timber, and that no monopoly was *de facto* created by excessive concessions. Maxwell was confident that this Bill would resolve the land problem:

> . . . the Native Chief, who will receive through the Government a reasonable share of the land revenue, will not be unduly prejudiced, the native peasant who is offered legal proprietorship will be a gainer, and the holders of concessions who intend to turn them to account will have an opportunity of obtaining a safe and marketable title on fair conditions.

> These are the classes whom it must be the object of the Government to encourage. For those who, by the enforcement of a fixed system of land administration lose the chance of irregular profits enjoyed under the old state of things, the Legislative Council is not likely to have any sympathy.[16]

As is well known (Kimble, 1963; Nworah, 1966; Omosini, 1972), Maxwell's prediction of easy success was not borne out and the Bill was eventually dropped in the face of combined opposition from the concessionnaires it was supposed to benefit, the African chiefs, and the lawyers who enjoyed some of the 'irregular profits'. The means by which the state sought to aid private capital were not universally welcomed by capitalists, and the London, Liverpool and Manchester Chambers of Commerce were less than enthusiastic over Maxwell's proposed reforms (Kimble, 1963). The colonial governments expected capital to pay a price for safer investments. Secure land titles would cost more than the fragile deals made before regulation. Moreover, the state expected some share in the profits of private enterprise if it was to accept responsibility for promoting its development. This had been a clearly articulated part of Chamberlain's policy. The state would carry out necessary infrastructural work, but would expect to extract the finance for this from the capitalists it was serving. As Chamberlain announced in a meeting with mining companies in 1899, 'I do not mean to oppress or in any way hamper this industry, but I do not mean all the profits to go to the private individuals'[17].

The insistence on a financial contribution was generally unpalatable to those investing in West Africa. Many British firms involved in the colonies were experiencing severe pressures from the 1880s onwards, when the process of concentration which was to produce one giant firm in the shape of the United Africa Company began (Hopkins, 1973: chapter 6). They were not prepared to pay extra even for changes which improved their long-term prospects. Thus, while firms complained of the uncertainties of the West African land market when they found themselves paying several times over for the same piece of land, they were unwilling to accept higher rents as the price for stable ownership. Negotiations with local chiefs meant purchases of land at derisory prices while negotiations with the state as referee might ensure greater security of tenure, but could also prove more expensive. The West African traders and mining companies were not enjoying colonial super-profits, and they regarded access to cheap land or *de facto* monopolies as the necessary compensation for their risks. Not surprisingly then, they greeted the 1897 Bill with some reservation, and in particular attacked the 5 per cent royalty clause. But it would be wrong to cite this as evidence that the legislation was anti-capitalist, or to suggest that the policies in the 1890s were already framed within the parameters of a thriving peasantry. Colonial policy in these years was firmly committed to the task of opening the colonies to capital, and the recurrent disagreements with capital were over the price to be paid for this. On the royalty question, the Colonial Office accepted an immediate compromise: the claim for 5 per cent was reduced to 2½ per cent, which was enough to quieten the complaints from this quarter.

In any situation, the policies pursued by a state to protect the interests of capital as a whole will bring it into conflict with individual firms. Nowhere was this more true than in the colonies, where firms frequently relied on under-regulated conditions for their profitability. The question of monopolies, for example, was always a thorny one. The state wanted as many firms as possible in the market. Existing firms wanted as few as possible. A persistent objective of state intervention in the land market was the prevention of monopolies by firms which took up vast concessions, thereby excluding competitors, but which delayed work on the land themselves. Fradulent investors must be discouraged, excessive monopolies controlled. Individual firms rarely welcomed such measures, which restricted the flexibility of their own operations. As one timber speculator asserted when faced with the not ungenerous restriction to 40 square miles, 'if small concessions are going to be the rule, I for one shall be tempted to cut my loss now and be done with it as the import can never be controlled with an indiscriminate number of people importing'[18].

The colonial states were of course criticized by the firms they tried to regulate; and the fact that land regulation ultimately aimed at improving conditions of accumulation was rarely acknowledged by those about to be brought in line. Hence capital's failure to rally behind Maxwell's land reforms tells us little about the objectives of the Public Lands Bill. The opposition of potential concessionaires cannot be cited – as it is for instance in Kimble (1963: chapter 9) – as evidence that the policy was designed to curb capitalist investment in the colonies. On the contrary, all the evidence from the 1890s confirms the view that colonial policy was to open up West Africa to capital[19]. Colonial administrators took it for granted that private capital would develop the mineral and timber wealth of the new estates, and their proposed reforms were designed to aid this process. In the 1890s there was little sense of the distinctiveness of British West Africa. The first Governors brought with them assumptions which contained no hint of a peculiarly West African dimension. Occasionally a

note of caution was sounded which anticipated the ideas of the 1920s and
1930s. The Acting Commissioner of the Niger Coast Protectorate, for
example, declared himself in 1898 as 'in favour of development by the
Natives themselves'[20]. But the consensus in the last years of the nineteenth century was for European capital as the agent of change. In land
policy as in labour policy, capitalist relations were taken as the criterion
of progress. The newly acquired territories were treated as a *tabula rasa* on
which entirely novel property and production relations could be
inscribed.

The contrast between the first attempts at land reform and the dream
of the inter-war years was later minimized by colonial officials, who came
to present British West Africa as a continuous haven for the African
peasant. Their rewriting of history was aided by the failures of early
radicalism. Since the legislation rarely reached the statute books, the
policy appeared more continuous than it was. And the contrast was
further mystified by the formation of the 'Third Party' of social
reformers, who proposed land nationalization for purposes quite different to those which activated the first land reforms (Nworah, 1966). The
public lands alternative, which in the 1890s meant the imposition of
private property in land, came under their influence to mean defence of
communal land tenure.

The Third Party alliance of trade and philanthropy brought together
Mary Kingsley, John Holt (of Holt & Company) and E. D. Morel, who
became famous for his denunciations of exploitation in the Belgian
Congo. In the 1890s they appointed themselves as the voice of the West
African merchants, though they were constantly frustrated by the
passivity of their constituents. They were to the fore in critiques of government interventions, and particularly of the Chamberlain-inspired
development policies, which they saw as merely a burden on the tax-
payer. As Nworah puts it, 'Holt disliked the "craze" for "development"', especially the then current mania for railway construction',
while Kingsley 'did not condemn railways generally, but there seems
to have been no particular railway route she supported' (Nworah,
1966:34–5). They saw themselves as critics of impractical missionaries
and colonial brutalities alike – hence the name of 'Third Party'.

Their vision was essentially that of mercantile capital. No need for
ambitious railway networks, the brutalities of concessionary companies,
the meddling of colonial states with property. Trade could proceed perfectly well through the self-interest of European traders and African
producers; the appeal of new manufactures alone would inspire Africans
to produce more. The prominence of alcohol among these imports was
unfortunate, but the civilizing impact of the trade was greater than the
degenerate effects of the commodity – a position which caused a breach
between them and the other European philanthropists concerned with
West Africa, the Aborigines' Protection Society (Nworah, 1966: chapter
3). It was this confidence in the role of commerce which unified the

strands in their policies: the indictment of the Congo concessions, the attack on slavery and forced labour, and the resistance to extravagant development projects. The state might assist in various ways, but trade was the key to expansion.

Official activity should in the main be limited to the construction with due regard to method and economy, of certain indispensable public works, collecting data concerning the native peoples and respective regions in which they dwell, strengthening native authority so rudely disturbed by recent events; in protecting commerce, encouraging capital, preparing the ground for others; in short a work of gradual, sure, systematic consolidation. It should be our object to intermeddle as little as possible with native institutions, abide with scrupulous exactitude to both the spirit and the letter of our treaties with the Chiefs; develop the native peoples along the lines of their own civilisation both in the case of Mohammedans and Pagans; use conciliation in preference to dictation, gold rather than the sword. Administrative extravagance should be rigidly held in check for fear of burdening new Colonies with a load of debt; the soldier and the policeman should be kept in the background, only to be used as a last extremity. Commerce, good roads and statemanship should be our preferable choice of weapons for mitigating evils . . . Patience, more patience, and again patience. That should be, ought to be, the corner-stone of British policy in West Africa. It was the tortoise that won the race; not the hare.' (Morel, 1968:15–16)

This group had little in common with the visions of the first colonial administrators, and it spoke more for a continuation of pre-colonial practice than a grand opening of colonies to capital.

In the 1900s, under the guidance of Morel, the group moved away from the disappointingly apathetic Liverpool traders, and gravitated towards British radicalism. With his new ally, Josiah Wedgwood MP[21], Morel became an advocate of the ideas of Henry George, a Ricardian thinker who saw landlordism as the source of all human misery[22]. The land, George argued, should be reclaimed as public property, a task which could be achieved through the imposition of a 100 per cent land tax. Landlords could continue to administer their 'property' and retain any rent which was due payment for improvements, but all rent deriving from claims to ownership should be returned to the community. The application of this to West Africa produced a policy which seemed to fit with the interests of mercantile capital. Land should remain the communally held property of the people of West Africa, and colonial states should abandon attempts to introduce the retrogressive relations of private property. Agricultural production should develop through African initiative, without the direct investment of European capital or the creation of large scale concessions (Nworah, 1966: chapter 5).

For Morel and Wedgwood, the evolution of private property in land was not only unnecessary to further expansion, but would indeed destroy those features of pre-colonial society which in their minds approximated to the ideal world of Henry George. Instead of intervening to promote individual property rights, the state should assume control over land sales and mortgages, and halt further erosion of the principle of public ownership. More concretely, their proposal was that all British colonies in West Africa should adopt the principle already embodied in the Land Proclamation (1902) of Northern Nigeria, which gave the Governor the right to proclaim areas as public land.

Nworah has documented in detail the path of their campaign, which proceeded through Parliamentary agitation, articles in Morel's paper, *The African Mail*, and a constant stream of letters to the Colonial Office drawing attention to fraudulent concessions. It is clear from Colonial Office minutes that many saw the campaign as a resurrection of the proposals for state control associated with Maxwell's Public Lands Bill[23]. Yet the strategy was almost a direct opposite. In the 1890s, public lands were to be proclaimed as a means to speed transition to individual ownership and smooth the way for private capital. Under the pressures of Morel and others, similar legislation was advocated as a means to prevent the emergence of private property in land, and secure agricultural development on the basis of African commodity production.

The superficial similarity between the Maxwell and Morel proposals has contributed to the false continuity between policy in the early years and the assumptions which came to dominate after the First World War. The arguments of Morel entered into the common-sense of post-1918 West African policy although, as will become clear, his specific recommendations were not implemented. Thus a continuous line was traced from the land reform efforts of the 1890s onwards. On this basis, Maxwell's attempts like Morel's, seemed designed to curb capital. The continuity was assumed in reverse by African opponents of Morel, who argued that his proposals were simply a devious reassertion of the strategy for state appropriation they attributed to Maxwell[24]. Yet there was no such continuity. In the first twenty years, 'developing the colonial estates' meant the creation of conditions favourable to private capital, the development of a transport network, the formation of a labour market, and the dissolution of communal land tenure to promote agricultural production by Africans and Europeans alike. There was little in common between this and the West African Policy as it was formulated in the twentieth century.

The reversal was dramatic, and the ultimate cause was the colonial state's inability to create a free labour market. As long as free labour was the objective, communal land tenure could only be regressive. It provided a safety net for Africans who might otherwise fall into the labour pool. It discouraged private capital by undermining labour supplies and threatening the security of its claims to land. But once the project of creating free labour was abandoned as a hopeless task, and the chiefs installed as the only safe guarantors of labour, customary land tenure emerged as the central plank of the West African policy.

African resistance to government interference with land of course played its part. The formation of the Gold Coast Aborigines' Rights Protection Society (ARPS) caused some dismay to colonial administrators, and the organization proved capable of raising substantial sums to finance its campaigns (Kimble, 1963). But the impact of such groups should not be exaggerated. In 1897 Maxwell pressed the Colonial Office to ignore their complaints, seeing them as the voice of unscrupulous chiefs and lawyers who sought only to enrich themselves at the expense of the community[25]. Later governors were more circumspect in their dealings with African opposition, but virtually all agreed that such groupings had dubious claims to represent 'African tradition'. And as events soon demonstrated, the Gold Coast ARPS was more concerned with the rights of African enterprise than with protection against the ravages of European capitalism[26]. The ARPS certainly played a role in halting Maxwell's schemes for land reform, but they cannot be credited with responsibility for the subsequent favouring of Morel's ideas.

The retreat on the land front coincided with the retreat on the labour front, and both converged on the new goal of a commodity-producing peasantry. Two developments within West Africa speeded this change in colonial practice: first, the rapid confirmation of early fears that West Africa would attract speculative capital, and second, the emergence of a sector of British manufacturing capital which preferred to mimic merchant's capital, and 'leave production to the natives'.

When the 1897 Bill was abandoned, the Gold Coast Government introduced a Concessions Ordinance (1900). This Ordinance set up a Concessions Court with the power to invalidate fraudulently obtained concessions, and to impose area restrictions of 5 square miles for mining and 20 square miles for agriculture. The Ordinance was, however, totally inadequate to the task of controlling speculation. It had no power to enforce the effective working of a concession. It instituted a two-tier system of validation which proved an easy target for devious companies, and it created a court which made little effort to ensure that the area limitations were respected. After 1900, sales of land were first 'proven' before the Stamp Commissioner – which meant no more than witnessing the execution of documents – and then validated before the Court, which in practice approved anything not challenged by a third party. In the gold boom of 1901–2, enterprising companies advertised leases which had been 'proven' as fully validated concessions, and a market in 'paper concessions' sprang up. Individuals rented land (often without consent of the paramount chief) at nominal sums, then sold the concessions in England for £1,000 or more[27]. The Governor complained that 'a concessions industry has grown up which is quite distinct from the mining industry, and threatens to ruin it and to permanently injure the future of the Colony'[28]. At the height of the gold boom, when the Commissioner was proving more than thirty-five mining concessions each week, only one

company was exporting gold from the colony, and overall output had
been declining for years[29].

Companies could easily circumvent the area restrictions by taking out
concessions under different names and subsequently amalgamating.
There was no legislation to control concentration of concessions already
validated. Concessions were taken out over vast areas, on the wildest
possibility of future gold wealth, and then remained locked up for generations. By 1913, the nominal area under concession in the Colony proper
was 25,000 square miles – greater than its actual area – and though
more than half of this had been struck out by the Court or allowed to
lapse, 12,000 square miles remained under notice of concession[30]. Colonial officials at this stage were not concerned with the potential
dispossession of Africans. They considered them sufficiently protected by
the clauses which allowed them to practise traditional agriculture within
the land granted to the concessionaire. But they did worry about the
evidence that capital was turning to the Gold Coast for speculation rather
than production. Doubts as to the validity of earlier visions were
inevitably raised.

Coincident with this booming concessions industry was the growing
interest of a sector of manufacturing capital which chose to operate in a
merchant role rather than engage directly in production. Throughout the
nineteenth century, relations between West Africa and Britain had been
dominated by merchants acting as middlemen between producers in the
two continents. The development of the legitimate commerce in palm
products had been consistent with European exclusion from production.
As Dike (1956) has shown, African rulers and merchants jealously
guarded the Niger Delta from European companies, sometimes to the
point of forcing them to conduct operations from off-shore vessels. One
task of colonialism was to break this African monopoly (Hopkins, 1973:
chapter 4) and guarantee greater access to the interior to such merchant
companies. But the Chamberlain-inspired visions went further than this:
it was hoped that the imposition of colonial rule would open up the
colonies to new kinds of direct investment as well as extend the older
merchant activities. Mining was the obvious example of a capital which
entered directly into production, but similar developments were projected for agricultural and forest products. As the discussion of early
attempts at land reform indicate, the first administrators accepted a
responsibility for encouraging direct investment by British capital. By
the turn of the century, however, it became clear that British industrial
capital might be content to continue the practices established in the first
decades of legitimate commerce. Two new sectors – cocoa and cotton –
emerged, both integrally related to British industrial capital, but neither
dedicated to direct investment in the colonies.

The first step was the formation in 1902 of the British Cotton Growing
Association (BCGA) on an initiative from the Lancashire Chambers of
Commerce (Nworah, 1971). The cotton industry had recently suffered

violent price fluctuations, arising partly from a world shortage of raw cotton and partly from American speculation. The objective of the BCGA was to promote cotton growing in the colonies as a protected source of raw materials, and West Africa became one of its main targets. All four colonial states agreed to contribute to the costs of its activities, though by 1907 only the Gold Coast and Nigeria were sufficiently committed to continue[31]. Though the Association did attempt plantation development (Nworah, 1971), it was soon convinced that the best future lay in encouraging production by Africans. The Association and Government would distribute free cotton seed, would experiment to improve potential varieties, would set up buying centres (with guaranteed prices), and would build ginning factories. Peasant production was thought to be cheaper than plantations. As the Association Manager said in 1913, 'my experience of the African is that he will take on risks that people in civilised countries will not'[32]. Africans working for themselves would work longer and for less return, than day-labourers. In a paper to the Royal Colonial Institute in 1907, one of the members of the BCGA explained that self-employed Africans were content with two pence a day return for their labour, while wage workers expected between six pence and one shilling.

> There are hundreds of thousands of the best type of native who would not go out and serve under a white overseer for a daily wage, but who, working in their own way, and in their own time, would accomplish far more than the average paid labourer, and would, in my opinion, be content with proceeds which give them even less than the equivalence of 6d. a day. (Birtwhistle, 1908:22).

Northern Nigeria was the Association's main hope, and expectations of future expansion contributed to Colonial Office support for a railway extension to Kano[33]. As with earlier hopes of a gold-miners' paradise in the Gold Coast, the expectations were ill-founded, and the Association soon shifted its attention to Uganda[34]. But in the years preceding the First World War, the BCGA put all the weight of a major manufacturing sector behind the peasant policy.

British chocolate manufacturers pursued a similar line. Cadbury Brothers faced a peculiarly embarrassing scandal in 1908 when it was publicly attacked for its reliance on plantations in Principe and São Tomé as the main source of its raw cocoa[35]. These plantations indentured labour from Portuguese Angola. Workers were taken on under five-year contracts, but once on the islands were treated as slaves and forced to re-indenture if they survived the rigours of plantation work. Any children born to them on the island were regarded as the property of the plantation owners. Cadbury Brothers had no role in the running of the plantations, since their general policy was to purchase raw cocoa on the market rather than engage directly in production, but their philanthropic image nevertheless suffered a severe setback. With some relief, they turned to British West Africa, where a thriving cocoa industry was developing without any forced labour. Like the BCGA, Cadbury Brothers experimented with small plantations, and like the Association came to the conclusion that they would rather leave production alone[36]. 'We would very much rather not have the responsibility. Let the natives bring it to the open market.'[37].

Thus two major sectors of industrial capital arrived in West Africa with interests quite different from those expected of concessionary companies in the 1890s. They did not want to invest directly in production and they did not require a mass of wage labour. They preferred to 'mimic' mercantile capital, and leave production in the hands of African peasants.

The rapid expansion of cocoa production effectively destroyed the case for English land law as a pre-condition for permanent cultivation of cash crops. Customary land tenure, till then associated in the minds of colonial officials with shifting cultivation, could apparently adapt itself with ease to settled agriculture. By 1912, the Governor of the Gambia, the colony which in 1895 had attempted forcible imposition of private property, could say, 'there is . . . no doubt in my mind that the tribal system of communal tenure of land is the most suitable for West Africa. The marked development of the cocoa industry in the Gold Coast during the last decade is a striking proof of what can be done by the West African under that excellent system.'[38]

Settled agriculture had created a new situation. As long as Africans were assumed to be engaged in shifting cultivation, gathering palm products from wild palmeries, the establishment of European concessions could be presented as perfectly compatible with the older trade. Mining concessions, and even concessions to timber or rubber produce, could permit this traditional cultivation to continue. Africans could carry on with subsistence farming, or collection of palm products, without interference from the new companies. Some might be displaced by the mining villages but as long as it was assumed that Africans were engaged in shifting cultivation, such displacement could be dismissed as relatively painless. The development of the cocoa industry forced a re-evaluation.

In 1910 an influential memorandum from a District Commissioner in the Gold Coast pointed to the potential conflicts between African production and private capital in the newly established cocoa industry[39]. The clauses guaranteeing 'traditional' rights did not protect cocoa farmers. They were not engaged in shifting cultivation and hence did not qualify. More than this, the establishment of a European company would inevitably mean demands on local labour, and cocoa farmers might well migrate to areas where they would be free from such constraints. Where a concessionary company was set up, it would press local chiefs to supply labour for its estates. And while the District Commissioner did not object to this on principle, he argued that a consequence could be depopulation, as Africans moved to areas where they could pursue their lives uninterrupted.

The native is very sensitive to anything partaking of the nature of enforced labour. Labour is always scarce, and it seems not immaterial that the Concession holder should expect chiefs to supply labour from among those subjects who may remain on the land over which the Concession rights have been acquired.[40]

In this perceptive comment, the problems facing the colonial states were laid bare. In the absence of a free labour market. European companies would have to rely on semi-compulsory labour. Chiefs would be drafted as labour agents, and local producers subjected to labour conscription. The effects on the rapidly developing cocoa industry, which by now offered more hope for the future than the gold mines, could be disastrous. Peasants and plantations began to appear as alternatives, rather than as complementary paths.

Certainly, the BCGA and Cadbury Brothers were beginning to draw this conclusion. Both had attempted their own experiments in plantations; both had given up and come to oppose plantations in general. Cadbury in particular gave substantial financial support to Morel in his campaigns[41], while the manager of the BCGA argued in 1916 that colonial governments would have to choose between plantation or peasant production:

> . . . if utmost and sustained endeavours be made to teach natives to grow economic products for sale for their own account on their own land, the success of that policy will almost certainly imply that natives will not care to go to work for wages on European plantations. Thus if lands are granted to Europeans by the Government in the present stage of native policy, the Europeans will bring pressure to bear on the Government to relax Government efforts to native industries and to thereby cease inducements to natives to work on their own instead of for Europeans. If the Government refuses and still continues to teach natives to plant for themselves, the European plantation owners will say that the Government has broken faith with Europeans, in that the Government has attracted Europeans into the country and to spend money on plantations, and then deprived the Europeans of cheap labour. So the Government should face this at the outset and declare their policy, if it be so, to make the native an independent farmer. Failure to do this i.e. confusion of policy in (a) granting lands to Europeans, while (b) pursuing the native economic policy, has already led to British East Africa becoming restless.[42]

The BCGA did not want African production of raw cotton disrupted by plantation agriculture.

The two roads to progress were beginning to diverge. The assumption of compatibility between European enterprise and African production now seemed naive. In the late nineteenth century, it had been thought that the two could coexist in harmony. Indeed, the introduction of plantation agriculture, hopefully using more sophisticated techniques, was expected to play an exemplary role, encouraging small farmers to adopt the more advanced methods of production. The emergence of the cotton and cocoa interests undermined this assumption. Even small model plantations set up by the state did not act as effective examples to small farmers, and capitalist enterprises would threaten their survival.

The arrival in the colonies of the cotton and cocoa interests thus created a climate less sympathetic to European concessions, and more favourable to the Morel/Wedgwood advocacy of independent commodity production. The tide did not, however, turn overnight. The first success of the Morel/Wedgwood campaign was the passing of the Land and Native Rights Proclamation, Northern Nigeria, in 1910, which declared all land public land. Even this, it can be argued, arose more from pragmatic revenue considerations than a firm commitment to a new peasant policy. With land declared public, and under state disposition, its revenues could be claimed for public purposes rather than disappearing into private pockets. Colonial administrators had long bemoaned the inequity of a situation where land values rose because of the colonial presence, but benefits accrued to private individuals[43]. Sir P. Girouard, Governor of Northern Nigeria, was determined to change this. Proceeds from land sales should go to public use and relieve the state of some of its financial burden. The ideas of Henry George struck a responsive note.

In 1911 the Colonial Office decided to look again at land policy in the Gold Coast, and appointed H. C. Belfield, an administrator who, like Maxwell, had experience in the Malay States, to investigate the workings of the Concessions Ordinance. This was occasioned partly by the Government's difficulties in introducing a Forest Ordinance to creat protected forest areas. All the influence of the Gold Coast ARPS was paraded to protest against this legislation, which it treated as yet another attack on African ownership (Kimble, 1963: chapter 10). The terms of reference given to Belfield did not, however, suggest that the Colonial Office was moving to unqualified opposition to European concessions[44], and his report in 1912 continued to affirm their merits. Belfield, at least, still accepted that a capitalist sector could play a positive and exemplary role and he gave no hint of a potential incompatibility between this and peasant production.

> The permanent cultivation of land on scientific lines and under European supervision seems to have made little or no headway in the Colony, but should the time arrive when the planter acquires and develops the land, it seems clear that his example will prove at least equally valuable to the native, who will have the opportunity of studying the method of preparing the soil, of planting the trees and of treating the crop for the market. The average native of the Colony cannot be credited with energy, or any real desire to improve his position by personal exertion, but the success which is attending the introduction of the cocoa industry seems to indicate that he will follow an example which holds out the prospect of profit, and may be expected to take an interest in any agricultural project if assured it will

pay. On the whole therefore, it is reasonable to assume that the presence of European industries in their midst is conducive to the material advantages of the people.[45]

The fact that the cocoa industry had developed without European assistance, whether public or private, escaped Belfield's attention. According to him, Ashanti chiefs shared his commitment to European concessions and were, if anything, disturbed by the relatively low rate of investment in their part of the Gold Coast:

> . . . the chiefs have expressed to me their distress at the lack of European enterprise in their territories, and have emphasised that the white man shall come in and open up their territory, explaining that it is only by means of his presence and example that they and their people can become more prosperous.[46]

The conviction that capitalist agriculture could play an exemplary role was apparently still shared by colonial officials who contributed evidence. Some pursued the argument to its logical conclusion, and belittled mining investment as offering no useful lesson to the African smallholder[47]. Sales of agricultural lands to Europeans were still seen as uncontroversial; if in conflict with African production, this would only be in some far distant future when aspiring African capitalists might resent the granting of 99-year leases to Europeans. The main recommendations of the Belfield Report were directed at the problem of speculation. It proposed that further area restrictions be introduced, not because concessions were innately undesirable, but rather so as to prevent monopolization by speculators. Conditions should be introduced to force investors to work their land or else forfeit their concessionary rights.[48].

The campaign for a new land policy continued. The mounting evidence of contraventions to the 1900 Ordinance had its effect[49], and the Colonial Office set aside the Belfield Report and established the West African Lands Committee (WALC) to consider the more fundamental issues. Morel and Wedgwood were invited to join this Committee[50], and under their influence it tackled not only the question of land sales to Europeans but also their especial concern, the relative advantages of communal versus individual land tenure.

The evidence presented established for the first time the extent to which land had been commercialized, particularly in the Gold Coast colony. Migration of Africans from one area to another was now a normal feature of life. Conventions had evolved in response to this, though in most cases they took the form of demands for rent or tribute rather than freehold sales of land. In some parts of Nigeria selling land to a stranger was still considered sufficient ground for deposition of a chief[51]. But a number of African representatives made their case for a clear recognition of private property in land. Some, like Mate Kole of Eastern Krobo, asserted that it was already well established and now 'an appreciable factor in the social life of the Gold Coast'[52]. Others, like Chief Adedeji of

Ilesha, regretted its absence and appealed to the Governmnent 'to recognise individual ownership of land in the country'[53]. Colonial officials were, as ever, divided in their evidence. One from the Gold Coast believed that 'there are many thousands of acres and thousands of pounds changing hands every year'[54], while the Governor maintained that individual ownership was still far off[55]. But all admitted that communal land tenure had been transformed by the development of permanent crops and the creation of a land market between European companies and African occupants. In all the voluminous evidence submitted to the Committee, the only group which consistently denied cause for concern was the Gold Coast ARPS. Casely Hayford, their chief representative, expressed what Committee members viewed as a suspicious complacency. He suggested that chiefs could comfortably sell up to half their stool land without ill effect, and reminded the Committee that many Africans – particularly those descended from slaves – were already working for wages[56]. He refused to acknowledge that there could be serious conflicts between chiefs and commoners, since the people could always destool a chief who offended them[57]. In contrast to the early years, it was now the ARPS who represented the 'progressive' force in British West Africa, pushing for private property in land as the historically proven basis for development. All the arguments for tradition came from the colonizers.

Morel and his supporters expressed their anxieties in a draft report[58] submitted in 1916. It was not destined to be adopted by the full Committee, but its contents were nevertheless highly instructive. Commercialization of land was a danger because (1) it tempted chiefs to use their traditional control over land to their own private advantage, and thereby undermined community confidence in them; (2) it led to land litigation and expensive court proceedings between chiefs with competing claims; and (3) it promoted migration of workers for European companies, and farmers for more fertile land, and thus drew Africans away from the authorities to whom they were traditionally subject. Essentially, the fear was that commercialization of land would destroy the authority of the chiefs through whom the colonies were controlled. The greed of the chiefs would bring them into disrepute and weaken their powers. In the Gold Coast Colony, the land market had plunged many parts of the country into debt. More disastrously still, it had led the chiefs

> . . . to set aside 'those rules and regulations of native tenure' which constitute the cement which holds native society together and to undermine the native system of government through the chiefs, which as we have seen, is the only way in which a country like the Gold Coast can be efficiently governed.[59]

The tendencies towards migration further weakened this cement. European concessions demanded a 'system of hired labour by natives not members of the community'[60]. The immigrants would fall outside the network of native authority and in the absence of a modern state, lawlessness would follow. Private property, in this argument, was incompatible with political order.

The authors of the draft report were prepared to consider alternatives to peasant smallholdings. They could wax enthusiastic over the development of large plantations by the chiefs, even when these employed some form of wage labour, but only because they considered such developments consistent with the chiefs' traditional powers. The establishment of wage labour, the report implied, was acceptable as long as it was mediated through the pre-capitalist relations of dependency. Free wage labour was disruptive, what was effectively semi-compulsory labour was preferred as a reinforcement of native authorities. Thus plantation development by 'progressive chiefs' was paradoxically employed to defend the vitality of the 'native system of tenure', and to strengthen the case against the dissolution of communal tenure[61].

In the deliberations of the WALC, the principles of the West African Policy took shape. It meant a sharp break with previous assumptions, a reassessment of the place for European concessions, and a rejection of private property in land as the basis for progress. The shift remained, however, largely at the level of intent, and barely influenced practice. It did involve significant changes in the terms of reference used to evaluate the future of the colonies, but required no dramatic reversal of legislation since the more radical dreams of earlier years had not been realized in law. The appearance of continuity was further sustained by capital's consistent indifference to plantation developments. With the one notable exception of Lever's efforts to transform the palm oil industry (see Chapter 5), lack of profitability alone kept capital out (Hopkins, 1973:212–14). There was no need for the state to make new laws to curb sales to concessionary companies when these companies showed little interest in West Africa. Changing attitudes to communal land tenure were similarly muted, particularly as even those converted by Morel's advocacy to the 'native system of tenure' found his proposals for legislation politically impossible.

The draft report of the WALC recommended sweeping state intervention to halt the transition to individual tenure. Except for certain urban areas where development was too advanced for reversal, it recommended state control of the land market. Governors should be able to enforce communal tenure, even against the wishes of the traditional rulers, by preventing the sale and mortgaging of land between Africans. In addition, they should impose far more radical restrictions on the sale of land to Europeans, with maximum concessions of one square mile.

But faced with the organized opposition of such groups as the Gold Coast ARPS, colonial governors could not implement such proposals. Clifford, Governor of the Gold Coast in 1914, considered such proposals political suicide. It

. . . would be regarded by the native population as a blow aimed at their inalienable rights in the lands, and as a direct breach of faith on the part of the Government. The loss of prestige which the Government would suffer were this action to be taken would be fatal to the efficiency of our administration, and would destroy the at present growing confidence of the chiefs and people in the bona fides of the Government.[62]

However prescient the report might be in its predictions for the future of unrestrained commercialization, it was impossibly naive in its prescriptions for saving the political order. Colonial governments could not use legislation to control the land market. They could not freeze commodity production at that ideal point where private property and traditional authority would remain in equilibrium. In the Gold Coast at least, attempts to intervene against private property would provoke a more immediate political crisis than that which they aimed to avoid. The draft report was not confirmed by the entire Committee, and its proposals sank virtually without trace in the course of the First World War. Many of its ideas lingered on to be incorporated into subsequent visions of the West African path, but its specific recommendations were not implemented. In this way, the shift in policy assumptions never found explicit expression in a new strategy for British West Africa.

It is not therefore surprising that few commentators have remarked on the contrast between policy in the first decades and policy as it developed in the inter war years. British West Africa could be presented as a model of enlightened colonial policy, where pre-colonial institutions were cherished, where agricultural expansion was based in the activities of independent peasants, and where colonial administrators worked to protect these Africans from the destructive influences of capitalist companies and modern 'individualism'. The past could be rewritten to provide a perfect continuum.

The continuity was little more than a cloak for inactivity. Old dreams of a radical rupture had died; new fears of political disorder had been voiced. But in neither phase could the colonial government act on its intuitions. The makeshift nature of the colonial settlement was already becoming apparent. The colonial states lacked the power to carry through their first visions of progress. They could not impose conditions which would create free labour without destroying communal land tenure, and they could not destroy communal tenure without weakening the chiefs on whom they relied in the interim for forced labour and political order. The fragility of their control made them dependent on pre-capitalist relations and thwarted their early attempts to impose the bourgeois order. Fortunately, the reluctance of capital to engage in direct investment and the discovery of the alternative of peasant production allowed them to retreat with honour from the task of transformation. They could even romanticize their failure into a success, and point to their policies as a model of colonial responsibility.

But the new model worked better in theory than in practice. Peasant production refused to conform to expectations. The peasants kept threatening to turn themselves into capitalist farmers, asserting private rights over their land, getting into debt, and challenging the authority of the chiefs. And the problems of political order which had prevented the colonial states from pursuing their own more radical schemes now prevented them from adopting the measures proposed to pre-empt this disintegration. Moreover, capital was not universally satisfied with the new model, and in the palm oil industry a major confrontation was brewing.

NOTES

1 In 1897, the C.O. published its first collection of correspondence over land concessions in the Gold Coast, covering the preceding decade. Over the next few years the correspondence grew in volume, and it provides clear testimony to the interest of private capital in the Gold Coast. See *Correspondence Relating to Land Grants and Concessions in the Gold Coast Protectorate*, African West 513, 1897; *Further Correspondence (January 1897–December 1898) Relating to Land Concessions and Railways on the Gold Coast*, African West 531, 1899; *Further Correspondence (December 1898–December 1900) Relating to Land Concessions and Regulations*, African West 578, 1900; *Further Correspondence Relating to Concessions and Railways, Gold Coast 1901*, African West 652, 1902; *Correspondence (November 1909–September 1911) Relating to Concessions and the Alienation of Native Lands on the Gold Coast*, African West 977, 1911.

2 Governor to Secretary of State, 25 June 1889, African West 513, 1897.

3 The Acting Governor finally acknowledged, 'Buried treasure, and Prempe's problematical reserve of gold dust must, I submit, not be regarded as probable assets to this Government'. Alternative sources of revenue would have to be pursued. Acting Governor to Secretary of State, 14 May 1896, *Further Correspondence Relative to Affairs in Ashanti*. African West 504, 1896. The Acting Governor suggested that the alternative might be simply to take over the mines which belonged to the Ashanti rulers, and claim a monthly share of the proceeds from the Africans who would continue to work them. The C.O. made no response to this suggestion.

4 Governor to Secretary of State, 27 June 1895, CO 87/149.

5 See the comments by the Chief Justice, 7 April 1891, who doubted the wisdom of a measure which would weaken the power and dignity of the chiefs, and simultaneously create hostility to the Government. African West 513, 1897.

6 Memorandum by Brandford Griffith, 21 January 1892, African West 513, 1897.

7 ibid.

8 Governor to Secretary of State, 28 September 1896, African West 513, 1897.

9 Governor to Secretary of State, 9 May 1895, African West 513, 1897.

10 Governor to Secretary of State, 15 July 1897, African West 531, 1899.

11 Secretary of State to Governor, 28 August 1895, CO 87/149.

12 Governor to Secretary of State, 8 February 1897, CO 87/153.

13 Governor to Secretary of State, 28 July 1897, African West 531, 1899.

14 See especially African West 531, 1899; African West 578, 1900; African West 652, 1902.

15 For details of the proposed legislation and opposition to it, see African West 531, 1899.

16 Governor to Secretary of State, 11 March 1897, African West 531, 1899.

17 Chamberlain at meeting with Gold Coast traders, 28 March 1899, African West 578, 1900.

18 James Irwine to C.O., 5 April 1899, African West 578, 1900.

19 The colonial state was prepared for example, to use considerable powers of persuasion to aid the prospecting mining companies. In 1898, the Colonial Secretary sent a sharp warning to King Amoaka Atta II of Akim, who had – with some justification – objected to the activities of the Gold Exploration Syndicate Ltd which was prospecting for gold inside the town boundaries: 'It is only by assisting the miners and prospectors in your country in every way that it will be possible to ascertain whether gold exists in your country in sufficient quantity to render it worth while for the Syndicate to spend money in getting it. You must therefore assist the Company . . . This is the Acting Governor's Order and he hopes to hear nothing more about opposition on your part.' Enclosure in Acting Governor to Secretary of State, 12 February 1898, African West 531, 1899. In a similar incident in 1899, the Resident in Kumasi wrote to the Chief of Ekwanta: 'I am sorry to hear from Captain Campbell that you and your people are not showing him all the workings in your district. This is to tell you once again I want you to give him every assistance, and show him everything in the way of mines that are in your district. You are to keep nothing back but tell him everything, or I shall be very displeased with your conduct.' Resident to Chief of Ekwanta, 6 March 1899, African West 578, 1900.

20 The full quote is as follows: 'I do not consider the time is yet ripe for concessions to be granted in the Protectorate, more especially in the Bini country. The applicants as a rule have no intention of investing their capital in the country. What they would probably do would be to work their concessions with great energy so as to get as much out of it in the shortest possible time, and having drained these resources to seek concessions elsewhere, which means that in a few years the Natives of the Protectorate, instead of having benefitted by the Government granting such concessions, would be left with their country very much poorer in certain products. I am personally in favour of development by the Natives themselves, by which means the country's capital is best retained in the country.' Acting Commissioner, Niger Coast Protectorate, to F.O., 28 July 1898, passed on to the C.O. for information 15 September 1898, African West 531, 1899.

21 Wedgwood was originally a member of the Liberal Party, but later became a Labour MP. As President of the English League for the Taxation of Land Values, he was to become the main British advocate of the theories of Henry George, and wrote a pamphlet on *Henry George for Socialists*, published by the ILP in 1908.

22 George's main work was *Progress and Plenty*, first published in 1881. His ideas were taken up by many who shared the socialist antagonism to contemporary society but resisted the conclusion of a necessary class conflict between capital and labour. In the late nineteenth century, the debate between socialists and 'single-taxers' achieved some prominence, and Wedgwood's pamphlet was a contribution to this debate. George himself toured Britain in the 1880s, and

debated publicly with H. M. Hyndman of the Social Democratic Federation. His ideas were sufficiently prominent in America for Engels to devote the preface of the 1887 American edition of *Condition of the Working Class in England* to a critique of his work.

23 See African West 977, 1911, for various C.O. comments on letters from Morel, calling for public lands legislation. When in 1910 a District Commissioner produced a memorandum warning of the growing commercialization of land in the Gold Coast, a C.O. official commented: 'If Sir William Maxwell's Bill vesting all Waste and Forest Lands in the Crown had been carried all would have been well' – a comment which revealed considerable misconceptions of the objectives of Maxwell's legislation. Eliot to C.O., 6 July 1910. CO 96/504.

24 See Hayford (1971). *The Times* published a letter on 6 June 1912, signed by E. D. Morel, Noel Buxton, J. Ramsey Macdonald, Philip Lorrell, Sir Albert Spiver and J. Wedgwood, which called for a Lands Act which could 'secure the threefold aim of legalising the rights of the natives to the occupancy and use of the soil, preventing the creation of monopolies in the soil's produce, whether natural or cultivated, and reserving the value of the land and freedom of access to it, for the future generations of our protected subjects'. The Gold Coast Aborigines Rights Protection Society responded in a letter to the *Times*, 18 July 1912, and attacked the proposed legislation as yet another attempt to deprive the people of their ownership of the land.

25 In reporting the emergence of an African opposition, Maxwell claimed that there was 'not the smallest reason for apprehending any disturbance of any kind', and commented, 'I have remarked that such opposition as there is has originated in the places where the native middlemen who negotiate concessions for English speculators carry on their business'. Governor to Secretary of State, 1 July 1897, African West 531, 1899.

26 In *The Truth About the West African Land Question* (1971) J. Casely Hayford of the ARPS quoted approvingly Sir William Geary's statement that the arguments in favour of land nationalization

> 'are twofold, i.e. that by nationalising the land the introduction of freehold individual tenure, which has already shown a tendency to creep in, is prevented, and the alleged communal system preserved; and secondly, the chiefs are stopped from improvidently alienating the tribal lands . . .
>
> Why should not individual ownership come in Northern Nigeria, as it has come in elsewhere? Politically a peasant proprietorship owning security of tenure to the British Government seems a valuable asset. Economically, to forbid by law the individual African ever becoming the owner of the land he occupies, removes the strongest inducement to thrift, good farming, and development of the country . . .
>
> The second argument is that by improvident alienation to Europeans, the tribe will be deprived of their land and reduced – the phrase is Mr. Morel's – to a landless native proletariat. Even assuming this to be either true in the present or a risk in the future, this is no reason for interfering with native land tenure and dealings between natives.' (p. 130)

27 Governor to Secretary of State, 24 September 1901, African West 652, 1902.

28 Governor to Cape Coast Chamber of Commerce, 20 September 1901, African West 652, 1902.

29　The Stamp Commissioner gave numerous examples of dubious concessions: 'I heard of a case a few months ago where a few "bookmakers" in England had purchased a "Gold Mine" and sent one of their number out to look at it. When the latter arrived he could not find the property. I was informed that the property did not exist. I saw the man myself and know that he went home very soon after he arrived; but I was under the impression, at the time, that he had found what *should* have been his property but that it had been sold so many times before that he thought it better to let the other parties fight out the title; he and his partners looked upon their speculation in the light of putting their money on the wrong horse, and retired from Gold Mining on the West Coast, and resumed their more lucrative employment of "laying odds" at home.' Enclosure 1 in Governor to Secretary of State, 24 September 1901, African West 652, 1902.

30　*West African Lands Committee: Correspondence and Papers laid before the Committee*, African West 1048, 1916:103.

31　Originally, the West African Governments agreed to pay the wages of the Association's cotton experts who would be sent out to West Africa. By 1904, this had become a general financial contribution: £1,500 a year from Sierra Leone; £2,000 from Lagos, £3,000 from Southern Nigeria. The Association agreed in return to spend £30,000 within three years in developing the experimental plantations set up in each of the three colonies, and to purchase all cotton offered by Africans at a minimum price of a penny (1d) a pound. By 1907, Sierra Leone and the Gambia had dropped out, and the remaining administrations contributed sums varying from £1,000 to £5,000 on condition that they were matched by the Association's contributions. By 1909, the colonial states preferred to take over the experimental/instructional work on the small plantations, and possibly to subsidize the ginneries and buying centres. For a summary of the relationship between the Association and the colonial states, see C.O. minute on BCGA to C.O. 5 November 1909, *Further Correspondence Relating to Botanical and Forestry Matters*, African 953, 1912.

32　BCGA to WALC, q. 9424, *West African Lands Committee: Minutes of Evidence*, African West 1047, 1916.

33　See for example W. S. Churchill, Memorandum on the Northern Nigeria Railway, 18 July 1907, *Further Correspondence Relating to Railway Construction in Nigeria*, African West 845, 1908.

34　The first agreement between the BCGA and the E. Africa Protectorate was made in 1907. From 1911 onwards, developments in Uganda came to dominate the correspondence between the BCGA and C.O., African West 953, 1911.

35　Cadbury Brothers were attacked in an article in the *Standard*, a Conservative newspaper which was delighted with this opportunity to undermine the pretensions of the Liberal Cadbury. Cadbury Brothers sued the *Standard* for libel and won. See Cadbury Paper 1(1–8), University of Birmingham Library; and Southall, 1975: chapter 2.

36　Cadbury Brothers were in fact encouraged by the Gold Coast Government to set up a small 'model' plantation as an example to African farmers, but the venture failed. Subsequently, they prided themselves on their resistance to approaches from land speculators with offers of cheap land for plantations. See W. A. Cadbury to WALC, q. 10669–10682, African West 1047, 1916. The BCGA had considered plantation development on a larger scale than required by the proclaimed objectives of experimentations, and defended this on the basis that costs for a 10,000 acre plantation were comparable to those for 500 acres. However, the Association soon dropped the plans for plantations. BCGA to C. O. 30 March 1904, *Correspondence (1902–1905) Relating to Cotton-Growing in West Africa*, African West 745, 1906.

37 W. A. Cadbury to WALC, q. 10682, African West 1047, 1916.

38 H. L. Galway, 22 July 1912, African West 1048, 1916.

39 E. C. Eliot to C.O., 6 July 1910, CO 96/504.

40 ibid.

41 William Cadbury financed Morel's tour of West Africa in 1910, and offered to pay a generous annuity if he entered Parliament to campaign for his ideas. (Nworah, 1966:79.)

42 W. H. Himbury to WALC, q. 9537, African West 1047,1916.

43 For example, Sir P. Girouard's *Memorandum on Land Tenure, 1907, Northern Nigeria Lands Committee: Minutes of Evidence and Appendices*, Cd. 5103, London 1910, where he argues that the 'practically unearned increment' from land sales should go to the Government – 'the legitimate and best trustee for the people in their dealings with aliens' – through land nationalization.

44 Belfield was asked to consider:

'How far the alienation of native lands to Europeans which is going on in the Gold Coast threatens – having regard to the probable increase of population – to deprive the natives of adequate land for their subsistence? Whether such alienation is beneficial to the natives by acquainting them with new and improved industries or enabling them to earn higher wages?

Whether the present system under which the alienation of native land is controlled only by the High Court is satisfactory, or whether the control should be transferred to the Executive Government?

Whether in practice, the condition of the Concessions Court that the proper parties must be shown to have agreed to the grant is fulfilled, or whether the chiefs alienate land without consulting the tribe as a whole?

Whether the consideration paid for the concession is actually adequate; and if not, whether it would be possible to lay down any general standard of adequacy?

Whether the consideration received is spent by the chiefs in the general interest of the tribe, and if not, whether any, and what, steps can be taken to secure this object?

Whether it is possible to take any better measures to secure better development of the lands granted, and to prevent them being mere counters for company promoters?' C.O. to H. C. Belfield, 12 September 1911, African West 977, 1911.

45 *Report on the Legislation Governing the Alienation of Native Lands in the Gold Coast Colony and Ashanti*, Cd. 6278, London 1912:13.

46 ibid., p. 14.

47 For example Francis Dove, a lawyer resident in the Colony since 1897, said, 'I do not think that the natives in this part of the Colony are much inclined to engage in mining work. They are primarily interested in agriculture, and they would reap more benefit from the example set by European planters than from the operations of a mining company', ibid. p. 50. H. C. W. Grimshaw, Acting Provincial Commissioner for the Western Province was even more dismissive: 'I think the mining industries are of very little advantage to the people, it is true that they afford opportunity of earning higher wages, but mining does not appeal to the natives', ibid., p. 63.

48 Belfield recommended that existing restrictions be reduced from 5 square miles to one for a mining concession, and from 20 square miles to two for an agricultural concession. Mining companies should begin operations within two years, or forfeit their concessions, while agricultural companies should begin work within a year and within five years should have 25% of the land under cultivation. The restrictions suggested meant a radical reduction, but the rationale as presented in the report was not to prevent concessions, but rather to scare off speculators.

49 The campaign reached its height in 1912 with the publication of a letter to the *Times*, 6 June 1912, signed by E. D. Morel, J. Wedgwood, Ramsey Macdonald and others.

50 The Committee was chaired by Sir Kenelm Digby, and included Sir F. M. Hodgson, Sir W. Taylor, J. C. Wedgwood, E. D. Morel, C. Strachey, W. D. Ellis, R. E. Stubbs and, later, Sir W. Napier.

51 Osho Eremese (of Ife) to WALC, q. 13470–13473, African West 1047, 1916.

52 Quoted in W. D. Ellis, Memorandum on evidence as to the existence and origin of private property in land on the Gold Coast, African West 1048, 1916:299.

53 Chief Adedeji (of Ilesha) to WALC, q. 13275, African West 1047, 1916.

54 W. H. Grey to WALC, q. 5345, African West 1047, 1916.

55 J. J. Thorburn to WALC, 22 July 1912, African West 1047, 1916.

56 Hayford to WALC, q. 677–690, African West 1047, 1916.

57 'Our people are so strongly attached to their customs that they would at once punish any attempt on the part of any chief to depart from them. Therefore there is no fear of any permanent danger at all. Two or three chiefs, as I have said, who have attempted to do things differently from native law have been actually destooled.' Hayford to WALC, q. 823, African West 1047, 1916.

58 *West African Lands Committee: Draft Report*, African West 1046, 1916.

59 ibid., p. 101.

60 ibid., p. 81.

61 'The results arrived at in the Krobo country . . . show that under an enlightened and progressive chief and with an industrious population some of the best results hitherto reached can be obtained.' (Comment on the cultivation of palm trees by Mate Kole in Eastern Krobo.) ibid., p. 87.

62 This was Clifford's response to a C. O. suggestion for emergency legislation to control land sales in the interim of the deliberations of the WALC. African West 1048, 1916:131.

5

Peasants versus Plantations: Cocoa and Palm Oil

It has been argued (Hopkins, 1973: 212–14) that the peasant road was more viable than the plantation alternative, and that whatever the reasons behind its adoption, subsequent events confirmed the rationality of the choice. Peasants enjoyed superior knowledge of tropical conditions, and this, combined with their lower overheads and lower labour costs, gave them a clear advantage over expatriate plantations. Moreover, as the representative from the BCGA argued in 1907, peasants would be prepared to work for rewards which wage labourers would dismiss as inadequate, a point which was reaffirmed in the 1920s, when the colonial governments had to make their case against plantation developments. Sir Hugh Clifford, Governor of Nigeria from 1919–25, produced in 1920 the following arguments for peasant production:

> . . . agricultural industries in tropical countries which are mainly, or exclusively, in the hands of the native peasantry:-
> (a) Have a firmer root than similar enterprises when owned and managed by Europeans, because they are natural growths, not artificial creations, and are self-supporting as regards labour, while European plantations can only be maintained by some system of organised immigration or by some form of compulsory labour;
> (b) Are incomparably the cheapest instrument for the production of agricultural produce on a large scale that have yet been devised; and
> (c) Are capable of a rapidity of expansion and a progressive increase of output that beggar every record of the past, and are altogether unparalleled in all the long history of European agricultural enterprises in the Tropics.[1]

Clifford's main argument was that no wage labour existed for plantation agriculture. He understood only too well the inadequacy of the labour market, and correctly perceived that European investment would involve forced labour. He claimed, however, that an acceptance of the peasant alternative was defensible on its own terms, and that the social and political constraints which had dictated the choice of the peasant road were reinforced by strictly economic considerations. There was in this

view no conflict between economic and political concerns: peasant production was the safest alternative for political reasons, but also the
cheapest and most productive.

What such arguments ignored was the key question of control. With
independent smallholders confirmed as the basis of agricultural development, neither state nor capital could dictate the conditions of production.
In the palm oil industry which, from the end of the First World War,
faced increasing competition from plantations in the Dutch East Indies,
the independence of peasants was to prevent measures widely favoured as
means to increased agricultural productivity. And even in the apparently
successful Gold Coast cocoa industry, peasant resistance to what were
considered improved techniques was a source of much anxiety. Though
the weight of colonial opinion was placed behind the peasant option, the
result was largely a makeshift. Neither palm oil nor cocoa production
collapsed, but both presented problems which could not be resolved by
colonial officials. This chapter examines these two key sectors as
exemplifications of the obstacles which peasant production presented to
the development of agricultural productivity.

1. Peasants refuse to comply: the case of cocoa

As has been indicated in the previous chapter, the vitality of the Gold
Coast cocoa industry was cited as the ultimate argument in favour of
peasants. From nothing to the world's largest exporter in less than twenty
years: if peasants could achieve this, why bother with the political and
economic risks of plantation production? This argument carried less
weight, however, with those directly concerned with the cocoa industry,
and from the first years of its success colonial administrators attacked it
for inefficiency and poor quality control. The Gold Coast producers were
regarded as 'natives in a most elementary state of civilisation' and not
'sufficiently intelligent to accept European methods'. Their sole aim
appeared to be 'the attainment of a maximum amount of money with a
minimum expenditure of energy'[2]. Under these circumstances, it was
feared the success of cocoa would be short-lived and the industry would
destroy itself in a combination of negligent cultivation, unchecked disease, and inadequate drying methods.

The dangers threatening the cocoa industry became a major topic
under pressure from W. S. Tudhope, Director of Agriculture in the Gold
Coast. 'I live in constant dread', he declared in 1915, 'of disaster
overtaking the industry through the careless or negligent practices
employed by the natives, and I have constantly advocated an increase in
the European staff of my Department and legislation to control these
anomalies'[3]. The main concern was that African farmers took few precau-
tions to counteract disease among their cocoa trees, and Tudhope's
anxieties were shared by the Director of the Botanic Gardens in
Kew:

Under existing circumstances the spread of blights is so marked and so progressive that it becomes every day more difficult to deal with their ravages, and if the Cacao (sic) industry in the Gold Coast is to escape a fate comparable with that which befell the Coffee industry in Ceylon, steps must be taken without delay . . .[4]

The output from Gold Coast cocoa farms was constantly compared with that from the West Indies or the African island of São Tomé, and the differences were implicitly attributed to the peasant relations of production in the Gold Coast:

. . . in making such a comparison it is necessary to take into consideration the facts that whereas the producers of the West Indian cocoa are either Europeans, of European extraction, or are sufficiently intelligent to accept European methods, the producers of cocoa in this Colony and Ashanti are natives in a most elementary state of civilisation, whose sole aim, as yet, appears to be the attainment of a maximum amount of money with a minimum expenditure of energy – however uneconomical the system, and whose lack of foresight for the future welfare of the industry – and consequently for themselves – has not yet been compensated by adequate legislative measures.[5]

The Acting Director of Agriculture, who made this comparison, went on to indicate that coercion might be the only solution:

It might be a fairer comparison to take São Tomé which produces a much higher standard cocoa than the Gold Coast with practically the same labour, but there decided methods of coercion obtain under European control.[6]

Under existing relations of production, it was not possible to dictate the methods adopted by cocoa farmers, or to impose standardization on the crop. Even Clifford, a strong advocate of peasant production, said in 1916:

. . . owing to the fact that the cocoa industry of this Colony and Ashanti is in the hands of small peasant proprietors, *a large quantity of cocoa of a uniform grade* is precisely the article which the local farmer cannot produce.[7]

Under peasant relations of production, government coercion seemed the only way to impose changes. Direct control of production was ruled out in peasant farming. Market incentives were never a real possibility when the buying firms refused to offer higher prices for better quality cocoa. The success of the industry seemed to depend on securing the assistance of local chiefs, who could then serve as agents of modernization. As far back as 1883, the Gold Coast Government approved the introduction of by-laws as a means of enforcing improvements[8]. Chiefs thereby had the powers to fine 'inefficient' producers who failed to keep their farms in order or allowed disease to spread unchecked. Further by-laws introduced in 1910 permitted fines of up to £5 for farmers who failed to report disease, or who abandoned their farms without action. These by-laws, officials complained, were 'universally adopted, but rarely enforced'.

> . . . their Chiefs, though readily acquiescing in the promulgation of the by-laws necessary to obviate such spread [of disease], almost universally refrain from enforcing them.[9]

At least one colonial official dealt with this by the 'rather rough and ready remedy'[10] of simply 'instructing' chiefs to fine offenders, a practice which was condemned in 1913 by the Commissioner of his Province. 'If it were possible I should like to see Agricultural Officers have nothing to do with prosecutions and the enforcement of penalties, otherwise the farmers will be disinclined to consult them or show them their farms.'[11] Tudhope was more sympathetic to the use of coercion and doubted the efficacy of 'friendly persuasion'[12]. His persistence came close to reward in 1916, when a Bill was drafted which would have given the Government power to impose fines of up to £50 on recalcitrant farmers. The Government would have the power to declare Infected Areas, within which the government inspectors would have free access and the right to dictate remedial measures. Failure to comply would mean massive fines or six months' imprisonment[13]. In the end the bill was not implemented, partly because so many Paramount Chiefs resented this threat to their authority, but more because it was no solution when virtually all farmers were potential offenders. Full implementation would have devastated cocoa production.

In the following year, Tudhope was asked to set up an enquiry into the industry, and predictably used this opportunity to press for stronger coercive measures. His reports are revealing, since they indicate that the problem was not so much the backwardness of peasants as the too successful introduction of capitalist relations. It was, in his view, precisely the failure of farmers to remain simple peasants that was plunging the industry into potential crisis. Greed was encouraging Africans to extend their farms beyond what the individual family could maintain; hence the tendency to abandon farms in the face of disease. 'It is generally found', he claimed, 'that each farmer has several distinctly separate plantations. This is invariably due to greed'[14]. Cocoa farming was no longer a purely peasant affair. Farmers had more than one farm, employed wage labour, bought and sold land as private property, and borrowed money at 50 per cent interest. The size of farms was hard to estimate, but annual loads (a load was sixty lb) varied from 10–2,000 – a clear indication of the emergence of capitalist farming[15]. Thus in the model sector for the West African Policy, 'peasants' were few and far between, and Tudhope's main recommendation was a restriction of cocoa planting so as to reimpose the ideal of

> . . . moderately sized plantations which can be maintained for the most part by the individual peasant proprietor with his own labour and that of his family.[16]

A Committee set up in 1919 to consider his proposals found them 'eminently undesirable' in their advocacy of direct state intervention [17]. As always, the colonial state was unable to introduce sufficiently stringent measures to prevent the anticipated dangers. The cocoa industry had produced unexpected deviations from the desired model, but it was impossible to act forcibly against it. The Committee's recommendations were more restrained. It suggested further use of fines, buying centres to assist standardization, licensing of buyers to control purchases of inferior cocoa, and police inspection of weights and measures. Tudhope's more far-reaching proposals were never seriously considered.

Concern about the cocoa industry re-emerged in the mid-1920s, when numerous shipments of Gold Coast cocoa were turned away by American customs officials as unacceptable. A further enquiry recommended grading certification but held back from making this compulsory, partly because it correctly assumed that buying firms would not pay a premium for higher quality cocoa. The only legislation which was introduced was the Cocoa Industry Regulation Ordinance (1934) which established minimum standards and mechanisms for government inspection, but its impact was undermined by this refusal of firms to pay a differential which reflected the new government grades[18]. In this campaign to control the cocoa industry, the state had few allies, since neither chiefs nor private firms were prepared to aid its efforts.

Colonial dissatisfaction with the peasantry shifted uneasily between attacks on peasant backwardness and complaints of the all too civilized behaviour of profit-maximizing cocoa farmers. The small size of plantations (in the 1930s still on average only four acres) discouraged improvements in cultivation and fermentation. But at the same time the success of the industry had dissolved the 'peasants' into a complex of money-lenders, absentee landlords, independent smallholders and migrant labourers. The 1931 Census confirmed Tudhope's early report on conditions in the Gold Coast cocoa industry: the proportion of the crop produced by smallholders was decreasing annually, some plantation owners were reported as paying as much as £400 a year in wages, and the vice of absentee landlordism had arrived on the scene. The Census Officer favoured the small peasant, and warned that:

> . . . the Gold Coast peasant-farmer, if he is to survive, must remember and be taught always to remember that the crops which produce small but certain profits are those on which his existence depends, since they do not draw upon him the envious eye of the usurer or the greedy one of the capitalist. (Cardinall, 1931:99)

The only long-term solution which the colonial state could propose to this double problem of inefficient production and disintegrating social relations, was that of co-operatives. In the 1930s, co-operative fermentaries and co-operative marketing agencies were widely canvassed as the means to save peasant production. The co-operative movement was explicitly defended as an alternative to 'destructive individualism' and came to be regarded as the necessary corollary to peasant agriculture. In terms reminiscent of those employed in the draft report of the West African Lands Committee, co-operatives were presented as a bulwark against the dissolution of traditional restraints. Lord Lugard, in his introduction to C. F. Strickland's *Co-operatives for Africa* (1933) made the case thus:

> . . . there is . . . an increasingly large illiterate class which by pro-longed contact with alien races has learnt a new individualism without its necessary restraints, and a licence which strikes at the very root of communal sociology. Domestic ties are broken and replaced by less binding relations. The *deraciné* has learnt that as an individual he can earn money and spend it as he likes. In some Dependencies it is a rapidly growing class, especially in the larger cities, to which the unattached native drifts and where he is often compelled to incur debts from which he seeks relief by theft. In the solution of this problem the 'thrift' and 'better living' co-operative society may well afford invalu-able help. (Strickland, 1933:ix)

The same moralism was expressed in C. Y. Shephard's lengthy *Report on the Economics of Peasant Agriculture in the Gold Coast* (1936), where the co-operative was presented as the last haven for the rapidly disappearing good peasant.

> . . . a co-operative system affords the industrious, intelligent, thrifty, and business-like peasant an opportunity of escaping from the eco-nomic bondage imposed upon him by his weaker neighbours. It should be regarded as an organisation open to individuals of good character, and not as a reformatory for the correction of those of ill-repute. Sound moral character is the foundation and not the super-structure. The success of the society will depend upon a strict obser-vance of sound business principles.[19]

The co-operatives were not a resounding success. In 1936 after many years of encouragement, only 9,000 farmers, accounting for 2 per cent of the crop, had been persuaded to join co-operative marketing societies. All too often, the maintenance of these societies depended on extensive aid from agricultural officers in keeping the books, collecting the crop, carrying out sales to the merchant firms, and distributing the proceeds.[20] Co-operative fermentaries were set up from the late 1920s with the aim of improving the quality of the beans to that achieved under plantation production, and though the quality of beans was undoubtedly improved, these fermentaries again accounted for only a tiny proportion of the crop. The stumbling block was the resistance of the buying firms to the demand for a premium for improved quality. Despite enthusiastic encourage-ment, the co-operatives only controlled 2.8 per cent of the cocoa crop in 1937–8 (Hancock, 1942:227).

The Gold Coast cocoa industry survived, and the more nightmarish prophecies of total collapse were not fulfilled. But even in this supposed model of the peasant option, problems had arisen and remained unresolved. The thrifty, conscientious, yet unambitious peasant was more a colonial dream than a reality. Attempts by officials to transform conditions of cultivation and processing were usually blocked by unco-operative farmers, and the direct coercion which peasant production was supposed to avoid seemed the only way to impose desired standards. In this case, however, the relative ignorance of colonial experts and the absence of a coherent alternative in the form of plantation production muted the conflicts. The recommendations of the Agricultural Department were often ill-advised, and the supposed inadequacies of African production were never sufficiently proven to produce radical proposals for change. Moreoever, the cocoa-buying firms continued to distance themselves from the process of production and did not campaign for government interference in cocoa production. It was only in the palm oil industry that the West African Policy faced an explicit confrontation with an alternative model of development.

2. Plantations versus peasants: the case of palm oil

At the time of colonization, palm products made up half the total value of exports from British West Africa. Palm oil had long been a staple of domestic consumption and internal trade, and processing methods were established before colonial rule. The men collected palm fruits from wild palm trees, and the women boiled and pounded the pericarp of the fruit to produce palm oil. Any attempt to transform production and processing techniques necessitated a challenge to this division of labour, and as subsequent events demonstrated, it proved remarkably resistant to change. The development of the palm kernel industry however, was less problematic. Palm kernels had little value within West Africa, and it was only with the invention of margarine and the development of processing methods which made palm kernel oil an appropriate substance for this new commodity, that the kernels became a major export. The processing of kernel oil developed from the outset under the control of capitalist manufacturers, primarily in factories in Germany and Holland, and proved relatively simple. By contrast the processing of the pericarp to produce palm oil had to be done locally, since the oil turned rancid on the long journey to Europe, and any policy for new processing techniques involved direct confrontation with established African production. As in the case of cocoa, colonial officials were deeply distrustful of African methods, and in this sector a viable alternative to ineffective official propaganda offered itself.

The initiative came from William Lever, founder of the vast soap and margarine empire of Unilever and the only significant representative of the process Lenin considered characteristic of twentieth century imperialism: the transition from export of commodities to export of capital.

From the beginning of the century, Lever replaced his selling agencies with overseas factories, initially in Switzerland and subsequently in Germany, Australia, Canada and the United States of America. In 1904 he set up a factory in Belgium, in 1910 he expanded to France, in 1911 to South Africa, and by 1913 he had penetrated Japan (Wilson, 1954). Within these more developed countries, the internationalization of production allowed a new strategy of market expansion. By creating factories within what had previously been export markets, it was possible to evade high protectionist tariffs and simultaneously to appeal to patriotic consumers who could now buy goods produced in their own country[21]. Lever was not a British manufacturer seeking markets for British goods. He was the forerunner of the modern multinational corporation which recognizes no national boundaries[22].

In British West Africa, Lever had little patience with the strategy pursued by the chocolate manufacturers of leaving production under the control of African smallholders. He wanted plantation production for more efficient cultivation of palm fruits and mechanized processing under capitalist relations of production. In pursuit of this vision he came into direct conflict with other firms involved in West Africa, not yet prepared or able to compete on this grandiose scale, and he provoked major tensions within the West African Policy.

Lever Brothers first turned their attention to Sierra Leone, and submitted in 1907 a scheme embodying this vision for the future of the palm oil industry. A visit to the colony, where the company faced a noticeably lukewarm governor, persuaded it to revise the proposal into a less radical suggestion for power mills to process the palm fruits, with collection of the fruits left in the hands of independent Africans. This began a series of negotiations with the Colonial Office, as Lever Brothers pushed for this and similar proposals for Nigeria and the Gold Coast[23]. The company argued for extensive monopoly rights as a condition for the capital investment. It wanted exclusive rights for 99 years to the erection of processing equipment within a twenty mile radius of each mill, exclusive rights to the construction of railways to transport the produce, preferential rates on government railways, rent-free sites for the mills, and remission of import duties on materials for the construction of the mills[24].

It is hardly surprising that negotiations were protracted and indeed occasionally suspended. The Colonial Office faced the antagonism of Lever's competitors, if such preferential treatment were agreed. As Hopkins argues, 'Other expatriate traders who lacked either the capital or the inclination to enter production feared that their more adventurous rivals would be in a position to undercut them by a considerable margin and to establish a monopoly over the supply of export crops' (Hopkins, 1973:213). The Sierra Leone negotiations provoked a spate of anxious enquiries from firms operating in West Africa and from Chambers of Commerce in England. The Manchester Chamber of Commerce declared itself opposed to any form of monopoly rights within the colonies[25]. The African Oil Mills Company and Liverpool Chamber of Commerce were deeply hostile to encouragement of a *kernel* processing industry inside West Africa, when factories already existed in Britain and Europe. The antagonism was further overlaid by Tory Party criticisms of Lever as an active member of the Liberal Party, and suggestions that Lever was being offered favourable consideration because of his support for the Liberals (Nworah, 1972). These complaints centred on the issue of monopoly rights, and though the Colonial Office was prepared to reduce the scale of the concessions to Lever, legislation was nevertheless introduced. The Palm Oil Ordinance (1912) permitted monopoly rights within a radius of ten miles and for a period of twenty years. Kernel crushing mills were, as a result of complaints from other firms, excluded from the terms of the Ordinance[26].

The first serious experiment under the Ordinance of 1912 was the erection of a processing factory at Yonnibanna in Sierra Leone, which was made ready for production by 1914 [27]. The fruit was to be supplied by independent African collectors, and after protracted negotiations with local chiefs over the appropriate price to be paid operations began[28]. Lever himself considered this dependence on African suppliers a shaky basis for factory production, and expressed his reservations in 1912 in comments on the parallel enterprise established in the Belgian Congo:

> All this river fruit buying is in its infancy, but I do not think we can rely on it as a permanent supply of fruit. We can only depend on our own gathering and cultivation. The fact is the native has few wants: a little salt and a little cloth are his indispensables; after this, beads, brass rods and other luxuries. Chief Womba of Leverville can be taken as an example. Twelve months ago he and his people were poor and few in number, and were keen to bring fruit. After twelve months or less of selling fruit he is rich and lazy, has ten wives, and his village is about four times the size it was; but he gathers little or no fruit. The palm-tree is in these parts the banking account of this native, and he no more thinks of going to his bank for money when his wants and ambitions are supplied than a civilised man would. His bank is always open when he wants to draw on it. (Lever, 1927:173)

In Yonnibanna such fears were fully justified, though for more complex reasons than those given by Lever. As the company saw it, the problem in Sierra Leone was the irrationality of the Africans. All they seemed to understand was that processed oil sold at £4 a ton, while unprocessed fruit could earn only 30/- a ton, and they seemed incapable of calculating that they could earn more money if they concentrated all their energies on collection alone. The company failed to perceive that existing methods of oil production were deeply embedded in a specific sexual division of labour. The men collected the fruit and the women processed it. If the palm oil producers of Yonnibanna accepted the new division of labour proposed by the factory, it could only mean that the women joined the men in the work of gathering, or that the men did twice as much work as before. The patriarchal relations within West African households made either alternative unlikely. As a Provincial Commissioner commented in 1925,

> If all palm fruit were carried to a mill the women would escape their share of the work and I cannot imagine the Sierra Leone native taking kindly to a system whereby he did all the work and his wife none. The women whose other duties consist of looking after their children, cooking food and weeding the farm, would not be able to assist in the transport.[29]

For Yonnibanna to survive on the proposed basis, a fundamental rupture in existing social relations was required. Yet to effect this radical transformation, West Africa Oils Limited had at its disposal only market forces: the somewhat unconvincing lure of 30/- a ton for fruit against the previous £4 a ton for oil. Depending as it did on peasants for the supply of material to the factory, the Company could not dictate a restructuring of the division of labour. It did not have direct control of the labour process.

In this case, a happy symbiosis of capitalist and pre-capitalist relations was impossible. Within cocoa production, the defence of an African peasantry involved tensions, but at Yonnibanna the entire enterprise would fail if it could not effect the necessary transformation. Without a regular supply of fruit, the capital invested in the mill could not earn an adequate profit. The factory operated below capacity, and eventually was forced to close down in December 1915[30]. The conclusion which many drew from this first experiment was that fruit production must be directly controlled. Factory processing (which all concerned favoured) would be feasible only if the supply of raw materials was guaranteed, and this meant either plantation estates worked by wage labour, or the imposition of factory requirements on the independent producers by the employment of extra-economic coercion.

In 1915 a Parliamentary Committee was set up to investigate the future of the West African oil trade, though its particular emphasis was on ways of promoting a kernel-crushing industry within Britain[31]. The report of the Committee dodged the difficult questions raised by the failure of Yonnibanna, saying that the issue of supplies to factories inside West Africa would depend on land policies, still under discussion in the West African Lands Committee[32]. It did however inspire the Gold Coast Government to set up a research project on the oil palm industry, which under Colonial Office pressure became a joint project between the Gold Coast, Nigeria and Sierra Leone[33]. In 1921 a central laboratory was established in Nigeria to co-ordinate work on improving seeds, methods of cultivation and of processing. After several years, two hand presses were developed which could be used by African producers themselves to improve their output[34], and the promotion of these presses became a major feature of the Nigerian response to the crisis of the palm industry.

The sense of impending crisis was meanwhile intensified by the emergence of the 'Sumatran menace'. Before the First World War the foundations of a palm oil industry had been laid in the Dutch East Indies, particularly in Sumatra which could draw on the heavily populated island of Java for indentured labour, and which could develop production on the basis of plantations and factory processing. After the war, this expanded rapidly – 6,500 acres were under plantation in 1915, 28,000 acres by 1922, and 60,350 acres by 1925[35] – and it seemed that the combination of systematic cultivation with mechanical processing permitted an output of oil which far exceeded that obtained in the wild palmeries of West Africa. Estimates of the advantages varied, depending largely on whether the evidence was being used to urge a new policy for West Africa or to deprecate the seriousness of the threat. But the Gold Coast Deputy Director of Agriculture claimed that in Sumatra the factories could extract 30–31 per cent of the weight of the fruits in oil, while Nigerian palm fruits only *contained* 16–25 per cent oil, with only half of this extracted under existing techniques[36]. The early collapse of the West Africa rubber industry in the face of more scientific cultivation was employed as a grim warning for West African oil, unless new policies were adopted[37].

In the face of the new threat the commercial world closed ranks, and the Joint West African Committee of the London, Liverpool and Manchester Chambers of Commerce pressured the Colonial Office to set up a committee to investigate the dangers. In 1923 their request was granted and a committee established, with five representatives nominated by the Joint West African Committee. Its report, published in 1925, concluded in favour of factory processing, and outlined five conditions for success:

(1) freehold, or at least 99-year leasehold, land for the mill;
(2) protection for 21 years against competitors;
(3) plantations of up to 5,000 acres;
(4) facilities for legally binding contracts with Africans over supplies;
(5) exclusive rights to the use of mechanical transport for fruit within a seven mile radius of the mill.[38]

The crucial proposals were (3) and (4). The Committee was convinced, with good reason, that processing factories could not survive on the basis of supplies from independent African collectors. Private firms should have the right to set up plantations beside their mills or, failing this, to engage the authority of local chiefs to guarantee supplies. They should be allowed to conclude agreements with chiefs, binding them to supply a specified amount of fruit within an agreed period. If the chiefs failed to fulfil their part of the bargain, the factories should be entitled to employ wage labour to collect the agreed quantity from African-owned palmeries. Market forces alone would not persuade local producers to sell fruit to the mill. The future of the industry demanded either plantations or coercion by chiefs to enforce adequate supplies.

The arguments in favour of peasants, apparently settled by the time of the First World War, had to be re-opened, and this time with private capital pushing for a genuine alternative. The economic argument for peasants was that they were cheap and likely to continue production despite falling world prices. As Ormsby-Gore reported after his 1926 visit to West Africa, even a very rapid development of plantation production in other colonies would not destroy the West African trade:

> . . . serious as is the necessity for the more scientific development and equipment of the industry we can at any rate be sure that any industry on a peasant proprietorship basis is far more resistant than would often appear. Even if the rapid development of the plantation industry in other countries succeeds in depressing the price and curtailing the market for the West African products, the native will continue to produce. In fact, while high prices are a great stimulus to increased production, however paradoxical it may sound, low prices may equally be a stimulus to native production. A native peasant having acquired certain wants and a certain standard of living will work harder to satisfy those customary wants if he has to produce more to obtain the same money. It will be very difficult for the competition of the plantation oil to eliminate him.[39]

Aligned with this were the political arguments against plantation estates. Large grants of land to European companies were considered ill-advised, and as the Governor of the Gold Coast said in 1929, 'the factors governing the ownership of land form serious obstacles to the introduction of the plantation system'[40]. Anxieties about potential land disputes were reinforced by concerns about labour supplies to plantations. As Clifford had stated in his 1920 Address to the Nigerian Legislative Council, 'European plantations can only be maintained by some system of organised immigration or by some form of compulsory labour'[41], an argument which was to be confirmed by those firms which did set up factories or small plantations in West Africa. 'Shortage of fruit cutting labour is our chief difficulty', complained the Lever subsidiary, West African Oils Limited of its Gold Coast mill in 1926, 'and the principal reason that we do not make profits'[42]. If this was true of the Gold Coast where wage labour was more fully developed than in Nigeria or Sierra Leone, the problem of labour supply was clearly a major one.

But against these arguments for peasant production was the generally agreed necessity for factory processing, which included even Clifford among its advocates. The experience of Yonnibanna had already shown that erecting a factory was useless without some strategy for ensuring adequate supplies. The Superintendent of Agriculture in Nigeria pointed out in 1926 that 'no cases have been placed on record of highly capitalised factories being regularly and stably supported from independent small holdings in the tropics, with the exception of cotton'[43], and there was little reason to expect West African palm oil to become the second exception.

Nevertheless, the 1925 Report was not well received, and a Colonial

Office memorandum cast doubt on the Committee's neutrality. Composed as it was of long-standing supporters of the factory system, the Committee could 'hardly be described as an impartial body'[44]. The Nigerian Government reaffirmed its opposition to plantations and suggested that the Sumatran menace was much exaggerated[45]. The Governor of Sierra Leone, however, was prepared to consider plantations; here the lessons of Yonnibanna had been taken most to heart, and legislation was passed in 1922 to permit European plantations of up to 5,000 acres[46]. The Committee's proposal for legally binding contracts with chiefs was however rejected as too obviously coercive, and only contracts with individuals were to be condoned. The Governor recommended in addition a model plantation set up by the state (of 5,000 acres) to provide an incentive to Europeans and Africans alike[47]. In the Gold Coast, where the development of cocoa had largely undermined palm oil production, the Governor also proposed model plantations, but on a smaller scale (250 acres) and with the objective of encouraging African cultivation. The Colonial Office was not inclined to enforce the more radical proposals of the Committee, and left each colony to pursue its own strategy.

i. *The Nigerian response*
In Nigeria, the state maintained its opposition to plantations and exclusive monopoly rights until the late 1920s. Lever's early negotiations for monopoly rights to mills in Southern Nigeria had foundered[48], and Nigeria made no application under the Palm Oil Ordinance (1912) for powers to grant exclusive rights to erect mills. Two mills were nevertheless established in Calabar Province, though neither with much success. The tension between Lever and the Nigerian state stemmed from these early negotiations, but was dramatically intensified during Clifford's period as Governor when it developed into a bitter personal feud between the two men[49]. At the height of this antagonism, when Lever had attacked the 'extravagant and inefficient management of expenditure and finances in West Africa'[50], Clifford responded with an idealization of the non-market nature of Nigerian society, and its virtual independence of world capitalism:

> Lord Leverhulme, in common with a good many other gentlemen interested in West African produce, would appear not yet to have digested the possibly unpalatable fact that, though European business in this country, together with the public Revenue for administrative and development purposes, are both almost entirely dependent upon the conditions of Nigeria's external trade with the outside world, the vast bulk of the eighteen odd millions of native Nigerians are in the singularly fortunate position of being able to regard that trade as nothing more than a useful and very acceptable adjunct to a livelihood which, without taking it into account, is already amply assured . . . In Nigeria . . . the bulk of the people can and do grow their own cotton, or at least spin their own thread, weave their own garments, provide

all their own food-stuffs, and even, when the occasion arises, forge their own tools and make their own pottery.[51]

In these sentiments, Clifford was taking the West African Policy too far: it was, after all, supposed to embody a vision of co-operation between capitalist and peasant production, and not idealize one at the expense of the other. The vehemence of his attacks on Lever were largely personal, and not fully representative of colonial thinking, but even when he was replaced in 1926 by a governor more alive to the Sumatran menace, the contradictions facing the colonial state prevented any dramatic change of direction.

There was some shift in emphasis in 1926 with the appointment of Sir Graeme Thompson as governor, and plantations were accepted as a possibility for the more under-populated areas of Nigeria. The Report of the Agricultural Department played down the change in policy:

> . . . the desirability of some plantations of this kind [i.e. large scale] as an object lesson to everyone in the country is obvious, and this has been a subject of much discussion during the year. There seems to have been a good deal of misconception on this subject, for it seems to have been thought by many merchants that Government is opposed to the starting of such plantations. This is not the case. The position is merely that it would, it is generally believed, be impossible for any one to arrange to lease large areas of land from the native communities in the densely populated parts of the palm oil belt, simply because the people cannot possibly spare the land. And it would be neither possible nor just for Government to exercise any influence to encourage these communities to give such leases. But it is believed by many, who should be able to judge, that there are large areas of land which is suitable for oil palms, in some cases actually bearing palms, which are still very thinly populated and which the native communities who own them would not be averse to leasing out.[52]

The announcement did not produce a rush of European firms for plantation leases, perhaps because it was felt that labour problems would be even more acute in under-populated areas. The United Africa Company did begin prospecting for possible areas in 1928, and in 1930 set up the Sapele plantation. But when it attempted in 1936 to extend the operations into the Provinces of Calabar and Warri, the state intervened, fearing a proletarianization of the peasantry in these areas (Hancock, 1942:191n).

European plantations remained marginal to the Nigerian strategy on palm oil. From the late 1920s, the govenment operated on three main fronts: (1) encouraging small African plantations and African-owned hand presses; (2) introducing a subsidy scheme for unprofitable processing factories; (3) introducing export duties to favour higher quality oil. The two hand presses developed in the Nigerian research laboratory became available in 1927, but the more efficient one cost over £17, and even the cheaper Duchscher press which was subsequently developed cost £11[53]. Clearly this was not compatible with the original vision of an African peasantry, so confidently used in arguments against plantation production. Only substantial farmers could afford to buy such presses, and these would almost certainly be employers of wage labour. The small numbers sold confirm this. In 1930 only 100 had been purchased, and by 1940 the total in use was estimated at 816 (Hancock, 1942:242). In many cases these presses became the basis of a thriving entrepreneurial activity, run by teachers or artisans, who employed wage labour on the presses and sold their services to local farmers (Hancock, 1942:242n). The supposed 'peasant' alternative to European plantations and factories turned out to have little to do with peasants. As with the Gold Coast cocoa industry, reality did not conform to the dream.

But if processing methods were to be improved, and a plantation alternative discarded, the Nigerian state had to swallow this contradiction. Indeed the Agricultural Department formed an alliance with the Lands Department in the 1930s, and pressed for a more 'realistic policy on individual land tenure' which would accept this deviation from the original norm (see Chapter 6). Much the same conclusion followed from the other side of the 'peasant' policy – the attempt to promote more scientific cultivation of palm trees. If Africans were to be encouraged to plant trees rather than rely on wild palmeries, it would be the richer farmers, pressing for secure individual titles to land, who would be most co-operative. The Agricultural Department attempted initially to persuade village communities in the central palm belt to thin out and replant their palmeries[54], but found communal and family land tenure an obstacle. All members of a family had to be persuaded into agreement with the proposals, and faced with the difficulties of convincing all involved, the Department became converted to a policy of encouraging individual farmers. It embarked on a programme of encouraging a few farmers to set up experimental plantations, cultivated according to Departmental recommendations, and discovered that only those Africans who had succumbed to modern individualism were prepared to respond. By 1928, twelve such experiments had begun, but the Department warned:

> Lest it be thought that all difficulties are now overcome, it should be explained that all these plots belong to rather exceptional men, who are substantially 'individual owners' of land, or to families in which there is a man of such exceptional personal character or energy as to be able to carry the other members with him. The difficulties to general progress arising from communal ownership still remain, and frequently negotiations for one of these experiments have broken down because all the members of the family would not agree to them, in spite of the head of the family or the majority being quite ready to go on.[55]

The number of African plantations did increase, but by 1938 there were still only 5,530 planters, occupying only 9,213 acres (Hancock,

1942:242). The Department felt itself battling against the odds, under 'the overwhelming handicap of the present unsatisfactory position of land tenure'[56].

The second aspect of the Nigerian strategy – the subsidies to processing factories – began in 1928, when a scheme to encourage European investment was drawn up[57]. The Government was prepared to cover up to 30 per cent of any short-fall from estimated output, with subsidies of up to £4,000. It was a full admission of defeat. Factory processing could not be profitable without regular supplies, and since the Government was not prepared to take steps to ensure supplies, it would simply foot the bill for resulting losses. The only firm to apply for a subsidy was the United Africa Company, and even this application was for their existing, unprofitable, mill at Ibagwa. In the absence of further enquiries, the Nigerian state became more circumspect and began to doubt the viability of any mill even after the maximum five years of government subsidy. The Director of Agriculture recommended rejection of the only request, and pointed to the Department's work in encouraging African plantations as the more promising venture. After protracted discussion, the United Africa Company announced the closure in 1931 of the Ibagwa mill[58].

The prospects for factory processing thus receded, and the Nigerian response to the potential crisis came to rest on the development of African cultivation and processing. In 1935 the activities of the Agricultural Department were reinforced by an Ordinance to favour palm oil from cultivated plantations: such oil would be eligible for remission of export duty. A combination of market forces and administrative advice would have to do, since the alternative of mechanized processing was doomed without radical changes in the production of palm fruit. It was not after all possible to superimpose a modern factory on peasant production, and future agricultural productivity would have to depend on changes in African production alone. But as was clear to the Agricultural Department at least, this was no victory for the 'peasant'. It involved, rather, the individualization of land tenure, class differentiation, and state support for larger farmers. The plantation project was squashed in Nigeria, but so too was the vision of the African peasantry as dreamt up by the West African Lands Committee.

ii. *The Gold Coast response*

In the Gold Coast the more extensive development of commodity production and wage labour produced different policies. West African Oils Limited (a Lever subsidiary) was allowed a concession in 1912 at Seysie, near Sekondi, where it employed a combination of fruit purchases from independent collectors, and wage labour to cut fruit within the area of the concession[59]. The decline of the palm oil industry meant that prices for locally-produced oil were lower than in Nigeria, and the contrast between the price of fruit and the price of oil was less dramatic than at

Yonnibanna. Moreover, the development of seasonal wage labour was relatively advanced, and the mill could see some prospect of solving its labour problems. The mill lasted longer than that at Yonnibanna, but even so was never able to produce at capacity, and put continuous pressure on the state for assistance in its labour difficulties. Colonial officials did their best, as the Commissioner of the Western Province explained in 1926:

> As regards labour, political officers have done all they can to help the Company, and will continue to do so. Efforts by the Company to obtain labour from Sefwi last year were unsuccessful, though the project was fully explained to the chiefs by the District Commissioner. Similarly, efforts to obtain labour from Ashanti have met with no better success . . . there has been a shortage of labour ever since the Company (or their predecessors) started about 1912.[60]

Labour remained, as the Director of Agriculture said in 1920, 'the fly in the ointment'[61].

As at Yonnibanna, the company had little understanding of the social relations which produced the labour problems. It was 'lack of comprehension' which led Africans to prefer processing their own fruit. The problems were intensified by the 'spineless and inept' Omanhene, who failed to come up with the necessary labour, and by the 'apathy' of the Africans who spent an 'excessive amount of time' on funerals[62]. The mill, which had the capacity for 6–12,000 tons of fruit of year, failed to sustain its 1923 peak of 3,600 tons. It could employ 1,000 workers, but in 1926 had only 400[63]. Even within the Gold Coast, European power mills had little chance of success.

In response to the labour difficulties, the state devised in 1920 a plan for the greater involvement of progressive chiefs in the finances of processing factories. Two alternatives were considered. The chiefs could set up a co-operative society and finance their own small factory, or they could enter into profit-sharing agreements with European firms and agree under bond to guarantee supplies of fruit[64]. The objective in both cases was to involve chiefs in the financial success of the mills, in the expectation that this would encourage them to exert all their authority over their people to ensure supplies. But even the favourite progressive chief, Mate Kole of Eastern Krobo[65] was reluctant to consider an investment of the order of £20,000, and threw the problem back at the Government with the suggestion that it undertake financial responsibility[66]. This the state was reluctant to do. When Mate Kole raised this possibility again in 1925, the Director of Agriculture responded that 'the provision of a factory is entirely a commercial matter and if private enterprise is not sufficiently attracted, it would be unwise for Government to go into the business'[67].

In the Gold Coast, as in Nigeria, the state had to acknowledge that processing factories could not survive on the existing basis. The Seysie mill made no profits until 1928, and even then had made little headway in persuading local producers to sell to the mill. It was only the possibility of employing wage labourers to collect fruit from the concession land which made the mill at all viable[68]. In 1928 the Government drew up a subsidy scheme similar to that introduced in Nigeria. It was prepared to subsidize mills which ran at less than five-sixths estimated capacity, but only where the failure could be directly attributed to problems in supplies of fruit[69]. On the basis of this scheme, an agreement was reached with the United Africa Company for the erection of two mills in the Krobo area. The Government was confident it would escape with less than £1,800 subsidies in the first year, since it had taken the precaution of concluding a prior agreement with local chiefs. Mate Kole was to receive a bonus of 3/- a ton on all fruit delivered to the factory, and the other six principal chiefs would get a bonus of 1/- a ton. The chiefs had no doubts of their abilities to persuade their people: 'Mate Kole, who intended calling a mass meeting of his people during the present week, said that he thought we need have no fears about the price not being accepted'. When one sub-chief complained that the boxes they were to fill seemed rather large for the proposed price, Mate Kole responded that he 'considered the box fair and would see that his people accepted it'[70].

This scheme, approved in its entirety by the Secretary of State in 1929, contained all the essentials of the labour contract proposed by the 1925 Committee, leaving out only the punitive clauses. Whatever the reservations about state involvement in processing factories, the Gold Coast Government was prepared to go into the business in a big way. It would cover financial losses and use its political influence with chiefs to coerce local suppliers into co-operation. In its solution to the problem of guaranteeing supplies to European mills, the Gold Coast Government relied on these alliances with chiefs – it accepted the formal independence of the producers, but employed administrative influence to aid the mills. Even more clearly than in the Nigerian case, the crisis of the oil palm industry produced policies which took the state far from the supposed defence of an independent peasantry.

In addition to its policies on European mills, the Gold Coast Government established in 1926 three small model plantations, designed to engender more scientific cultivation among African farmers[71]. As with the strategy pursued in Nigeria, the object of these lessons was not the small peasant, secure in communal owership of land. Rather it was the progressive chiefs, such as Mate Kole, who could be encouraged to turn their stool land – and the labour of 'their people' – to productive use. The encouragement, again, of hand presses for use by African farmers was necessarily directed at a stratum of larger farmers employing wage labour. Though the terms of the debate had been set up in the 1920s as 'peasants or plantations', the Gold Coast ended up poised between the two. The palm industry was not transformed along the lines first laid down by Lever. European plantations were not encouraged, and the few processing factories set up continued to suffer labour shortages, and operated below capacity. But the failure of Lever's project to produce palm oil under capitalist relations of production did not entail a successful peasant alternative. Africans were drawn in as wage labourers on the Seysie concession, their effort were supplemented by supplies from local collectors under the control of their chiefs, and the future development of the industry was seen to depend on the activities of the more 'progressive' large farmers.

iii. *The Sierra Leone response*

Sierra Leone was remarkable as the one colony converted by the early 1920s to the development of plantations. The 1922 legislation providing for European estates of up to 5,000 acres was not however acted upon, and in 1925 the Government set aside £16,000 for the creation of a state-owned and state-run plantation[72]. The experience at Yonnibanna had induced a severely practical assessment of the conditions for factory processing, and a report by the Agricultural Chemist in 1925 summed up the alternatives:

> This fruit could be supplied by any one of the following methods:-
> (a) By a plantation of suitable size under European control
> (b) By an African owned plantation of suitable size
> (c) By fruit being brought in by natives from the surrounding bush provided the bush were sufficiently rich in palms
> In my opinion (b) may not be looked for for many years, and (c) did not prove successful in Sierra Leone. The reason for the non-success of (c) is, I think that by carrying the fruit to the factory the men are depriving their own women of a job and their own supplies of palm oil disappears since it is doubtful if the factory would undertake local retail; (a) is then left as the only means by which a factory can be supplied with fruit.[73]

Even (a) was recognized as involving a 'revolution' in social life, since it would involve 'some slight migration of the population' to clear land for a plantation, and further migration of workers to the plantation[74]. In the face of this, it was felt that private firms might be too disruptive, and that the initial experiment should be undertaken by Political Officers[75].

The Masanki plantation established by the state turned out extremely costly. Only 2,000 acres were brought under cultivation, and by 1927 a further £26,000 had to be set aside to cover the escalating costs[76]. The Empire Marketing Board and United Africa Company (UAC) provided small subsidies but when, in 1931, the Government tried to persuade UAC to take the burden from them, UAC were unimpressed by the concern, and offered only to take over without compensation[77]. By 1934 the experiment was admitted a failure. Work on the plantation had effectively stopped, and only a small gang of prison labourers remained to collect fruit from 200 acres, the rest having reverted to bush[78]. Even the

2,000 acres brought under cultivation at so much cost would not have been adequate to supply a substantial mill, and if its output had to be supplemented by supplies from local collectors, the old problems would have arisen again. By the mid-1930s, the only suggestion for the Masanki plantation was that land could be divided into small plots for a land settlement scheme, with Political Officers providing advice on scientific cultivation, and tenants processing the fruits with small hand presses[79]. By comparison, the mill at Seysie was considered a great success, and this was attributed to its employment of wage labour to collect from wild palmeries.

3. Conclusion

As can be seen from both cocoa and palm oil production, colonial administrators doubted the efficiency of existing techniques and favoured changes in methods of cultivation and processing so as to raise productivity. In both instances, the autonomy of the farmers blocked their efforts. In the palm oil industry, all three colonial states accepted the arguments for mechanical processing, and all three took the Sumatran menace sufficiently seriously to devise ways of encouraging the erection of power mills. Yet such mills were not established on any significant scale, and ironically the greatest success was the mill at Seysie on the Gold Coast, the colony which was, of the three, the least dependent on palm oil exports. The independence of peasant farmers proved a major obstacle to the desired changes. Processing mills could be profitable only with regular supplies of fruit, and this meant a revolution in existing relations of production. Supplies had to be tailored to the requirements of the mill, through the use of wage labour to collect the palm fruits, or through a radical restructuring of the sexual division of labour among palm oil producers. With the partial exception of the Gold Coast, the first alternative was impossible, since it entailed both appropriation of palm-bearing land and the formation of an agricultural proletariat. The second alternative proved equally difficult, since in all three colonies existing fruit collectors were reluctant to sell fruit to the mills. The sexual division of labour provided sound material arguments against co-operation with the mills, and even insistent political pressure from colonial officials and allied chiefs failed to shift this. As long as producers could sell locally-processed oil at prices which compared favourably with those offered for unprocessed fruit, the dominant gender relations would sustain for any foreseeable future this reluctance to comply with the new conditions. In this case, peasant production was a definite obstacle to proposed improvements in agricultural productivity. The erection of the power mills, even with considerable financial and political support from the colonial states, was not enough to effect the necessary transformations.

Within the parameters of the West African Policy, the only solution was to encourage African producers to adopt more efficient techniques.

Hand presses were developed for sale to local farmers, and model plantations set up to encourage the cultivation of palm trees. Success in this field
was premised, however, on a destruction of the peasantry as originally
conceived by the West African Lands Committee. Colonial officials
turned their attention to the wealthier farmers, who had little in common
with the supposed peasantry. Improved methods of cultivation and processing demanded a progressive elimination of the family and communal
encumbrances on economic activity, a demand which potentially undermined the authority of the chiefs.

The same constraints appeared in the cocoa industry, though on a less
dramatic scale. Here too the autonomy of the farmers blocked the efforts of
agricultural experts. Africans could not be made to tend their farms along
the lines preferred by colonial officals. The success of the industry was a
testament to African initiative, but as a result, it remained under African
control. It could not be revolutionized to accord with colonial preferences.

It has been argued (Green and Hymer, 1966) that the inefficiency of
the cocoa industry was largely a delusion of colonial officials, and that the
proposed changes were neither necessary nor desirable. Agricultural
experts constantly confused the Gold Coast cocoa with the finer quality
bean grown in the West Indies, and mistook what was a difference in kind
for a difference in techniques of production. In this view, many of the
efforts to improve the quality of cocoa in the Gold Coast were fundamentally misconceived, as were some of the proposals for countering disease.
When faced in the 1930s, for example, with serious outbreaks of swollen
shoot disease, colonial experts had no other solution to recommend than
the cutting out of diseased trees. The 'unintelligent' Africans resisted
destruction of their trees, preferring to abandon the affected farms to the
cures of time. It emerged that their solution was less disastrous than that
demanded by Agricultural Officers, whose favoured policy of cutting out
was later described as 'inefficacious and actually harmful'[80]. The cutting
out of diseased trees reduced the forest canopy, which provided much
needed shade and high humidity. A report in 1937 concluded that swollen shoot developed in precisely the less humid conditions created by a
programme of cutting out[81].

These arguments have some validity, and there can be no doubt that
agricultural 'experts' were extremely ill-informed of the conditions
appropriate to West African agriculture. What is important to my argument, however, is the fact that the experts did view the relations of production as a constraint on agricultural productivity. Whether their worst
fears were realized in the subsequent history of cocoa farming is a subject
for another study. What matters here is that the colonial administrators
came to regard their 'thriving peasantry' as an unsatisfactory compromise. They believed agricultural productivity was suffering, yet found
themselves powerless to effect change.

Moreover, the arguments of Green and Hymer are aimed, like those of
Hill (1963), against the recurrent complaints of African irrationality.

Their argument is a defence of African ingenuity against colonial incompetence, an argument which can all too easily become one-sided. Extracted from the terms of this debate, the issue is less clear. However ill-informed colonial officials were in their prescriptions for agricultural development, they were right to view the independence of the peasants as a constraint.

In the case of palm oil, the fears of colonial officials were more definitely grounded in an alternative which was technically superior. The plantation developments in other colonies produced more oil per acre than was possible in the wild palmeries of West Africa. Hopkins's defence of peasant production is inadequate here. Though he rightly points to the high failure rate of plantations in British West Africa, this serves as evidence for the dilemmas facing colonial officials rather than as proof of the vitality of the peasant alternative. In the absence of an agricultural proletariat, plantations were not a real option – a point which appears in Hopkins's analysis only in the technical guise of relatively high wage rates due to labour shortages. Since the colonial states were unable to resolve the labour shortage through proletarianization, they chose to remain within the boundaries of peasant production, but by doing this, they eliminated the prospects for factory processing.

The strategy pursued in the palm oil industry has been explained by Hancock as a sacrifice of economic progress to political security. Lever's strategy was proved right, he argues, by the subsequent contrast between British West Africa and the Belgian Congo. The export of oil and kernels from Nigeria doubled between 1909 and 1936, while in the Congo it increased ten-fold between 1909–14 and 1924–8 (Hancock, 1942:195). The refusal to contemplate developments like those in the Congo stemmed, he argues, from the colonial states' concern for political stability. However, as the examples of both cocoa and palm oil indicate, the West African Policy could guarantee neither economic progress nor political security. The result, it can be argued, was a failure on both counts. In the palm oil industry, attention was increasingly directed at the wealthier farmers, freed from those constraints of communal tenure which supposedly ensured political order. In the cocoa industry, farmers refused to fit the mould of peasant production, and all the 'vices' which communal tenure was meant to pre-empt – wage labour, landlordism, and money-lending – came to characterize the industry. For a long time, colonial officials were too mesmerized by their ideology of peasant farming to admit the capitalist nature of the cocoa industry, but this archetype of peasant production eventually produced a class of capitalist farmers sufficiently organized to challenge the power of the cocoa-buying firms in a series of cocoa hold-ups (Howard, 1978: chapter 6). In these two key sectors, the West African Policy was less successful than contemporaries suggested. The dictates of agricultural productivity conflicted with the peasant basis of production, and produced a middle way which was neither economically efficient nor politically stable.

NOTES

1 Governor's Address to Nigerian Legislative Council, Lagos: Government Printer, 1920:186.
2 Acting Director of Agriculture, 21 December 1915, Papers Relating to the Cocoa Industry:, *Gold Coast Sessional Paper II of 1916–17.*
3 Director of Agriculture to Colonial Secretary, 3 July 1915, *Gold Coast Sessional Paper II of 1916–17.*
4 Director of Botanic Gardens, 25 March 1915, *Gold Coast Sessional Paper II of 1916–17.*
5 Acting Director of Agriculture, 21 December 1915, *Gold Coast Sessional Paper II of 1916–17.*
6 ibid.
7 Clifford to Secretary of State, 1 August 1916, *Gold Coast Sessional Paper II of 1916–17.*
8 Enclosure A in *Gold Coast Sessional Paper II of 1916–17.*
9 Acting Governor to Secretary of State, 10 September 1915, *Gold Coast Sessional Paper II of 1916–17.*
10 Comment by Clifford, 30 January 1913, Enclosure C in *Gold Coast Sessional Paper II of 1916–17.*
11 Commissioner of Eastern Province, 14 January 1913, *Gold Coast Sessional Paper II of 1916–17.*
12 Director of Agriculture, 8 February 1913, *Gold Coast Sessional Paper II of 1916–17.*
13 Cocoa Plant (Diseases and Pests) Ordinance 1916, *Gold Coast Sessional Paper II of 1916–17.*
14 W. S. Tudhope, Enquiry into the Gold Coast Cocoa Industry: Interim Report, *Gold Coast Sessional Paper IV of 1918–19*:7.
15 W. S. Tudhope, Enquiry into the Gold Coast Cocoa Industry: Final Report, *Gold Coast Sessional Paper II of 1918–19*:11.
16 W. S. Tudhope, Enquiry into the Gold Coast Cocoa Industry: Interim Report, *Gold Coast Sessional Paper II of 1918–19*:7.
17 Report of the Committee Appointed to Consider the Conditions of the Cocoa Industry, *Gold Coast Sessional Paper XVIII of 1918–19*:5.
18 For details of these later discussions on the cocoa industry, see Report of the Committee on Agricultural Policy and Organisation, *Gold Coast Sessional Paper XVII of 1927–28*; Memorandum on the Creation of a Fund for Improving the Quality and Marketing of Cacao, *Gold Coast Sessional Paper XVIII of 1930–31*; and C. O. File on Cocoa Industry 1927, CO 96/675/4442.
19 C. Y. Shephard, Report on the Economics of Peasant Agriculture on the Gold Coast, *Gold Coast Sessional Paper I of 1936*:47.
20 ibid. chs. III and IV.
21 In 1902, Lever told the representatives of his Belgian and Dutch subsidiaries, 'I want you to continue your efforts a little longer until we can put a Works down in your country and you are able to call upon your customers and say to them, "This soap is made in Belgium for Belgian people" or "This soap is made in Holland for Dutch people." ' Wilson, 1954:100.
22 This brought him under attack from both Tory Tariff Reformers and socialists, who accused him of taking work from British workers. See Wilson, 1954:98; and Nworah, 1972.

23 *Correspondence respecting the Grant of exclusive rights for the extraction of oil from palm fruits*, Cd. 6561, London 1913. See also Nworah, 1972.

24 Lever Bros. to C.O., 6 July 1908, Cd. 6561, London 1913.

25 See various letters, May–June 1912, Cd. 6561, London 1913.

26 *Palm Oil Ordinance*, Cd. 6512, London 1912. The Ordinance permitted the granting of exclusive rights, but individual colonies had to apply under the powers granted in the Ordinance. Sierra Leone and the Gold Coast applied in 1913, but not Nigeria.

27 For a resume of the Yonnibanna experiment, see Despatches relating to the Sierra Leone Oil Palm industry and the Establishment of Oil Palm Plantations, *Sierra Leone Sessional Paper 12 of 1925*: Appendix E. For the correspondence between Lever Bros. and the C. O. see *Correspondence (December 9, 1912–March 13, 1915) relating to Palm Oil Grants in West Africa* African West 1023, 1915.

28 The chiefs originally insisted on £3 a ton, but were forced down to the factory offer of 30/-. *Sierra Leone Sessional Paper 12 of 1925*: Appendix E.

29 Acting Provincial Commissioner, Southern Provinces, quoted in Governor to Secretary of State, 28 September 1925, *Sierra Leone Sessional Paper 12 of 1925*.

30 *Sierra Leone Sessional Paper 12 of 1925*: Appendix E.

31 *Report of Committee on edible and oil-producing nuts and seeds*, Cd. 8247, London 1916.

32 ibid., p. 20.

33 Correspondence relating to the Scientific Investigation of the Oil Palm, *Gold Coast Sessional Paper III of 1920–21*.

34 Annual Report of the Nigerian Agricultural Department, 1927.

35 C. G. Auchinleck, *Notes on a Visit to the Netherlands, Indies and the Federated Malay States*, Accra: Government Printer, 1927:10.

36 ibid., p. 13.

37 For example in *West Africa: Palm Oil and Palm Kernels*: Report of a Committee appointed by the Secretary of State from the Colonies, September 1923, to consider the best means of securing improved and increased production, Colonial 10, 1925.

38 ibid.

39 *Report by the Honourable W. G. A. Ormsby-Gore on his visit to West Africa, during the year 1926*, Cmd. 2744, London 1926:109.

40 Governor to Secretary of State, 6 September 1929, in Despatches Relating to the Oil Palm Industry with particular reference to a subsidy scheme for Oil Palm Mills. *Gold Coast Sessional Paper III of 1930–31*.

41 Governor's Address to Nigerian Legislative Council, Lagos: Government Printer, 1920:186.

42 Memorandum by West African Oils Ltd. for visit of Ormsby-Gore in 1926, CO 96/662.

43 Superintendent of Agriculture, Report on a visit to the East Indies in 1926, filed in CO 583/146/75, p. 69.

44 Memorandum by A. J. Harding on the Report of the Committee on Palm Oil, in *Correspondence (September 20, 1924–April 16, 1932) Relating to the Palm Oil Industry in West Africa*, African West 1113, 1932:5.

45 Governor's Address to Nigerian Legislative Council, Lagos: Government Printer, 1925: 217-19.

46 Governor to Secretary of State, 28 September 1925, African West 1113, 1932.

47 ibid.
48 *Correspondence respecting the Grant of exclusive rights for the extraction of oil from palm fruits*, Cd. 6561, London 1913.
49 The conflicts reached the point at which Clifford refused an invitation to dine with Lever unless he withdrew the allegations he had made concerning financial mismanagement by the Nigerian Government. Lever refused. See Lever, 1927:315.
50 Governor's Address to Nigerian Legislative Council, Lagos: Government Printer, 1924:26.
51 ibid., pp. 22–3.
52 Annual Report of the Nigerian Agricultural Department, 1926:9.
53 Annual Report of the Nigerian Agricultural Department, 1931.
54 Annual Report of the Nigerian Agricultural Department, 1926.
55 Annual Report of the Nigerian Agricultural Department, 1928:14.
56 Annual Report of the Nigerian Agricultural Department, 1930:13.
57 *Correspondence (September 20, 1924–April 16, 1932) Relating to the Palm Oil Industry in West Africa*. African West 1113, 1932:71.
58 For the details of the negotiations see ibid., pp. 110–31.
59 For details of the operation of the Seysie mill, see Correspondence Relating to the Development of the Oil Palm Industry, *Gold Coast Sessional Paper IV of 1924–25*; and Memorandum by West African Oils Ltd. for visit of Ormsby-Gore in 1926, CO 96/662.
60 Report of Agricultural Department for visit by Ormsby-Gore in 1926, CO 96/662.
61 Director of Agriculture to West African Oils Ltd., in *Gold Coast Sessional Paper IV of 1924–25*; 6.
62 Memorandum by West African Oils Ltd. for visit of Ormsby-Gore in 1926, CO 96/662.
63 ibid.
64 *Gold Coast Sessional Paper IV of 1924–25*.
65 The Governor pointed out in his despatch to the Secretary of State, 6 September 1927, that 'Sir Emmanuel Mate Kole is a chief who has a very unusual influence over his people, that he is an enthusiastic farmer himself, and that his people are some of the best farmers in the country.' CO 96/690/6511.
66 *Gold Coast Sessional Paper IV of 1924–25*.
67 Report of Director of Agriculture, 18 January 1926, on visit of Ormsby-Gore in 1926, CO 96/662.
68 *Gold Coast Sessional Paper III of 1930–31*.
69 ibid.
70 ibid., p. 34.
71 *Correspondence (September 20, 1924–April 16, 1932) Relating to the Palm Oil Industry in West Africa*, African West 1113, 1932:40–1.
72 Despatches relating to the Sierra Leone Oil Palm Industry and the Establishment of Oil Palm Plantations, *Sierra Leone Sessional Paper 12 of 1925*.
73 Report by Agricultural Chemist, *Sierra Leone Sessional Paper 12 of 1925*: Appendix A.
74 *Sierra Leone Sessional paper 12 of 1925*: 170–2.
75 ibid.
76 *Correspondence (September 20, 1924–April 16, 1932) Relating to the Palm Oil Industry in West Africa*, African West 1113, 1932:104–5.

77 ibid., pp. 130–2. In 1932, UAC dropped out of the negotiations, saying they would wait till conditions became more propitious.

78 Report by F. A. Stockdale, Agricultural Advisor to the Secretary of State for the Colonies, on his visit to Sierra Leone in January 1936, *Sierra Leone Sessional Paper 2 of 1936.*

79 The Sierra Leone Government asked two visiting experts – F. A. Stockdale, and C. Y. Shephard, Professor of Economics at Imperial College of Tropical Agriculture – to make suggestions for the future of Masanki. Shephard's report on his visit to the colony in 1934 was published as *Sierra Leone Sessional paper 4 of 1935.*

80 Report on Mr H. A. Dade's visit to the Gold Coast, Swollen Shoot of Cacao, *Gold Coast Sessional paper V of 1937.*

81 ibid.

6
Land Policies in the Inter-war Years

By the time of the First World War, colonial land policy had apparently crystallized into a set of guidelines which reflected the peasant road. Extensive alienation of land to private capital was not encouraged, a policy which remained relatively consistent even under Lever's energetic campaign. African rights to the land were acknowledged, but claims to private ownership by individuals were not. The government was entitled to appropriate small areas for railway work or other public purposes, compensating the occupants only for their crops or buildings, and not for the value of the land. If any of this land was subsequently leased to private firms, the rents from it were the due reward of the government, whose endeavours in developing the colonies were responsible for the increase in land values.

These principles were not consistently reflected in legislation. Land legislation presented the bewildering complexity of local variation which was typical of British administration in Africa. As a legacy from the earliest days, the Crown claimed full ownership over some of the coastal land, though the legitimacy of even these claims was effectively challenged in the case of Lagos, where African opposition mobilized from 1912 onwards (Crowder, 1968:423-4). Apart from this, the state had accumulated, through 'compensation' to previous owners, some small tracts of Crown Land in most of the major cities. Successive ordinances gave the governments the right to appropriate land for railway development – again with the obligation to compensate owners only for cultivated land, and not to pay the value of the land itself. The resultant Crown Lands were tiny in proportion to the colonies, and apart from these, the only serious claims to control over land were in Northern Nigeria. Here the 1910 Proclamation remained in force, establishing the Government as sole trustee with extensive powers over the public land. Colonial control was most limited in the Gold Coast, where the Concessions Ordinance (1900) acknowledged African ownership – though still not as individual property rights – and restricted government action to the judicial approval of the terms on which Africans leased land to

Europeans. Apart from these two cases, no significant land legislation had been passed, and government practice was ruled by decree rather than by law. The continuing attempts by the colonial states to assert administrative control over forest land remained a source of tension, the full tale of which has been told elsewhere (Kimble, 1963).

The ambiguities and inadequacies of the peasant road meant that debates over land policy continued into the inter-war years. The arguments for communal tenure had never been accepted by all colonial administrators. Lord Lugard, for example, was a firm believer in private property as the source of thrift and hard work, and with all his ceaseless propaganda for indirect rule, could not resign himself to communal tenure as the corollary (Lugard, 1922). In the 1920s and 1930s developments in the palm oil industry forced a reassessment of the supposed advantages of communal tenure, and the continuing expansion of commodity production raised the further question of African rights to mortage land. The model colonial policy as articulated in the proceedings of the West African Lands Committee (WALC) seemed increasingly inadequate for conditions in West Africa, and in the inter-war years was frequently challenged as anachronistic. In this period, officials in London became the main advocates of the ideals of Morel and Wedgwood, while those faced with the burden of implementation were more inclined to view these ideals as anachronistic. On the two important issues of this period – how to regulate even those limited sales to private capital which were condoned, and how to impose relations of communal tenure on Africans who persisted in claiming individual rights – a gap opened up between the relatively isolated officials in London and the increasingly doubtful administrators in the colonies

1. Land values and private capital

One recurrent theme in colonial debates was the assertion that land had no value before the colonial conquest. It might have owners, though not individual ones, with rights of cultivation, and these were entitled to compensation if their land was taken over for public or private use. But since no land market existed, African 'owners' could not claim the monetary value of the land. In the Gold Coast Colony it had proved impossible to insist on this, and legislation recognized the rights of African owners to the proceeds from land sales. In Nigeria, however, Lugard tried to apply this principle, and suggested in 1914 that any leases to private capital in Southern Nigeria be mediated through the state[1]. The Government should acquire freehold title to such land, paying only compensation to the occupants, and then sub-let it to European merchants. In this way the benefits of rent would accrue to the state. The proposal was based on the assumption that existing African land tenure was not individual freehold. On this assumption land both belonged to the Africans and did not. The government could appropriate it with only minimal compensation, claiming that it was acting as the new 'paramount chief' of West Africa, with overall responsibility for land affairs.

On this occasion the Colonial Office retreated in horror, and sent Lugard a stiff letter of reprimand[2]. But in 1917, when bauxite was discovered in the Gold Coast Colony, officials in London proposed precisely the same scheme for this most touchy of West African colonies[3]. The Secretary of State advised legislation to vest all mineral-bearing land in the state. Africans could, he suggested, claim compensation for the agricultural value of the land they occupied, but all rents from the new mines should go to the treasury. Within the assumptions of customary land tenure, as interpreted by colonial officials, the proposal seemed perfectly straightforward. Africans lost only access to farming land, and could be duly recompensed for this. The mineral value of the land arose from the colonial presence, and why should the state not enjoy some benefits from this? Local administrators, who recognized the extent to which 'customary tenure' had dissolved, were totally opposed to the proposal.

Governor Clifford's lengthy (sixty-three printed pages) rebuttal included a reassessment and critique of all previous attempts to establish state ownership of the land[4]. He insisted that in the Gold Coast Colony the rights of Africans to their land had been finally acknowledged in the dismissal of Maxwell's Public Lands Bill, and could not now be challenged without serious political repercussions. The 'suspicion of profiteering on the part of Government will inevitably arise and the relations between the Government and the people will be very considerably affected', said the Chief Assistant Colonial Secretary[5]; the proposal would cause a 'recrudescence of distrust and resentment that will far outweigh the comparatively trifling pecuniary advantage', claimed the Colonial Secretary[6]. All the influential officials agreed with Clifford on the impossibility of such a scheme. In the Colony at least, private property in land was too far advanced for such legislation. Colonial Office minutes on this despatch indicate a sharp divergence of opinion between administrators in London and those on the spot, and although the suggestion was dropped in the face of such powerful opposition, the Colonial Office refused permission for the printing of the despatch[7]. Local doubts were considered excessive, and opinion in London continued to favour such proposals.

When the colonial government was taking over land for public purposes as, for example, in the construction of railways, there was little disagreement. The general principle that Africans could get compensation but not the value of the land was broadly practised. Successive ordinances to legitimate government claims to land embraced this principle that Africans could claim payment only where land was actually cultivated, or where public works destroyed their improvements to nearby land. In these cases the philosophy of Henry George was willingly applied: no-one owned the land itself, but only the crops or buildings.

The disagreements arose when the state assumed more extensive powers. In 1927, legislation similar to that applied in Northern Nigeria was at last extended to another part of British West Africa with the introduction of the Land and Native Rights Ordinance for the Northern Territories[8]. As with the Nigerian legislation, land was declared public, and the Governor given supreme powers to validate land titles. He could decide the rentals appropriate for leases to Europeans. Within the larger towns he could decide the terms for leases between Africans. He could determine whether or nor mortgaging would be permitted. All rents outside the towns would go directly to the treasury, while town rents would be divided equally between the chief of the town and the treasury. The new Governor, Slater, who arrived in the colony when the legislation was already agreed, was firmly opposed to it. In an argument similar to that of Clifford's despatch, he communicated in 1930 his amazement at the 'radical change' from Chamberlain's statement in 1899 that the state would not claim ownership of African lands[9]. He was not averse to some action to regulate leases to private capital, but considered the proposed legislation unnecessarily provocative. The Secretary of State defended the Ordinance as an extension of the 'very successful' Northern Nigeria Proclamation, and summed up general Colonial Office opinion of such legislation:

> The primary object of that legislation was to protect the native occupiers in the use and occupation of their land. Secondary objects were to prevent the evils of expensive litigation over land rights and to secure that the community instead of private individuals should benefit from increases in land values due to communal effort.[10]

The language here was heavily reminiscent of that used by Morel and Wedgwood.

The attitudes of Governors varied considerably and often shifted in the course of their administration. But the Colonial Office commitment to the assumptions of the draft report of the WALC remained surprisingly consistent up to the early 1930s, and was only occasionally moderated by a reminder that the report was never accepted by the entire Committee, and not approved as the official policy for British West Africa[11]. On the related issue of the rates charged to private capital for the land they leased in the colonies, there was often a similar contrast between opinion in London and local views. Under the Northern Nigeria Land and Native Rights Proclamation (1910), rising land values were regarded as a product of government work in improving communications and developing towns. Leases to private capital should be arranged in such a way as to maximize government rewards for this work. Thus land was publicly auctioned, and rents were revised at frequent intervals (preferably seven years), a procedure which promised high rents. Lugard complained about this system in 1913, and proposed an amendment to allow revision of rents at twenty-year intervals, since 'revision at more frequent intervals than this would act as a bar to the development of the country and prevent capital from entering.'[12] An unconvinced official in London commented, 'We are never told it *has* acted as a bar: on the contrary, we know that there has been a brisk demand for sites along the railway, and especially at Kano'[13]. The Colonial Office was prepared at this point to compromise by permitting twenty-year revisions for building sites, but did not accept the proposed amendments to the Proclamation, which Lugard subsequently dropped.

The dispute was re-opened in 1917, when Lugard suggested he might have discretion to offer land to mining companies at reduced rents, fixed for the term of their occupancy. On this occasion the response was firmly negative[14]. The matter was not simply a preoccupation of one governor. In 1919, Clifford was the next to take up the cudgels on behalf of the merchants, and supported their repeated requests for freehold tenure and lower rents[15]. The eventual reply from London explicitly referred Clifford to the draft report of the WALC as the embodiment of the principles he should consider in deciding land policy[16], and though he was allowed to abandon public auctions of land, his suggestion for more lengthy periods of rent revision was resisted[17]. Clifford was at this stage unimpressed by the land policy adopted in Northern Nigeria, and he commented in a later despatch:

> There can be no doubt, I think, that the Land Laws in force in the Southern Provinces are more favourable to the native population than are those which are embodied in the Land and Native Rights Ordinance of 1916 [of Northern Nigeria].[18]

An official in London noted hopefully that his experience in Nigeria was already modifying his views, and that he was now 'rapidly becoming a very fair Northern Nigerian'[19]. The fact that Clifford became a clear advocate of the peasant road, and one of the most vigorous opponents of plantation development, only confirms the complexity of the issues raised by land affairs in West Africa. Caught between African claims to land and European complaints of unfavourable treatment, even the most committed supporters of the West African Policy found the land proposals emanating from London unsatisfactory.

The conflict between the Nigerian Government and the Colonial Office reached its high point in 1928 when the Deputy Governor sent a lengthy despatch, approved by Governor Thompson, which once again suggested an extension of revision periods for private rents (to twenty years in the Northern Provinces, and thirty years in the Southern). The despatch recommended 99-year leaseholds, a restriction of public auctions to special cases, and a guarantee that new rents would never involve more than a 30 per cent increase on the previous one[20]. As ammunition, the Deputy Governor enclosed a report from the Lieutenant-Governor of the Northern Provinces, which directly attacked the principles of the 1910 Proclamation, and indeed the Wedgwood-inspired Northern Nigeria Land Committee:

. . . it was only a small minority of the Political Staff who agreed with the section of the committee, including one or two of our own officers, which wished not only to legalise the *de facto* African conception of land tenure, but to use it as a mechanism for imposing *in perpetuo* a some-what Utopian form of land tenure in the country. So far as Nigeria was concerned, Mr C. L. Temple, then Chief Secretary of Northern Nigeria and afterwards Acting Governor for a considerable period, was the protagonist of the Utopian influence which was dominant from 1908–1913. Mr Temple was a firm believer in the Marxian doctrine that labour applied to land constitutes wealth. [Flood of the C.O. here interjected in the margin, 'I don't believe it!'] He was a disciple of Henry George and wished to administer Northern Nigeria on a single tax basis, i.e. by putting into the revenue of the state the whole of what was termed the 'true rent' or 'incremental value' of land. Mr Temple instilled the theories of Marx and Henry George into his subordinates and acted on them whenever possible.[21]

Fortunately, the report continued, Residents and District Officers did not act on the Proclamation. And when Lugard returned to the colony in 1913, 'he was far from being in agreement with the Utopian ideals which animated in part its provisions, and was still less in agreement with the administrative action by which Mr Temple had sought to carry out the theories of Karl Marx and Henry George among the Native Administration'[22]. Officials in London found these allegations of revolutionary infiltration unconvincing, but since three successive Governors – Lugard, Clifford, and now Thompson – had agitated for change, they finally conceded to the arguments.

Temple was certainly one of the most convinced exponents of the ideas of Henry George, and in his period in Nigeria (Resident in Northern Nigeria 1901–10; Chief Secretary 1910–14; Lieutenant-Governor of Northern Nigeria 1914–17) he developed a version of colonial administration which rested on a profound distrust of modern 'civilization'. Indirect rule, for Temple, meant protection against the vices of this civilization, and he warned against the dangers of throwing the African 'like a crab without a shell amongst a horde of ravening sharks' (Temple, 1968:54). The 'question of land tenure', he argued in *Native Races and Their Rulers* (first edition, 1918) 'is connected in the closest possible manner with the burning question of labour' (1968:147), and the alternatives as he saw them were private property in land, the creation of a landlord class, and the emergence of a 'large thriftless population', or the African peasantry based on communal ownership of land. Private property could only mean expropriation of the poorer Africans and would start the downward slide towards proletarianization. The Northern Nigeria land legislation was, in his view, explicitly and correctly anti-capitalist, and in this he pursued the implications of the West African Policy beyond many of his contemporaries. But whatever views can be attributed to Charles Temple, it can hardly be argued that the Colonial Office was staffed in the early twentieth century by advocates of Marx and Henry George.

The recurrent conflicts between London and Nigeria have a more mundane explanation. The problem was that the model colonial policy, with its happy integration of expanding commodity production and traditional methods of social control, was from its beginnings inadequate to the complex conditions within West Africa. And not surprisingly, it was the administrators in London who were able, in their relative isolation, to sustain for longer the anachronistic visions of Morel and Wedgwood. The theories of Henry George had articulated a number of pressing colonial concerns. The doctrine of fair rents reduced the costs of administration without seriously hampering merchant activities. The restraining influence on individual land rights seemed to promise continued political order through local chiefs in the face of rapidly expanding commodity production. The (almost) universal preference of European firms for leaving production in the hands of Africans seemed to combine with this, to project a good public image of the colonial states as protectors of their African subjects from the worst excesses of capitalist exploitation. This model colonial policy rested fundamentally on the assumption that 'native customary tenure' was a direct opposite to individual freehold. On this assumption the colonial states could legitimately appropriate land for public works, and even for rental to private capital, without any significant interference with African rights. They could claim that they were acting as the new paramount chiefs of British West Africa, and that they were employing the accepted powers of chiefs to allocate land in the interests of the community. This was the argument that underlay the 1910 Proclamation for Northern Nigeria, and this was the assumption that justified the 1927 extension of similar powers to the Northern Territories of the Gold Coast. No-one could accuse the colonial states of seizing land from its rightful owners if the land had no private owners. The state was merely pursuing the traditional responsibilities of chiefs to 'protect the native occupiers in the use and occupation of their lands'.

As long as this version of traditional land tenure could be sustained, proposals such as the one for appropriation of all mineral-bearing land could be presented as a perfectly legitimate extension of African tradition. The same argument could be applied to the vexed question of forestry reserves. If it was assumed that no individuals owned the forests and that land was traditionally administered by public authorities, then surely the colonial state could establish forest reserves without any interference in existing African rights? In this argument, only the unrepresentative 'new' Africans, who made their living from land litigation and adopted Western concepts of land tenure, would offer any resistance. The true voice of West Africa would understand that the colonial state was simply fulfilling its social responsibilities to the community.

Thus the reforming vision of Morel and Wedgwood had provided a justification for denying African land rights, and it is not surprising that their ideas lingered on despite the failure to ratify the draft report of the

WALC. Many administrators within the colonies shared this vision, but it is noticeable that successive governors challenged its validity. Faced as they were with the practical task of implementing the proposals which arose from this conception of 'native customary tenure', many came to the conclusion that the concept was either incorrect, or at least out of date, when ideas of land tenure had changed so rapidly. Hence Clifford's refusal in 1914 even to consider implementation of the dreams of certain members of the WALC that the colonial state could halt further land sales[23]; hence the rejection of the 1917 suggestion that mineral-bearing land be nationalized; hence the recurrent criticisms of attempts at forestry legislation[24]. Contrary to the official version, the notion that Africans did indeed own their land was widespread, and the potential opposition to such legislation would not be restricted to a few unrepresentative African lawyers. Similarly, the objections within West Africa to the policy of extracting maximum rents from private capital expressed the greater sensitivity of the local governments to the political opposition of merchant companies. Their dealings with private capital were more continuous and direct than those of the Colonial Office, which faced at the most the occasional recriminatory letter[25], or a carefully stage-managed consultative meeting.

2. Peasants and private property

Land transactions with private capital challenged assumptions of African custom and undermined official versions of communal tenure. But the real problem was the peasants themselves. 'Native customary tenure' reduced even pre-colonial land relations to a false simplicity, ignoring the extent to which land was already bought and sold. In the inter-war years, the gap between the official version and rapidly changing reality became more striking, and the principles of the WALC proved an inadequate guide. Property relations in West Africa did not fit the proposed model, and as commodity production was further developed, a number of complex issues emerged. As in their dealings with private firms, it was the administrators on the spot who first admitted the outmoded nature of existing land policy. The Colonial Office clung longer to the dream of happy peasants, protected and encouraged by relations of communal ownership.

Three main problems arose. Firstly, how should communal tenure adapt to the introduction of permanent cash crops like cocoa, where trees took seven to twenty years to reach fruition? In particular, how should it deal with migration? Before colonization, migratory strangers were widely accepted into a community if they were of 'good character' and acknowledged the authority of the local chief by payment of tribute. But chiefs in some areas were reluctant to approve the planting of permanent crops, like cocoa, when it seemed to imply outright control of the land by the new occupants. The colonial states were here caught between a commitment to the new cash crops, and a concern to sustain customary tenure. Obviously, they wanted to support the right of strangers to culti- vate the crops on which colonial economies relied. Lugard, for example, tried in 1918 to persuade judicial councils and native courts in Southern Nigeria to adopt a rule which allowed strangers to erect permanent build- ings, plant permanent crops, and pass on land to their sons[26]. But the corollary of this was that a previous system of tribute would develop into demands for land rent, and customary tenure be correspondingly trans- formed. In this case, Lugard attempted to moderate the changes by insisting that any such rent be paid to public bodies and used for public purposes. It was impossible to enforce this requirement. In the Gold Coast, land rent had already developed: strangers were welcome to plant crops on stool land and paid a rent of 1d per bearing cocoa tree to the chief, who usually accepted it as a private income. As the Acting Chief Commissioner for Ashanti commented, the rent 'goes in theory to the community, but in practice to the Chief and elders only'[27].

This was the second problem associated with the development of commodity production. How could colonial governments prevent chiefs from asserting themselves as private landlords? And how were they to deal with the increasing conflicts between lesser and higher chiefs, as each competed for the right to land rent? Paramount chiefs were frequently grieved by the refusal of subordinates to share out the proceeds[28], and as the Secretary for Native Affairs in the Gold Coast noted in 1926, 'the forces of disintegration and degradation are hard at work', with lesser chiefs constantly flouting the demands of the superiors[29]. The state could not afford the consequences when the practice of indirect rule made political order so dependent on the authority of chiefs. Recurrent litiga- tion between chiefs interfered with colonial administration, and the transformation of chiefs into landlords hastened the decay of tribal authority. In the Gold Coast Colony, where commoners traditionally had the right to dismiss chiefs who acted against their interests, the number of depositions rose sharply in rhythm with the commercializa- tion of land.

	Number of stool depositions in Gold Coast Colony[30]
1904–8	10
1909–13	22
1914–18	39
1918–23	32
1924–25	16

The Secretary for Native Affairs who reported these figures did not attribute them to 'de-tribalization' of the commoners; the problem rather was the de-tribalization of the chiefs, who pursued private gain at the expense of community progress.

The third problem was how should the colonial governments respond to the mortgaging of land? African producers continued to press for full control over the land they occupied, and particularly for the right to sub-let and mortgage. In the inter-war years, some officials came to approve this development as the necessary price for agricultural improvement. In Nigeria the Head of the Agricultural Department formed an alliance with Rowe, the Commissioner of Lands, and campaigned for greater 'security of tenure' for individuals: in other words, for more rights to sub-let, mortgage and sell. The custom of referring decisions over land usage to the entire kinship group was regarded by such officials as a constraint on 'progressive farmers', and the denial of mortgages as as restriction on the credit which might otherwise be used for purchase of improved equipment. Such arguments inevitably shattered the assumption of 'native customary tenure', and officials in London were constantly shocked by the divergence between local proposals and the principles on which they had assumed land policy was formulated.

In the Gold Coast and Nigeria, the main proponent of change was Lieutenant-Colonel Rowe, Surveyor-General in the Gold Coast from 1920–27, and subsequently Commissioner of Lands in Nigeria until his death in 1933. Rowe interpreted these problems as heralding the end of the dreams of the WALC. Only a decisive move in the direction of individual property rights could ensure satisfactory conditions for development in British West Africa. Private property would guarantee security for migrants and undermine the devious transformation of chiefs into landlords by challenging the communal property which gave chiefs their powers. It would also provide access to credit for the progressive farmers who should be the backbone of any agricultural policy. Rowe's first success was the formation of a Committee on Land Registration in the Gold Coast in 1923, comprising himself, the Attorney-General, and one other political officer, to investigate a system of land registration to establish individual titles[31]. The report recommended procedures for the registration of titles for Europeans and Africans alike, and for the establishment of an insurance fund to compensate any dispossessed who might subsequently challenge the titles. In this way registered titles would be secure from litigation, and on the basis of these titles, mortgages could be arranged. The Committee did not yet press for compulsory registration, but expressed the hope that registration on a voluntary basis in more developed areas like Accra would encourage Africans throughout the Colony to adopt the practice[32]. The Attorney-General demurred, pointing out that under customary tenure individual property reverted to the community when the occupant died without heirs. How was the system of registration to deal with that? The honest answer was that the point of the system was precisely to destroy this custom. Rowe's objective was not simply to register existing individual rights but to dissolve communal tenure and introduce private property. The Acting Governor supported the Attorney-General, and the matter was laid aside, like many others, until the visit of Ormsby-Gore in 1926.

At this point, the Acting Governor drew up a detailed report, but focussed on the less vital issue of guaranteeing land titles to European firms. He favoured 99-year leases rather than freehold titles since:

> . . . in the present stage of development of the Gold Coast indiscriminate grants of freeholds to non-natives are not advisable. It would lead, as it has done elsewhere, to the creation of a class of absentee landlords, and as is well known, the existence of such a class has always caused trouble.[33]

On the more radical proposals for promoting individual rights among Africans he was equally discouraging, suggesting only that where individual freehold titles already existed, they should be more effectively registered. His arguments were much more firmly in line with the supposed principles of West African land policy than those of the Surveyor-General.

Rowe meanwhile had hardened his position, and called for compulsory registration of titles in the urban centres of Accra, Sekondi, Kumasi, Koforidua and Cape Coast. His ultimate objectives were made clear in the following extract from a 1926 memorandum:

> Sometimes administrators who are justly proud of a native administration based on native customs (which they are doing their utmost to preserve in their purity), view with alarm the idea of the encroachment upon the native customary methods of modern legal and technical processes, and it is often asserted that modern methods cannot be properly applied to land held under native custom. It must however, be recognised, that the gradual attainment of individual ownership and civilised forms of owning and leasing land is an advance brought about by economic necessity and must inevitably be introduced with the full development of any country. Land becomes scarcer and dearer with the increase of the population, with the building of railways and the inauguration of large enterprises. Semi-permanent crops such as cocoa are introduced, necessitating a semi-permanent and secure form of ownership of land, and commercial undertakings of any magnitude require long and good leasehold before capital will commit itself. This change to definite individual ownership of land may be delayed, but its ultimate establishment everywhere is inevitable, unless development of the country's resources and its commerce is to be hampered and retarded.[34]

This declaration of intent set the scene for a sharp confrontation between the cultural imperialism of Rowe and the cultural dualism of those like Rattray who clung, like Temple before him, to the image of a separate path of development for Africa:

> I postulate [declared Rattray in 1937] as the ideal for these people, a race, the bulk of whose population is settled on the land; the maintenance of the revenues necesssary for the advancement of their country and countrymen secured by agricultural pursuits, not as paid labourers, but by each man working his own holding; and finally the

possession of all land safeguarded by trusts as constituted by the Tribal Stool.[35]

The debates were published in two weighty collections by the Gold Coast Government: in 1927 the *Proposed Reforms in respect of Land Legislation of the Gold Coast primarily in order to promote security of title*, and 1930 the *Land Legislation of the Gold Coast, Vol II*, which brought together memoranda by various Gold Coast officers consulted on the subject[36]. Rattray, whose ideas were treated with considerable respect at the Colonial Office, thought the effects of Rowe's various recommendations would be as follows:

(a) Break up of the Akan Constitution
(b) Finally destroy the already dwindling power of the Chiefs
(c) Lead to a scramble by everyone who had acquired land by native customary methods, to rush to register an absolute title to what, under the law which alone had put him in possession of a valuable asset, could never have become his freehold property
(d) Lead to the rapid alienation of land, and facilitate it falling into the hands of capitalists (European and African)
(e) Bring about the eventual impoverishment of the tribal and family units and the creation of a landless class, who would in time become African paupers – a section of civilised communities familiar to us, but hitherto unknown in West Africa.[37]

Rattray knew very well that Rowe's proposals would gain the support of Africans, and argued that it was the responsibility of colonial states to prevent them escaping from the control of tribal authorities.

Opinion at this time was varied and, as Passfield commented, the 'marked divergence of opinion' suggested necessity for 'the utomost caution'[38]. The problem was not so much how to guarantee titles for European companies; on this issue all agreed that existing legislation was unsatisfactory and provoked excessive litigation. Debates here were only over the kind of legislative or executive action required to remedy agreed defects.

It was the question of private property for peasants that aroused passions. Rowe's proposals sometimes appeared as no more than a worthy attempt to control land disputes. But what was at stake was the reversal of existing land policy. The commitment to communal tenure which had evolved out of the first decades of colonial rule, and found expression in the draft report of the WALC, was fundamentally challenged by Rowe's campaign. He rejected the image of the undifferentiated peasantry, tilling the soil under the guidance of their chiefs, and secured in access to the land by customary tenure. For him the future lay with progressive farmers, freed from kinship constraints, able to raise mortgages for agricultural improvement, and presumably – though he did not insist on this – employing wage labour. The chiefs he saw as an obstruction, and in his arguments against them, he cleverly deployed the threat of landlordism:

> The Commissioner of Lands discovered that the system whereby under nebulous and uncodified so-called 'Native Law and Custom'

the rights of individuals were suppressed and attempts made to regard all land as vested in the Chiefs (so-called communal land), not only was great injustice inevitable but that in some places the Chiefs were, as a direct result of the policy, beginning to charge economic rents and that the people themselves would undoubtedly be, in the course of time, reduced to landless wage slaves on their own land. The same mistake (as has been made in other countries) of vesting the land in the Chiefs was being gradually introduced into Nigeria, but subtly disguised as 'Native Law and Custom'.[39]

In arguing this, Rowe revealed a glaring inconsistency in the West African Policy: the advocacy of peasant smallholders, secured in the communal ownership of the land, could all too easily turn into its opposite and encourage incipient landlordism among the chiefs. Rowe's ideas questioned much of what had become commonplace in British West Africa, but without a frontal attack on the principle of peasant farming. Rather, he emphasized inconsistencies between this supposed objective and current practices in land affairs. His ideas shattered much of the dominant consensus, but this consensus was already in some disarray, and Rowe found himself a surprisingly ready audience.

Guggisberg, in his period as Governor of the Gold Coast, gave Rowe considerable support, and established in 1925 a Lands Department separate from the Survey Department, with responsibility for overseeing the changes Rowe proposed. Slater, who suceeded him in 1927, was opposed to Rowe's suggestions. Like Rattray, he 'believed their effect would be to increase the number of land suits in the colony, as Africans fought with one another for rights over the land. The remedy', he suggested, 'seems worse than the disease'[40], a comment which indicates that for Slater the only point of further land legislation was to settle existing land disputes. As already mentioned, legislation similar to that of Northern Nigeria was introduced for the less developed Northern Territories, but no final solution was agreed for the more controversial Colony and Ashanti. By 1930, the Colonial Office was prepared to consider some modification of the previous basis of land policy, and Flood of the Colonial Office wrote an influential minute which began a process of distancing from the draft report of the WALC:

> I might perhaps add a word of caution in regard to the W.A.L.C., to which so much reference is made. That Committee was established at a time when the desire of people in this country was to prevent the poor native being robbed of all his lands for the benefit of the unscrupulous European and the exciting cause of its appointment was the scramble between Brunner Mond & Co. and Levers, for agricultural concessions in the Gold Coast. The circumstances are now changed and there is not now so much demand for permission to alienate native lands, and the problem before the Government is rather to regularise, so far as can be done, the existing situation, which is not satisfactory.[41]

The proposed resolution was nonetheless influenced by the draft report. Passfield suggested in May 1930 that the Government proclaim all lands as tribal or stool lands, and put the onus on claimants of individual property rights to establish the legitimacy of their claims before a quasi-judicial commission. Slater, who had already demonstrated his reluctance to modify existing land rights, rejected this suggestion and proposed that the discussion of registration of titles be discontinued[42].

The debate thus lasted from 1922 to 1931, with no ultimate results. The process of transition to private property in land was to be neither retarded nor speeded up, but left to develop at its own momentum. It is significant however, that with the exception of Rattray and a relatively small number of Political Officers who echoed his views, the explicit criticisms of Rowe's proposals were mainly that they would promote endless land litigation. This had been the cornerstone of Slater's objections. And significantly, he dealt with the argument that private ownership in land was needed to allow Africans access to credit, not by challenging the development of credit itself, but by pointing out that European companies seemed quite willing to lend money without mortgages, merely on 'personal guarantees by persons of substance.'[43]

Rowe meanwhile had transferred to Nigeria, where he was to participate in very similar debates during his period as Commissioner of Lands. The issue of private property rights had become a source of concern in Nigeria in the early 1920s[44], and indeed it was because of the emergence of these problems that Rowe was appointed to his new post. In the area around Abeokuta in Southern Nigeria private property in land had developed on a significant scale. This was partly because the Egba United Government, which ruled this area at the time of the colonial conquest, was less rooted in traditional African chieftaincies than were other parts of Nigeria, and pursued more Western concepts of land tenure; partly because the proximity of the town to the port of Lagos meant a greater integration into commodity production; and partly because the area had been one of the centres for the cotton production sponsored by the BCGA. From the beginning of the twentieth century land sales were sufficiently common to provoke the Governor to impose a restriction on land transactions to those between people of Egba descent, and by 1922 there was agitation among Egbas for the removal of these restrictions. A petition was drawn up by the 'people of Egbaland' and presented to the Alake of Abeokuta and his Council. This contrasted the rapid development of Lagos, where sales, leases and mortgaging of land were unrestricted, with the stagnation of Abeokuta where Egbas were prevented from selling land to either Europeans or non-Egba Africans[45]. In forwarding this petition to London, Clifford drew a similar contrast between the two towns, but in his case, to the detriment of Lagos, where he understood that

. . . the descendants of the original landowners have been reduced to the position of labourers on large estates which have been acquired by wealthy Lagosians.[46]

Clifford expressed the conventional antagonism to private property:

> . . . the present tendency, then, in Abeokuta is toward individual ownership of land, with the inevitable result that natives who acquired wealth by trade will form large estates to the exclusion of the uneducated peasant farmer. In my opinion this tendency should be checked, as it is not in the interests of the Egbas as a whole to allow a state of affairs to continue which can only benefit a few thousand literate natives.[47]

He was prepared to allow some concessions in the town of Abeokuta, and would accept leasing and mortgaging of any property which could be demonstrated as fully individual property – but only to other Africans, and only with the consent of the Alake and his Council. The control of the Alake should be further re-established, with all existing land transactions made dependent on his approval. The Alake was understandably in favour of this compromise.

In the course of the next two years, during which no decision was reached, Clifford's position modified to a clear advocacy of the rights to sell, lease and mortgage land within the boundaries of the town. Local opinion was unanimous in support of this. Private property was firmly established, as was perhaps inevitable in the process of development, and the institution of mortgaging already existed in the practice of mortgaging of crops[48]. Officials in London expressed the usual reservations. Mortgaging was considered by one official a very dangerous development for an 'improvident people'[49], while the discovery that crop mortgaging existed aroused fears that the owners of the land would soon be 'reduced to the position of serfs bound to till their own land for the benefit of the mortgagees'[50]. Approval for the mortgaging of *town* property was conceded, but faced with such reluctance from London, Clifford decided to delay action.

This uncertainty over the policy appropriate to Abeokuta led, in 1926, to a request for a post of Commissioner of Lands and the creation of a Lands Department to deal with land problems for both Northern and Southern Provinces of Nigeria. The decision over Abeokuta was laid aside pending the appointment of Rowe to this position, and it was hoped that the formation of a Lands Department would facilitate resolution of this issue, while also settling the confusions about land titles and boundaries in the Colony of Lagos.

Rowe's reception in the homeland of indirect rule was, as might be expected, somewhat mixed. What is remarkable is not that he faced opposition from Nigerian administrators, but that a man of his reputation was chosen by the Nigerian Government against the advice of the Colonial Office[51]. His first disappointment on arrival in Nigeria was exclusion from the Northern Provinces. The Lieutenant-Governor of the North was not prepared to co-operate with him, and the activities of the Lands Department were restricted to the South[52]. Even in the Southern

Provinces, he came up against strong opposition. In 1929, for example, the Lieutenant-Governor of the South declared that

> . . . any extension of the individual proprietary right would completely destroy native administration . . . Government cannot, I think, hope to be successful with its policy of rule by indirect methods if it gives much support to an extension outside Lagos of freehold tenure.[53]

Rowe found a valuable ally in the Director of Agriculture, however, whose attempts to deal with the palm oil industry by promoting the introduction of experimental plantations by African farmers had come up against the obstacle of family tenure. In 1931 Rowe could proclaim:

> The Director of Agriculture and the Commissioner of Lands are of the opinion that full progress in agriculture in Nigeria cannot be obtained under a system of land tenure which does not provide for security of the individual proprietary right.[54]

He pursued his campaign for a realistic land policy through accumulating evidence of already existing individual rights. In a lengthy memorandum of *Land, Planning and Development*[55], produced in 1931, he listed the example of Abeokuta, where public auctions of land averaged one hundred each year; Calabar, where the local Deeds Registry witnessed numerous transactions by individuals claiming virtually freehold rights; Kano, where the usufruct of farms was widely bought and sold; and Ijebu Province, where 'the greater part of the land is privately owned and is constantly let or sold outright'[56]. He challenged the claim of the defenders of 'native customary tenure' that they were protecting African rights by pointing to evidence that chiefs were abusing their position to become landlords. He managed to get the annual Conference of Residents 1929 and 1930 to discuss his proposal for registration of titles, though with little success at this stage, since the overwhelming opinion seemed to be in favour of preserving the 'supposed communal system'[57].

The Lands Department, like many others, suffered severe retrenchment in the early 1930s, when five of the European officers were dismissed in the financial stringency of the depression. But against all odds, an ordinance for the registration of land titles was finally approved in 1933 (Rowe died just before its final approval), which established the principle of compulsory land registration and accepted the practice of mortgaging and foreclosure. The Ordinance applied only to Lagos and the Southern Provinces, but within this area registration districts could be declared within which titles must be registered for any lease of over forty years, and any land transaction involving money also had to be registered. Registration of titles would be permitted for shorter leases, but with the qualification that applications would be rejected if the land was shown to be family land[58]. The acceptance of private property in land was thus hesitant, and fell far short of challenge to family property, but the principle of individual ownership was approved.

It was against this background of rapidly changing opinion that the decisions over Abeokuta were made. In 1928, Governor Thompson declared:

> I hold the view that the idea that the raising of a mortgage is in itself a doubtful proceeding in which the natives should not be allowed to indulge owing to their unsophisticated nature, which has to a large extent permeated our policy in regard to this subject in Nigeria, is now out of date.[59]

It was inconsistent to promote commodity production but deny the right to mortgage. In particular, Thompson suggested continued refusal of mortgages might undermine the position of the African middleman, who mediated between European merchant companies and African producers. Mortgaging could be safely permitted as long as it was only of leasehold land. Amery, in his response, correctly pointed out that this was no protection against possible expropriation from the land, but by now agreed that 'absolute protection against such a state of affairs apparently puts a check on the legitimate development of Nigeria'[60]. Approval was reluctantly given to the principle of mortgaging.

The framework of debate had thus shifted considerably. At the time of the WALC, free land sales had been associated with the policy of development through European plantations, and the alternative of African commodity production had been identified with the maintenance of 'native customary tenure'. By the late 1920s, it was increasingly admitted that even this 'legitimate development' through African smallholders demanded some relaxation in previous land policy. Policy remained varied, with the simultaneous extension of the principles of Northern Nigerian land policy to the Northern Territories of the Gold Coast, and a relaxation of restrictions on mortgaging in Southern Nigeria. There was no longer a simple model for British West Africa.

The shift in opinion was strengthened by new evidence of the conditions of 'native customary tenure'. For example, a comprehensive survey of land tenure in the four Yoruba Provinces of Southern Nigeria, commissioned in the early 1930s, revealed that land was not after all vested in the chiefs as trustees of the people[61]. The land belonged rather to the family groups who had settled it. The family heads who administered this land might often be chiefs, but their authority over the land derived from their membership of the family and not from their office as chiefs. The survey thus established, at least to Governor Cameron's satisfaction[62], firstly, that the chiefs did not own the land; secondly, that the only clear restrictions on land transactions within customary tenure were the obligations of members of a family to obtain the permission of chiefs before accepting strangers into the community; and thirdly, that customary tenure seemed to permit both individuals and families to sell their land. In Yorubaland, strangers who were permitted access to virgin land would be expected to make gifts to the head-chief of the family group, and also to the owners of the land – who might themselves be chiefs, or merely family heads, or even individual members of a family. In neither case was the gift a rent proper but whereas the gift to the head-chief was a recognition that 'he was the administrator of the group, the advisor on points of custom, and the chief judge in cases of dispute' (Ward-Price, 1933:28), the gifts to the actual grantors of the land were an acknowledgement of their rights of ownership over the land. Thus chiefs who claimed rights of ownership were acting outside the original custom, and Ward-Price, the author of the report, criticized attempts made by chiefs in previous decades to present themselves as owners of the land[63].

The report described the process whereby pre-colonial forms of tribute had been replaced by a simple monetary exchange. In the case of Ibadan,

> . . . in former days, town sites were granted rapidly because a grateful adherent was thereby added to the family, and the family's prestige and power increased. Sites were granted in perpetuity so long as they were occupied, which really means, except in rare cases, an outright grant.
>
> In modern times, the head of a family realises that such a grant really amounts to an outright grant, and that, under the new administrative and judicial systems, there is not much advantage in possessing grateful adherents of the family. He therefore comes to the conclusion that it is wise to make the occasion an opportunity of adding to the family's financial resources, as he stands to gain nothing by not doing so. (Ward-Price, 1933:44)

The establishment of colonial states meant a separation of politics and economics. The political advantages of 'grateful' tenants were increasingly minimal, and if the economic advantages of rent were denied to the owners, they would be reluctant to agree to an influx of new farmers. In this context, colonial restrictions on land sales or rents would actually reduce the opportunities for strangers to take up land outside their country of origin. The effect would be a greater inflexibility than that of pre-colonial society. A similar process was taking place in grants of virgin land in the country around Ibadan. Forest land, which had previously been freely granted to any new occupant who took on the task of forest clearance, was now regarded as valuable cocoa-growing land. The owners demanded a small annual payment from the new tenants, and a labour obligation to work on the grantor's farm at various periods during the year (Ward-Price, 1933:45). Again, if this form of tenancy were prevented by colonial legislation, migration to previously uncultivated land would be halted, to the detriment of agricultural expansion. Furthermore, as Cameron argued in forwarding the report, the custom of permitting strangers access to family land provided a mechanism whereby descendants of slaves, who owned no land, could establish themselves as farmers. Constraints on the practice would eliminate this possibility. In other words, Yoruba societies prior to the colonial conquest had evolved customs which encouraged mobility and migration to agri- culturally productive land. Under the conditions of colonization, the previous forms of tribute inevitably came to take the form of clear land sales and rentals. And if the traditional horror of such developments were to lead the colonial governments into preventative action, obstacles would be created to the expansion of agriculture.

The potential of expropriation from the land was not denied, but in a significant shift from the earlier terms of debate it was now hinted that the landless could be accommodated through working as wage-labourers for more successful farmers. Ward-Price commented on the extent of mortgaging of crops which had developed in Abeokuta Province, where 'there are numerous young men who are unable to redeem the trees their fathers pawned'. This, he suggested, 'may be one reason why there is always a large number of young men without work to do or farms to work on'. However, rather than simply deploring this development, he went on to point out that 'there are also farmers who are in need of labour to cultivate their holdings. The young men do not always trust that the farmers will pay them their wages regularly' (Ward-Price, 1933:79). The implication here was that the solution to the problem might lie in a more firmly institutionalized wage labour relationship, rather than in a doomed attempt to guarantee all farmers equal access to ownership of land.

As a result of this report, Cameron was prepared to give final approval to land sales and rentals in Abeokuta, and clung merely to the two safeguards that only the leasehold of town land could be mortgaged to non-Africans, and that only the crops on farming land could be mort- gaged. By this point officials in London were prepared to allow the West African Governors a free hand in decisions about land tenure, which was now considered 'such a tedious subject'[64]. The last vestige of Colonial Office anxiety was to occur in 1934, when Cameron proposed a new bill to regulate the 'kola' (peppercorn) tenancies which had developed among the Ibo people in the Southern Provinces[65]. The problem again arose from the development of land values. In the Onitsha Province, 'kola tenants' who paid a nominal tribute to the owners of the land, for exam- ple occasional presents of kola nuts, could now sub-let the land for as much as £200 per annum. The proposed bill would give the original grantors the right to reclaim the land on payment of compensation to their tenants, or alternatively give the tenants the right to purchase the land outright. Colonial Office officials were predictably horrified by this evidence of ground landlordism, and the precedent of India was once more brought out as the cautionary tale. But as with the Abeokuta deci- sion, it was accepted that the Governor should now decide on the appro- priate action, and the bill was approved. The Kola Tenancies Ordinance ws accordingly enacted in 1935.

Thus in the case of Nigeria the principle of private property in land was conceded, and institutionalized in legislation which permitted the registration of individual proprietary rights. This acknowledged the right to sell land without the constraints of native law and to charge an economic rent; and accepted, albeit with some restrictions, the right to raise mortgages on private property. This principle was not of course practised throughout the colony of Nigeria. The Registration of Titles Ordinance was only applied to the major urban centres, and the concessions of the late 1920s and early 1930s involved more the recognition of existing private ownership rights than the grandiose vision of Rowe, which pushed for an enforced introduction of private ownership throughout Nigeria. The change in policy stopped short of any deliberate campaign to promote private property rights. And the continued ambivalence was demonstrated in the failure of Rowe's propaganda for registration of titles in the Gold Coast. The principle of African proprietary rights in land had been conceded in the Concessions Ordinance, and any more explicit move in the direction of individual freehold was deprecated by the Governor in the late 1920s. The growing divergence between the supposed philosophy of West African land policy and the actual practice of colonial govenments testifies more to the inappropriateness of the original philosophy than to a dramatic conversion to its opposite.

The starting point of land policy at the time of the First World War was the concern to dampen the effects of change. It had been assumed that production could continue within largely pre-capitalist relations, and that the effects of merchant capital would ensure only a change in the nature of the products themselves. Africans would be encouraged to bring more land under cultivation merely by the lure of money rewards from the merchant companies; they would not have to change the relations under which they produced. The success of the West African Policy was that the transformation to commodity production did indeed occur mainly through the market. The colonial states in West Africa were not generally forced into the use of taxation or direct administrative coercion to 'persuade' their subjects to produce for the world market. But the second assumption, that in the process pre-capitalist relations could be preserved in relative purity, was not to be fulfilled. Administrators in London were slow to admit this, and administrators in the colonies varied in their perception of it. But by the time of the Second World War 'native customary tenure' no longer seemed so straightforward.

The clearest transformations occurred where land was required by the merchants (as in the urban trading centres), and where migration of strangers from another lineage group had preceded colonialism or developed in response to the new conditions of commodity production (as with the migrant cocoa farmers studied in Hill, 1963). In the former case land came to have a clear exchange value, and in the competition for the proceeds individual proprietary rights were almost universally established. In the latter, the cultivation of what the colonial administators termed 'economic crops' led the owners of the land to demand an economic rent. Ironically the imposition of the colonial state fostered this process by undercutting the politics of patronage. The land-owners demanded a money rent instead of the increasingly worthless 'gratitude' of their tenants.

Underlying these processes was the dependence on credit implicit in the transition to commodity production. The farmers, who came to live by production of a commodity which could be realized only once or twice in the course of the year, usually relied for their subsistence on advances from African middlemen who organized the purchase of the crops for the merchant companies. A complex system of indebtedness rapidly developed, the extent of which only became fully understood in the proceedings of the Commission on the Marketing of West African Cocoa in 1938[66]. The mortgaging of crops, the discovery of which had caused such consternation in Abeokuta, was widespread throughout the cocoa-producing districts of the Gold Coast, and inevitably placed the mortgagee at risk of expropriation if the crop failed or the output fell below expectations. The potential for class differentiation within this process worked itself out, to the extent that the 1931 census in the Gold Coast had to classify those involved in agriculture into the following five groups: (a) peasant proprietors cultivating crops solely for themselves and their families; (b) peasant proprietors cultivating crops for sale and export; (c) hired labourers; (d) employers of labour and non-working landholders; (e) distribution agents, buyers, middlemen, transport owners, transport employees, porters (Cardinall, 1931:201). This was not the vision articulated by the writers of the draft report of the WALC, though it arose from the fundamental principle advocated by those writers: that agricultural production should remain in the hands of the Africans, and not be developed through large European estates. What had emerged was that this principle was not enough. The exclusion of European capital did not of itself guarantee that pre-capitalist relations of production would be preserved against the forces of dissolution.

By the 1930s, the claim that British West Africa represented an alternative to capitalist agriculture was seriously discredited, and the colonial governments were engaged in little more than a holding operation. The commitment to peasant production had some effects, but from the emerging 'development' perspective, these were largely negative. It had enough force to hamper Lever's attempts to transform palm oil production, but not enough to ensure alternative ways of promoting productivity. It could force land transactions underground, and disguise the number of land sales, but could not eliminate them. It delayed regulation of the land market, and thereby limited access to bank loans, but could not prevent African farmers from turning instead to money-lenders, who charged exorbitant interest. It constrained investigation into the use of wage labour on African farms, and so hindered the regulation of this labour market, but could not stop the formation of capitalist agriculture. The policies, which at the time of the First World War seemed a coherent package of philanthropy, economic progress and political order, did not work. By the outbreak of the Second World War, the colonial states were merely adjusting themselves to conditions over which they had marginal control.

In this sense, the war was a watershed for colonial policies, and in subsequent years colonial administrators began to occupy themselves with a new set of problems. As one analyst of colonialism prophetically remarked in 1942:

> Different generations choose different aspirations and concepts to guide them in their political endeavour: 'indirect rule' was the watch-word of the decade which followed the last war; 'development and welfare' will probably be the cry of the generation which follows the present one. (Hancock, 1942:267)

The war served merely to mark this shift, and cannot be held responsible for it[67]. The crisis in colonial practice was rooted in the impossibility of the task the colonizers had set themselves, and the war only accelerated forces of dissolution already at work. Significantly, the inter-war attempts to regulate property relations and settle, once and for all, the vexed question of communal land tenure, came to nothing. The 'uncertain financial outlook' delayed investigation into land registration in the Yoruba Provinces[68], and by 1940, only three registration areas had been declared in Nigeria[69]. Land questions receded into the background, and by the end of the war the problem of labour came once again to the fore. Tinkering with property rights was no solution to the inadequacies of the peasant option, and a more immediate crisis was looming with mass migration to the towns. Moreover, decolonization was at last on the agenda, and the colonial states had to cope with new constitutional issues which absorbed much of the energy previously devoted to manoeuvring around the peasantry. The post-war years witnessed a further radical shift in the terms of colonial debate, a shift which can be traced through examination of labour policies from the late 1930s onwards.

NOTES

1 Governor-General to Secretary of State, 13 March 1914, CO 583/11.
2 ibid. The Secretary of State replied on 11 May 1914, urging caution pending the deliberations of the WALC.
3 Secretary of State to Governor, 23 May 1917, CO 96/583.
4 Governor to Secretary of State, 26 December 1917, CO 96/583.
5 Enclosure ii, in above.
6 Enclosure iii, in above.
7 The Governor's despatch was in fact filed as secret.
8 Ordinance 1 of 1927, Gold Coast.

9 Governor to Secretary of State, 15 March 1930, CO 96/694/6688.

10 Secretary of State to Governor, 21 November 1930, CO 96/694/6688.

11 C.O. minutes on Governor to Secretary of State, 10 February 1930, CO 96/693/6665.

12 Governor to Secretary of State, 7 March 1913, CO 446/111.

13 C.O. minutes, CO 446/111.

14 See Governor-General to Secretary of State, 8 August 1917, CO 583/59.

15 Governor to Secretary of State, 31 October 1919, CO 583/78. He reported that 'this Government, rightly or wrongly, has earned a reputation for driving hard bargains, and for claiming the last ounce of its pound of flesh, which Shylock might have observed with envy; and Europeans and native investors are persuaded that, not only are hard terms imposed upon them, but that no liberal interpretation is likely to be placed upon these conditions by the Colonial Administration.' For C.O. minutes on his proposal, see West African Merchants' Association to C.O., 24 March 1919, CO 583/82.

16 Secretary of State to Governor, 16 February 1921, filed in CO 583/82.

17 ibid. The despatch suggested that even the original modification, made under pressure from Lugard, of seven years revision to twenty, was a mistake.

18 Governor to Secretary of State, 24 June 1920, CO 583/89.

19 C.O. minutes, CO 583/89.

20 Deputy Governor to Secretary of State, 12 March 1928, CO 583/158/182.

21 Enclosure in above, p. 32.

22 ibid., p. 33.

23 African West 1048, 1916:131.

24 As in Clifford's lengthy despatch, 26 December 1917, CO 96/583.

25 For example, West African Merchants' Association to C.O., 24 March 1919, the letter which prompted Clifford's declaration of support for the merchants' demands for more favourable treatment. CO 583/82.

26 Governor-General to Secretary of State, 23 April 1918, CO 583/66. The notice was published in the Nigeria Gazette on 14 March 1918.

27 Report on Land Tenure in Ashanti by Acting Chief Commissioner, Enclosure 1 in Governor to Secretary of State, 31 May 1918, CO 96/590.

28 The Omanhene of Akwapim, for example, complained in 1901 that 'nowadays the people are unwilling to do as it is customary to be done' i.e. to give him a share of the proceeds of land sales. Quoted in Hill, 1963:147.

29 Memorandum by Secretary for Native Affairs, for the visit of Ormsby-Gore in 1926, CO 96/663.

30 ibid.

31 The memorandum Rowe wrote in 1922, which prompted Guggisberg to set up this Committee, is enclosed in Governor to Secretary of State, 31 January 1923, CO 96/637. Guggisberg was already at this stage convinced of the need for a separate Lands Department, and persuaded the C.O. to agree to the financing of a land survey which would create the cadastral framework for precise descriptions of registered lands. At this stage he presented the case as relatively uncontroversial – contrasting it with the very different conditions in Nigeria, where land issues were a major source of debate – and desirable simply to settle ownership disputes.

32 The Majority and Minority Reports were forwarded to London in Acting Governor to Secretary of State, 7 June 1923, CO 96/640.

33 Part of the report was filed in the documents relating to Ormsby-Gore's visit,

CO 96/663. The full version was reprinted in pp. 52–63 of the *Proposed Reforms in Respect of the Land Legislation of the Gold Coast primarily in order to promote security of title*, Accra: Government Printer, 1927.
34 Memorandum by R. H. Rowe, 28 September 1926, ibid., p. 76.
35 Memorandum by R. S. Rattray, 22 December 1927, printed in *Land Legislation of the Gold Coast*, Vol. II, Accra: Government Printer, 1930:27.
36 Both publications are filed in CO 96/693/6665.
37 *Land Legislation of the Gold Coast, Vol. II*, 1930:5.
38 Secretary of State to Governor, 2 May 1930, in CO 96/693/6665.
39 Notes by R. H. Rowe on Governor's Memorandum on the Land Department, pp. 25–6, CO 583/179/1154.
40 A. R. Slater, Confidential Memorandum, 1 October 1927, CO 96/671/4173.
41 C.O. minutes on Governor to Secretary of State, 10 February 1930, CO 96/693/6665.
42 Governor to Secretary of State, 10 October 1931, CO 96/700/7086.
43 ibid.
44 The issue was first raised even earlier than this. In Lugard's despatch of 7 March 1913, when he suggested a relaxation in terms for European merchants, he also suggested that 'rights of occupancy' for African farmers be introduced, so that they could have absolute rights of ownership over improvements to their land, but pay rents to the Government, revisable at four-yearly intervals (Lugard's objections to too frequent rent revisions apparently only applied to Europeans). The Government could then impose restrictions on sub-division of land at the death of the tenant, and thereby promote the principle of primogeniture. This proposal, which prefigured many of Rowe's concerns, was dropped without comment when the C.O. rejected his simultaneous proposals for better terms for the merchants. CO 446/111.
45 Enclosure i, Governor to Secretary of State, 31 January 1923, CO 583/117.
46 Governor to Secretary of State, 31 January 1923, CO 583/117.
47 ibid.
48 Governor to Secretary of State, 30 December 1924, CO 583/128. On this occasion, Clifford particularly antagonized the C.O. by asking for a reply by telegram, implying an urgency which did not accord with normal C.O. practice.
49 C.O. minutes on Governor to Secretary of State, 31 January 1923, CO 583/117.
50 C.O. minutes on Governor to Secretary of State, 30 December 1924, CO 583/128.
51 When the Governor asked for a Commissioner of Lands, the C.O. response was that one could be appointed, but only for the Southern Provinces, not both North and South as originally requested. Rowe was considered too senior for the post, and the appointment of an officer from within the Nigerian service was suggested as an alternative. See Governor to Secretary of State, 15 January 1926, CO 583/139/1190.
52 Rowe's complaints against this exclusion were vehemently presented in his Notes on His Excellency's Memorandum on the Lands Department, 21 October 1931, enclosed in Governor to Secretary of State, 21 March 1931, CO 583/179/1154.
53 Quoted by Rowe in the above document.

54 R. H. Rowe, Memorandum on Land, Planning and Development, Appendix III. CO 583/180/1232.

55 ibid.

56 ibid., p. 6.

57 ibid., p. 8.

58 Registration of Titles Ordinance, 1933. A C.O. minute on the new legislation commented on the unfortunate death of Rowe, just before his work reached fruition. CO 583/190/1115.

59 Governor to Secretary of State, 6 June 1928, CO 583/160/260.

60 Secretary of State to Governor, 11 March 1929, CO 583/160/260. Flood of the C.O. recommended acceptance of the Governor's proposals, but 'with a great deal of misgiving'.

61 H. L. Ward Price, *Land Tenure in the Yoruba Provinces*, Lagos: Government Printer, 1933.

62 Governor to Secretary of State, 13 April 1933, CO 583/191/1144.

63 He referred particularly to the case of the Bale of Ibadan and his Council, who in 1903 published this notice: 'The Bale and Council of Ibadan desire it to be made publicly known that all land in the town of Ibadan is vested in them as the chiefs and representatives of the people. They also declare that such land cannot be alienated from the native owners, but may be leased for a term of years on payment of a fair annual rent. Such leases can be issued only by the Bale and Council, and to them the rent must in every case be paid.' (p. 52) Ward Price's comment on this was that the Bale and Council had acted outside their rights; they did not own the land.

64 C.O. minutes on Governor to Secretary of State, 13 April 1933, CO 583/191/1144.

65 The discussion of the 'kola tenancies' is in CO 583/199/21202.

66 *Report of the Commission on the Marketing of West African Cocoa*, Cmd. 5845, London, 1938.

67 Bowden (1980) argues that 1939–40 marks the break point in British colonial policy for Nigeria and the Gold Coast, and stresses the impact of the war itself in precipitating greater emphasis on planning and development. But even in her argument, the impact of the war is to heighten Colonial Office sensitivity to political questions rather than to create entirely new conditions.

68 Governor to Secretary of State, 15 January 1938, CO 583/230/30267.

69 CO 583/250/30267.

7

The Emergence of an African Working Class

It was the unintended arrival of an African working class that finally torpedoed the West African Policy. The peasantry refused to meet colonial expectations, and under the pressure of circumstance, land policy never achieved a consistent pattern. The resultant ambiguities revealed the inadequacies of the original policy, but as long as African workers were absent from the scene, the peasant road retained some credibility. For as long as was possible, colonial officials treated wage labour as a peripheral activity, and it was not until the late 1930s, when the existence of African workers had to be acknowledged, that the Policy finally collapsed.

The resistance to plantation estates kept down the numbers of wage-labourers[1], and the main private employers were the mining companies. Even here, the use of migrant, and sometimes non-waged, labour sustained the illusion that wage labour was marginal to the colonial economy. In Nigeria, tin- and gold-mining were still alluvial, and though a 1935 report on the Nigerian goldfield suggested that this stage must soon end, most of the work remained in the hands of 'tributers', who collected mineral ore from the river beds and sold their findings to the companies[2]. In the gold mines, and the less significant diamond mines of the Gold Coast, the labour force was still substantially migrant, and as late as 1950, 50 per cent of the workers for the southern mines came from the Northern Territories or the neighbouring French colonies[3]. Again, the future of this labour system was under question from the 1920s as the mining companies discussed the possibilities of a more stabilized work force[4], but the work remained sufficiently casual to justify denials of a working class. A few small factories were set up in the 1920s and 1930s, but here too the work was of a casual nature. Rose's lime juice factory in the Gold Coast, for example, employed only seventy daily-paid labourers, and these were discharged at the end of each season (Greenstreet, 1972a:42). The Nigerian government retained control of the coal mines at Enugu, and operated under similar conditions to the private companies. The mine kept far more workers on its books than it could employ at one time – 3,400 on the books against 2,700 normally employed – and clearly considered its workers as temporary refugees from peasant production, rather than permanent wage-labourers[5]. Thus, where wage labourers were employed, it was on the basis described by Lord Hailey in *The African Survey*:

> In Africa the organisation of wage labour has proceeded on the assumption that, except where farms are worked by squatter labour, the homes of the labourers will continue to be in the native areas, and that responsibility for them will be discharged if they are remunerated at rates suitable to the single man and are adequately fed and housed in their temporary places of employment. (Hailey, 1956:710)

Recruitment to these jobs remained on an ad hoc basis. Pressures for a private recruiting agency had been rebuffed[6], and no alternative existed in the form of a labour exchange. When labour supplies were inadequate for public or private employment, the government resorted to the chiefs and did not enquire too closely into the methods used to produce the desired work-force. Conditions for the workers were subject to little regulation, and for most of West Africa the main labour legislation was a version of the Masters and Servants Ordinance, which regulated the terms on which migrant workers were employed. There was no factory legislation and no provision for trades unions. In these unregulated working conditions, companies were able to evade such minimal condition as regular payment of wages. In 1930, for example, the Gold Coast Prestea Mine was unable to pay wages for two months, and in the resulting confrontation, eight miners were shot and wounded by the mine staff[7]. Wage employment on African farms was almost totally ignored by colonial officers, and again the lack of regulation produced casualized working conditions. As Ward Price's report on *Land Tenure in the Yoruba Provinces* (1933) indicated, landlessness was on the increase among so-called peasants, but the victims of this were reluctant to work for local farmers when so many of the farmers failed to pay the promised wages. As long as the extent of wage-labour in agriculture was denied, and the illusion of peasant production maintained, such questions could not be faced. According to the principles of the West African Policy, wage-labour was a minor phenomenon which could be left to regulate itself.

The world recession of the 1920s and 1930s served initially to reinforce commitment to the West African Policy. Its first impact was to strengthen the case against wage dependency, and add weight to the peasant alternative. The crisis in world employment indicated the fragility of jobs, and the argument was that Africans who became dependent on wages for their subsistence would present a challenge to the political order when their jobs inevitably disappeared. One consequence of this was the disparagement of schemes for colonial development as creating more problems than they were worth. In the 1920s, such schemes were canvassed as a solution to Britain's growing unemployment problem: the colonies would get assistance in their development efforts, while Britain would benefit from the increased orders for equipment and machinery. These schemes, which found expression in the Colonial Development Act (1929), were not always welcomed by the colonial beneficiaries. Governor Clifford of Nigeria, for example, argued in 1925 that any 'sudden, brief spasm of intensive development' could be disastrous for the colonies themselves:

> Any attempt to force development by violent artificial means is bound to produce results which will be found to be quite tragically disconcerting.[8]

The problem was that solving unemployment in Britain might generate unemployment in Nigeria:

> Even if unemployment had been sensibly relieved in Great Britain, which might or might not be the case, would it be very satisfactory if each of the more backward Tropical Dependencies of the Crown was required to face an unemployment question of its own, as the price of the relief thus afforded?

He feared a 'premature' (recurrent colonial phrase) dissolution of peasant society, particularly when the new wage labourers might subsequently have to retreat to agricultural production:

> The Colonial Governments concerned would only be able to hope that the men whom they had seduced from agricultural work in order to fur- nish the means of promoting this sudden spasm of intensive develop- ment would sink back into the class of cultivators from which they had been prematurely drawn; but all experience in the Tropics proves that such reversions are in the last degree difficult to effect, and that angry discontent invariably kindles in the man, who having been lifted out of his 'natural' sphere, is incontinently dropped back into it by a Govern- ment which cannot find a use for the training or the skill which he has acquired through its agency.[9]

When the Colonial Development Act (1929) put these notions into prac- tice, and made available £1 millon per year for development projects, the funds were under-utilized, and few colonial governments took full advan- tage of the new opportunities for cheap loans. In Nigeria, the most popu- lated of the African colonies, a bare £ ¼ million was requested in the decade preceding the Second World War. Colonial resistance to the scheme arose partly from the fear that extensive development programmes would impose too great a burden on the finances of the local state, which would have to foot the bill for recurrent expenditure, and could expect assistance only for ini- tial investment[10]. But in addition to this was the reservation expressed by Clifford, that such projects would accelerate proletarianization beyond what the colonial economy and state could sustain.

The implications of world unemployment for Africa were stated most forcibly in Orde-Browne's *The African Labourer* (1933)[11]. Like the Governor of Nigeria, Orde-Browne saw future unemployment as the central danger. His study was written at a time of mass unemployment in Britain, when the state was facing considerable difficulties in devising social security schemes adequate for the large numbers out of work. With this in mind, Orde-Browne argued for the 'retention of the connection between the worker and the land', as the only way to avoid the vast machinery of welfare benefits which was in crisis in Britain. Wage-labour should remain an adjunct to peasant society, and in this way, the obligations of the state would be kept within acceptable limits:

> As long as the displaced worker can if necessary be re-absorbed into tribal life, provision for unemployment, old age pensions, and similar obligations of modern industrialised society will be largely superfluous; if, however, a considerable class of landless manual workers is created, and European conditions reproduced the government concerned will sooner or later be compelled to recognise the inevitability of appropriate measures to meet the attendant problems. (Orde-Brown, 1933:116)

If the colonial governments permitted wage dependency, yet resisted the claims to welfare provision, the results could be disastrous:

> . . . the detribalised worker must face destitution if he loses the employment from which he draws his wages, and will become a homeless wanderer picking up a precarious living for himself and his family as best he can. The danger of creating such a class is very real, for they must form a miserable and discontented body almost inevitably inclined to crime, while their misfortunes will render them peculiarly responsive to any agitator or mischief-maker. (ibid, p. 113)

Beyond the more pragmatic revenue considerations, any generalization of wage labour could threaten the political order of the colonies. In his foreword to this work Lord Lugard, never a principled opponent of wage labour, warned:

> . . . the problem of today is to ensure that service with Europeans shall not result in the premature disintegration of native society. For the illiterate worker who has lost faith in the approval or the anger of the spirits of his forebears, who has renounced his tribal loyalties and his claim to a share in the family or clan land and the ready help of his fellows in time of need, has now no motive for self-control and becomes a danger to the State. (ibid, p.v.)

Orde-Browne echoed this vision of the working class threat:

> For practical purposes . . . such workers are without any real standard of behaviour, and obey only such police or company regulations as may be effectively enforced. The ease with which such people may drift into the criminal classes, or the fertile ground which they will provide for inflammatory political progaganda, must be obvious. (ibid, p. 104)

139

In such an atmosphere it was only to be expected that West African administrators would continue to discourage or deny the formation of a proletariat. The peasant road was leading in a different direction than envisaged, and the journey was fraught with unanticipated dangers; but it retained enough credibility for the disparagement of wage employment as peripheral to the colonial economy.

The world crisis thus strengthened the case for the peasant road, but simultaneously, it spelt the end of its possibility. The processes which the colonial states had set in motion, could not be frozen at the desired point, and the recession intensified the process of proletarianization. As Berg (1965) has pointed out, the problem of labour shortage, which character-ized virtually all African colonies until the 1920s, was transformed into a new problem of labour surplus. World prices for primary commodities collapsed in the 1930s, and Africans who had become dependent on money earnings now found themselves unable to survive on the proceeds from their farms. Migration to the towns and mining compounds increased, but at a time when both government and private firms were cutting back on employment. The numbers of unskilled Africans seeking wage employment soon exceeded the available jobs, and in the Gold Coast, colonial administrators began to dissuade migrants from the Northern Territories from seeking work in the mines (Silver, 1981:103). Initially, these new conditions simply reinforced the commitment to casual labour, since the assumption that Africans did not rely on wage earnings justified mass lay-offs of workers. The crisis was taken as a demonstration of the correctness of colonial practice. If a working class *had* existed, the redundancies would have created serious problems for the colonial states, but as it was, it could be asssumed that the dismissed workers were simply reabsorbed into peasant society. The accumulation of Africans in the towns was treated as a problem of vagrancy, and the proposed solution was forcible repatriation. It was many years before colonial officials would dignify this new phenomenon with the term 'unemployment'. But through the 1930s, the problem of 'derelict labour' or 'so-called unemployment' emerged on to the scene. It was not until work was no longer available that the existence of a class of wage labourers was finally admitted.

An early attempt to investigate unemployment was made by a 1935 Committee set up to 'enquire into the Question of Unemployment' in Lagos[12]. The Committee issued notice that all those without jobs or means of subsistence should report to a government office, and 4,000 people (over 3 per cent of the population of Lagos and the surround-ing area) presented themselves for inspection. The unemployed divided almost equally into those born in Lagos and those born elsewhere (2,180 and 1,764 respectively), and the solution proposed for the latter was simply to send them back to their 'homes'. Nearly one quarter (969) had never had a job, which was interpreted as evidence of 'higher aspirations than are warranted by their abilities'[13]. For these, a land settlement scheme was suggested. The unemployed could be offered 4-acre plots of land, loans to cover them for the first two years, and if they deserted before repayment, they would be blacklisted from future employment by either government or private firms. The penalty made sense only within a much more regulated labour market than that which existed in Nigeria, a weakness which Committee members overlooked. The other main category of unemployed was those hitherto engaged in the building trades (919), and their plight was readily dismissed as one which would be solved in the expected resuscitation of the economy. The report was not considered important enough for submission to the Colonial Office, though it was published as a Sessional Paper in Nigeria, and the problem was set aside with hopes that it would simply resolve itself.

However, the existence of wage-labour as a reality which could no longer be ignored was confirmed by other developments. The 1930s was a period of growing labour unrest, particularly in the gold-mines of the Gold Coast, the coal mines of Nigeria, and among the railway workers employed by the state (Hughes and Cohen, 1978; Greenstreet, 1972b; Silver, 1981). Trades unions were formed and although usually short-lived, they indicated African refusal to remain within the boundaries of casual labour. It was becoming increasingly difficult to insist that these workers were merely temporary migrants, particularly as male workers began to bring their wives and children with them to the mining villages. According to Greenhalgh (1975), the diamond mines in the Gold Coast wanted a more stabilized work-force from the 1920s, and from 1923 began to provide free housing, churches, and non-profitmaking stores in the mining compounds so as to encourage more permanent employment. The 1938 Report on the Enugu coal mine showed that a similar stabilization was being pursued there[14]. A daily roster was set up to ensure more regular employment for the senior men, and in 1939 the practice of keeping more on the books than could be employed was broken as 600 employees were laid off. The changing conditions were described in the 1939 Report:

> At the commencement of mining operations great difficulty was experienced in securing labour and in training the primitive men for the work. That period has passed and today there is considerable competition to work in the mine. A system of labour supply has grown up which is now proving uneconomic. Under it the men have worked at the Colliery as and when they liked and absented themselves at will to return to their villages to pursue their normal activities. Free housing for a considerable number of men was provided to enable those who wished to stay on to do so. But the freelance system persisted, with the result that a great many more men than were actually needed obtained a place on the Colliery register. This in turn has led to an uneconomic sharing of the available work to the dissatisfaction of these men who prefer to work more regularly.[15]

The move towards a more permanent labour force was uneven, particularly when the labour surplus of the 1930s offered periods of exceptionally cheap unskilled labour[16]. In the Gold Coast mines, stabilization barely entered into discussion until 1945, and even then was not consistently pursued (Silver, 1981: chapter 5). Thus it is not surprising that within the space of a single decade, the arguments for retaining the connection with the land existed side by side with a new concern for settled wage labour, as providing more 'economic' conditions. It was a decade of transition, as the migrant labour system, based on a predominantly peasant society, began to emerge as an African working class.

The gradual shift in colonial perceptions was speeded up by developments in other colonies. In 1935, largely in response to Parliamentary questioning, the Colonial Office sent a circular to all governors, requesting information on their provisions for inspecting of labour conditions[17]. The West African colonies, still regarded as essentially peasant economies, were not the prime target of this circular, and the Colonial Office accepted the negative replies of the various governors without complaint[18]. But the 1937 strikes and riots in Trinidad introduced a greater urgency into colonial labour policy, and a meeting of the Colonial Labour Committee decided to press for the formation of Labour Departments wherever possible. In August 1937 a second circular was sent out, advising the creation of such departments for any colony with a 'substantial wage-earning community', and advocating the registration of trades unions[19]. The concern now was to regulate and moderate the development of incipient workers' organizations[20], and the complacency of those Governors who denied the existence of wage labour came under scrutiny. In 1938, Orde-Browne was appointed to the new post of Labour Advisor to the Secretary of State, and pressures on the West African colonies, among others, increased. The Colonial Office became impatient with local resistance, and the pattern of the earlier years, when colonial governors pressed for more adventurous land policies against Colonial Office conservatism, was reversed. By the late 1930s, it was the Colonial Office, with its sensitivity to developments in other colonies, which argued for change.

The Gold Coast government was the most responsive, and agreed that 'nothing short of the creation of a Labour Department will be adequate to the needs of the Gold Coast'[21]. In this most developed of the West African economies, a skeleton Labour Department was inaugurated in 1938, while the other colonies continued to question its necessity. The Gambia set up a Labour Advisory Board as an alternative; Sierra Leone resisted pressures from London, claiming that the 'wage earning community is largely casual and of insignificant proportions'[22]; and the Nigerian government reiterated the claim that the colony was based on small peasant farmers and had no urgent need for a Labour Department[23]. The outbreak of war heightened Colonial Office fears of labour unrest, and led to increased pressure for action, until the Gambia accepted the creation of a Labour Officer, Sierra Leone agreed to set up a Department from 1941, and Nigeria consolidated its existing Labour Inspectorate into a full Labour Department in 1942.

The more ready response from the Gold Coast was attributed by the Governor to the wave of strikes which occurred in 1937 and 1938[24], and concern with labour conditions was sufficient to generate both a series of committees to examine wage levels, and an extensive *Report on Labour Conditions in the Gold Coast* (1938)[25]. The committees were asked to consider (a) social conditions in the mines (b) wage levels for government labourers and (c) starting salaries for African civil servants. On the basis of their reports, the Governor argued for wage rises. Government employees in particular could no longer be paid as casual workers on rates of pay for single men. They lived with their families at the place of employment, and wage levels must reflect this. The Colonial Office demurred at his proposed increases, but on the basis of financial restraint rather than opposition to the changed conditions[26].

The *Report of Labour Conditions in the Gold Coast* argued for further modifications in labour policy. It estimated the number of wage labourers at 120,000, and recommended formal contracts for workers on the African farms so as to avoid the problem of unpaid wages. Reflecting the new conditions of labour surplus, the report pressed for fully voluntary recruitment, with only a labour exchange to provide information on availability of work. It condemned those practices which had been the basis of recruitment in previous decades and, in particular, the employment of headmen. Trades unions, it argued, should be recognized, if only because 'if such recognition is made there will be less danger from the agitators and the secret societies'[27].

The report did not break decisively with earlier assumptions; it continued, for example, to view 'detribalization' as undesirable, but questioned the claim that this necessarily accompanied wage labour. Conditions in the mines, particularly in the 'dreadful mushroom villages' around them, were considered appalling, and tribal headmen were recommended as a solution to this. Thus while their recruiting activities should be curtailed, their role in imposing discipline among mineworkers, and in 'keeping the village clean', should be strengthened. The problem, the report argued, was not wage labour itself, but the mushroom villages, and the Inspector of Labour hoped that 'something can be done to *re*-tribalize them'[28].

When in 1941, Orde-Browne published his *Labour Conditions in West Africa*[29], he confirmed the devastating effects of the world crisis on West Africa, but continued to identify the problem of unemployment with vagrancy. The fall in commodity prices had proved disastrous for the many Africans now dependent on the money economy, and meant that even with the considerable expansion in mining in the 1930s, there was no problem in recruiting labour[30]. There was, however, no serious danger of 'de-tribalization', and any unemployed person was to be dealt with through vagrancy laws:

. . . evidence of lack of means of support should enable the necessary action to be taken to return them to the agricultural community from which they have originally come.[31]

This reluctance to admit the full implications of the new conditions appeared also in the Annual Reports of the new Labour Departments, which nevertheless documented the rapidly changing situation. Labour was still presumed sufficiently casual to accommodate the large numbers of redundancies which accompanied the Second World War. In the Nigerian Cameroons, for example, 14,000 workers were sacked from the banana plantations in 1940, and the Labour Inspectorate considered this no 'undue hardship' when most of these workers were seasonal[32]. When thousands were re-employed over the next two years, the casual nature of the labour was cited as an advantage:

> There is a constant coming and going of labourers, a system which has its advantages in an industry of which the economic condition fluctuates as much as it does in the plantations, and in which the labour force can be increased or decreased without provoking labour difficulties.[33]

Similar arguments were employed when the Gold Coast Public Works Department cut its programme of work in 1939, and threw 2,000–3,000 men out of work: 'We are fortunate in this country in having a sufficiency of land to which our labourers can return when unemployed'[34]. The fact that many Africans could no longer make an adequate living from the land, as later demonstrated in Orde-Browne's report, was not considered relevant. Redundancies in the mines, where labour was not entirely casual were, however, viewed with greater foreboding. In 1943 the Gold Coast Labour Department predicted some unemployment problem when the Tarkwa mines laid off 6,000 men[35]. Fortunately for the colonial state, this coincided with a railway construction project in the next province, and the skilled craftsmen at least were assumed to be capable of finding alternative employment[36].

The problem of unemployment was thus initially discounted, though the 'derelict labour' which accumulated in Kumasi caused some concern. A Welfare Fund was set up to aid these victims of the migrant labour system, and the Medical Department had to deal with 1,469 cases of starvation in 1939–40[37]. A combination of vagrancy laws and repatriation remained the favoured solution. Magistrates' courts in Kumasi were given the powers to send young boys to approved institutions if they had no visible means of support, and in 1943, a subsidized transport scheme was set up to convey unemployed people in Kumasi back to the Northern Territories[38]. The 1944–5 Report of the Gold Coast Labour Department admitted a great excess of workers seeking employemnt in Accra, Sekondi and Kumasi, many of whom, it was feared, would soon become 'unemployables'[39]. Colonial officials continued however to view this phenomenon as reflecting the lure of the towns rather than genuine unemployment: work was available in agriculture if the migrants could only be 'persuaded' to return to it; and as late as 1950, they were described as only 'seemingly unemployed'[40].

The first reference to unemployment in the Nigerian Labour Department Reports came in 1942[41], when it was considered a problem restricted to Lagos. Again, the assumption was that these were only 'so-called unemployed', and the solution was to return them to the agricultural employment from which they came. In 1943, and employment exchange was set up in Lagos, temporarily raising the hopes of these unemployed:

> There is somewhat naturally the impression among the unemployed at present that it is the duty of the Exchange to guarantee them jobs and that the mere act of registration represents a promise of employment: but this conception is already disappearing and a more realistic view is gradually being taken.[42]

The numbers registered at the exchange quickly rose so that in February 1944, 7,800 were registerd as out of work, while only 350 found employment through the exchange. The numbers became alarming, and within a year of its creation, the Labour Exchange had to falsify the figures by restricting registration to those 'normally' resident in Lagos. This brought the numbers down to around 2,000, and indicates the 'back to the land' attitude of colonial officials. The problem of unemployment was thus blamed on the unemployed: it was their fault for leaving the countryside to seek work in the towns.

> Unemployment due to people crowding into towns with no particular employment in view is a growing evil and it is unnecessary to emphasise the harm it does. Labour leaves the land where it is most needed, there are more unproductive people to be fed in the towns, and if wages are increased, higher wages do not raise the standard of living if the increase if merely used to support a larger number of indigent relations and friends. Lastly if the unemployed remain unemployed for long they tend to become unemployable, and to form a discontented group of useless hangers-on to society. They sever their connection with the country, but never succeed in establishing themselves in town.[43]

There was little expectation that the problem would be solved by an increase in wage employment. The only hope lay with improved attractions in the countryside:

> It is difficult to venture any suggestion which might provide a solution to this grave problem. It will however be interesting to watch the effects of the proposed development policy which aims, amongst other objects, at the provision of good water supplies in rural areas and at a general improvement in the standard of living in the villages. Perhaps the improvement of conditions in the country will in some degree help to arrest the drift of the country people to the towns.[44]

In the Gold Coast, a 'back to the land' policy meant not a return to peasant agriculture, but an acceptance of wage employment on the African farms. The failure to regulate this labour market in those years when its existence was denied, now bore bitter fruit. It became difficult to persuade unemployed Africans to take up alternative employment with farmers who could not even guarantee regular wages. Wages on these farms were normally paid at the end of the season, and the 1937 cocoa hold-up dramatically increased the numbers of farmers who refused to pay[45]. As a result, labour for the farms was in short supply, even when there was a surplus of labour for other jobs and large numbers of unemployed in the towns. The cocoa farmers used the Kumasi labour exchange (set up after the 1938 *Report on Labour Conditions*) to recruit workers, but most migrants were suspicious, and now preferred the dangers of mine work to the irregular conditions of agricultural labour. The Labour Department tried to ease the situation by aiding workers to recover their wages and in this way restore confidence in the industry, but its efforts met with only partial success, and successive Annual Reports referred to the shortage of workers for the Ashanti cocoa farms[46].

The difficulties in persuading the unemployed to work in agriculture were intensified in the years after the war, when the colonial states faced the problem of demobilized soliders. Nigeria had to deal with 100,000 ex-soldiers, many of whom had technical training and expected skilled or semi-skilled wage employment. With numbers of wage earners still as low as 300,000, it would be impossible to find jobs for all of the soldiers, and a return to the peasantry was the preferred solution.

> Strong representations were made through the Secretary of State to the War Office in early October [1945] to impress on the minds of serving Nigerian troops the correct state of affairs in order to eliminate from their minds any false impression that there was sufficient employment for all.[47]

The Gold Coast faced 45,000 ex-servicemen, and although opportunities for wage employment were in principle more encouraging, with vacancies on the cocoa farms, the soldiers had no intention of taking up unskilled farm labour[48]. As is well known, this problem was to contribute to growing nationalist agitation (e.g. Austin, 1964).

By the end of the war, wage labour was acknowledged as a permanent feature of the colonial economies, and the concern if anything, was to establish 'normal' trade union practices. Labour Departments with a substantial staff now existed to monitor conditions; trade union registration was regulated by Trade Union Ordinances (passed in 1939 in Sierra Leone and Nigeria, and in 1941 in the Gold Coast); and labour exchanges operated at Kumasi and Lagos. The war ended with widespread worker agitation over wages and the cost of living, and the Nigerian state was forced to set up a number of commissions to examine wage levels[49]. Here, a general strike was organized in 1945, and significantly, it was difficult to find workers to replace the strikers, even with unemployemnt in Lagos running in several thousands. Neither the ex-servicemen nor the registered unemployed were prepared to break the strike, and it became necessary to recruit 2,000 from those 'non-residents' of Lagos who had previously been refused work, or the right to register as unemployed[50].

The colonial governments were by this time convinced that modern trade unionism would be an advance on what they considered the irrationalities of the African workers. The 1945 Gold Coast Report complained that strikes were difficult to settle when the workers had no clear demands[51], and there was concern in both the Gold Coast and Nigeria over the growth of 'unofficial' action. The 1946 Nigerian Report commented favourably on the development of the Nigerian Trades Union Council (TUC), which was, it believed, composed of

> . . . sober thinking men, disseminating sound Trades Union principles, and . . . gradually taking over the functions of various mushroom and rival bodies, both rational and irrational, which grew up as a result of the 1945 General Strike and the presence of the Tudor Davies Cost of Living Commission.[52]

The Department was encouraged when the TUC began to organize a summer school for trade unionists with lectures on the functions of trade unions, and trusted that this would help dissolve the misconceptions over the range of issues appropriate to union action. The Labour Departments became increasingly involved with the establishment of formal trade unionism. Trade Union Officers were created with responsibility for 'organisation of existing trade unions on sound lines'[53]; and when the unsuccessful general strike in the Gold Coast in 1950 produced a temporary decline in union organization, the Labour Department set about the re-establishment of the Gold Coast TUC[54]. The time for denial of wage labour was over; it was now necessary to regulate the working class. The colonial governments preferred to deal with national trade unions, rather than the multiplicity of transient local organizations, and they wanted to ensure that these unions would restrict themselves to purely industrial affairs.

They were remarkably unsuccessful in their aims. In both colonies, nationalist parties allied themselves with the trade unions, and worker resistance to low wages fuelled the agitation for independence. The 1950 general strike in the Gold Coast was officially in support of a strike by government meteorological workers, but more importantly was part of the campaign of 'positive action' declared by the Convention People's Party against the proposed constitution (Austin, 1964). The Nigerian government faced in the same period extensive labour unrest. Fifty thousand workers were involved in strikes in the fifteen months between January 1949 and March 1950, and 577,000 working days were lost[55]. A dispute at the Enugu colliery ended with twenty-one miners shot by the police, and nationalist parties lost no time in capitalizing on such events[56]. The emergence of wage labour confirmed Orde-Browne's earlier fears that such workers would be fertile ground for 'inflammatory political propaganda', but by the end of the Second World War, it was no longer possible to ignore their existence.

The attempts to regulate those in employment coincided with continued efforts to control unemployment by restricting migration to towns. The restrictions on registration at the Lagos labour exchange remained until 1952. By 1947, the Labour Department reported that the exchange was operating seriously as a regulation of the labour market, with 7,621 vacancies notified to the office, and most of them subsequently filled[57]. Non-residents however were still not permitted to register, and despite their assistance in breaking the 1945 general strike, they were not supposed to take up employment in Lagos. The system came under increasing press criticism in the following years, and a Labour Department Report confirmed the traditional arguments about peasant society:

> Nigeria is essentially an agricultural country and, whatever developments take place, the mass of the population must continue to gain its livelihood from the soul. For this reason the continued migratory movements of peasant farm workers who tend to be attracted to urban, mining and plantation areas in the belief of the existence there of plentiful wage-earning opportunities constitute a serious problem. The retention in the employment exchange areas of orders restricting registration and making registration a condition for employment, has made it possible for a measure of control to be exercised over these movements, and schemes for the establishment of labour control centres in the Eastern and Western Provinces are also being considered. But a real and permanent solution can be found only in developing the agricultural resources of the country and in improving the economic and other living conditions of the villages to such an extent that the peasant farmer will be content to remain at home and realise that his lot is no worse or, may be, better than that of the wandering wage-seeker and detribalised fellow countryman. The fulfilment of the Development Scheme now being operated should play a big part in bringing this about.[58]

The system did not, however, work. Migration to the towns continued to increase, and the non-residents were forced into either destitution or, for the more successful, bribery as a way of getting on to the register. A committee was set up in 1950 to investigate the workings of the registration restrictions, and two years later the system was discontinued as an ineffective solution to the problem[59]. It was not possible to stem migration in this way, and mass unemployment in the West African cities was to become a permanent feature in the post-war years (Gutkind, 1967).

The failure of the colonial dream was all too apparent. Peasant production could not be sustained as a permanent alternative to wage labour. Wage employment inevitably grew, if only in the towns and mining enclaves; peasant farming itself generated wage employment and extensive migration and thus failed to conform to the colonial image; returns from those small farms which did still fit the image were unattractive as compared with the rewards from wage earning. On all sides, the political economy of colonialism was in crisis. Stagnation in the countryside promoted migration to the towns, but employment in the towns could not expand rapidly enough to absorb it. Workers in more permanent employment were, as predicted, increasingly antagonistic to the colonial order, and provided much of the support for nationalist mobilization. And as a final irony, the migrant labour which had appeared an ideal compromise in a world which could be neither capitalist nor exclusively peasant, was becoming a constraint on development. It did offer the advantages of a dispensable work-force, which could be taken on and thrown off at will. But set against that were problems of labour discipline and irregular attendance, problems which were to preoccupy many of the later development theorists.

In 1948, the Gold Coast mines still relied on migrants from the Northern Territories and French West Africa for 50 per cent of their labour force, and of these, less than 5 per cent came to settle permanently in the south. A Labour Department Report from this period continued to support the principle of migrant labour, but with more reservations than previously:

> This constant changing of labour may not be economically sound for the mining companies but its effect on the agricultural communities is more beneficial than the converse, and it is questionable whether a stabilised industrial population engaged in mining would be a permanent benefit to West Africa and its people. The example of other more advanced countries is not particularly encouraging.[60]

A 1951 committee on migratory labour returned to the question of the 'economic soundness' of such labour, and argued that steps must be taken to ensure healthy migrants as a counter-balance to their inbuilt inefficiency[61]. Similar concerns were being voiced in Nigeria, where 'an undesirably high rate of labour turnover' was mentioned in the 1950 Labour Department Report as a problem; the solution would not come until 'the new idea of regular wage-earning employment is more widely acceptable'[62]. Annual turnover in the tin-mining industry was particularly acute, with as many as 175,000 employed in only 50,000 jobs, and here the Report argued for a stabilized work-force as the 'desirable long-term aim'[63]. Migrant workers were regarded as 'unstable', difficult to subject to labour discipline, bad at time-keeping, and too inclined to abandon their work for religious or family celebrations. The novelty of wage employment, in addition, contributed to an 'obscurity of the relationship between work and wages'[64]. Colonial officials in the early 1950s were beginning to express the anxieties which were summed up in the International Labour Organization (ILO) *African Labour Survey* (1958):

> What has emerged is that . . . by tradition and background the African is singularly ill-adapted for assimilation as an effective element in

a wage economy on the modern pattern, that the reason that leads him to seek wage labour heavily influences his attitude to work and his response to incentives and that his reactions differ widely from those of the European worker, whose background and aims are so different. It has also emerged that the African's work performance is at present unsatisfactory in many respects by European standards; that in quantity and quality it is often inferior; that the African sometimes lacks pride in his work; that he is often unstable and restless and prone to absent himself apparently without valid reasons.[65]

As long as West Africa was viewed as an alternative to the 'wage economy on the modern pattern', migrant labour seemed a godsend. But by the time of decolonization, its advantages were more ambiguous.

Perceptions of wage labour thus changed rapidly during the 1940s. The image of the casual labourer was finally discarded, and the colonial states took on the new task of regulating the working class they had inadvertently called into existence. The traditional concepts of peasant society remained mainly in the treatment of the unemployed, who were for many years defined as misplaced peasants who should be despatched home as soon as possible. But with this exception, post-war practice finally admitted the African worker as part of the political economy of colonialism.

By the end of the war, the colonial project had been redefined in the new terms of development and welfare. Annual reports no longer debated the issues of peasants versus plantations, or agonized over the ambiguous consequences of civilization. Instead, the technicalities of development increasingly dominated. The process of transformation dated back to the late 1930s, when a number of prominent colonial administrators attacked the complacencies of previous policy. Notable among these was Lord Hailey, formidable member of the Indian Civil Service and author of *An African Survey* (1938), who questioned the extent of colonial achievments. Capital investment, he pointed out, was abysmally low, and largely concentrated in the mining enclaves. The raw materials exported from Africa were often irrelevant to modern industry, and substitutes could be found for most of them. Industrial production was virtually non-existent, yet no country could survive in the future world economy without some industrial base. On present patterns of development, the colonies had no future. Contemporaries went further, and argued tht 'real development has been positively hindered' by colonial practice (Macmillan, 1938:291).

Based partly on the arguments of Hailey and Macmillan, Governor Bourdillon of Nigeria produced a scathing attack on the doctrine of individual self-sufficiency, which for decades had constrained colonial states to work within a balanced budget and to cut their development work to fit their (often declining) revenues[66]. The Colonial Development Act (1929), he argued, was 'doomed to failure from the outset', since a colony like Nigeria could not afford the risks of indebtedness which any major development scheme entailed. Casual assistance was not enough. Colonialism in Nigeria had generated little capital investment and no real market for British goods. Set against this was an actual decline in soil fertility under British rule. 'Both socially and economically', he argued, 'progress has not gone very far, and is being unduly retarded at the moment'[67].

Officials in London expressed some sympathy with this critique, but trusted that the Colonial Development and Welfare Act (1940) would meet his demands. This provided up to £5 million each year for colonial development schemes, and was amended in 1945 to provide £12 million. The real change, however, came in 1947 with the formation of a Colonial Development Corporation (CDC), which was designed to promote investment in industry and trade, rather than the welfare projects which swallowed up so much of the earlier development fund. The CDC had authority to raise up to £100 million in long term, and £10 million in short-term loans, and then devote these resources to development schemes in the colonies. The formation of the CDC marked the major shift in colonial thinking. From this point onwards, a machinery existed for the promotion of industrial capitalism within the colonies.

Governors in West Africa were encouraged to draw up ten-year plans, though only the Nigerian Government responded fully to the new spirit. The Governor of 'the Gold Coast published in 1944 a *General Plan for Development in the Gold Coast*[68], which promised only an expenditure of £5 million over five years, and seemed if anything to reveal a 'loss of confidence' in the face of anticipated post-war difficulties (Kay, 1972:44). In the following year, both Sierra Leone and the Gold Coast drew up official plans, projecting expenditure of £5 million and £11 million respectively (Greensteet, 1971). In Nigeria, however, an entire development machinery was created, beginning in 1943 with the creation of an Advisory Committee on Economic Development and Social Welfare. Development Committees were set up in each of the twenty-four Provinces, and in 1944 a Development Branch of the Secretariat was instituted[69]. In 1945, a *Ten Year Plan of Development and Welfare of Nigeria* was published[70], which proposed investment of over £55 million (£23 million to come from the Colonial Developent fund, £16–17 million from loans, and the rest from revenue). A panoply of development institutions was brought into existence: a Central Development Board; Local Development Boards; Area Development Committees; Provincial Development Committees. In Nigeria at least, the post-war preoccupation with development made its mark.

This sudden conversion to a new paradigm had little effect on subsequent economic development, and the decade following the Second World War was necessarily taken up with debates on constitutional matters. But in the few years left to them, the colonial states had to discard the once treasured West African Policy. They had sought a middle way between subsistence production and capitalist development; they had promoted commodity production but tried to contain this within the confines of small peasant farming. The process had got out of hand, and by the end of the war it was impossible to ignore the gap between image and reality.

The Watson Commission (1948) was a last-ditch attempt to restate the West African Policy. Set up to enquire into the post-war disturbances on the Gold Coast, it was forced to consider the question of industrial development. 'At every turn,' the commissioners reported, 'we were pressed with the cry of industrialization'[71]. Nevertheless, the report argued, prospects for heavy industry must remain a dream in such an enervating climate, and with the traditional warnings of 'unbridled private enterprise' and its potential for 'future social strife'[72], it reaffirmed the advantage of co-operatives as the best basis for secondary industrial development. The report carried no conviction by this stage, and its proposals for further moderate adjustment were swept aside in the rapidly changing conditions of post-war Africa.

By the early 1950s it was clear that the colonizers intended to abandon their West Coast possessions and extricate themselves from a situation they could neither control nor turn to their advantage. The most fervent nationalist could hardly claim that it was the political strength of the nationalist movements which dislodged the British from West Africa. More fundamentally, the colonial holding operation had reached its limits; the West African Policy was in shreds; and the construction of a stable polity which could contain the process of accumulation was so far beyond the resources of the colonial states that they were happy to relinquish the task to their successors.

NOTES

1 The main exception to this was in the Nigerian Cameroons, formerly a German colony, where plantations already existed when the British took over trusteeship after the First World War. In 1938, these plantations employed 25,100 workers (Orde-Browne, 1941:79).
2 The Nigerian Goldfield, *Nigeria Sessional Paper 17 of 1935*. In 1934, 10,450 of the 13,440 workers were 'tributers'. See also Orde-Browne, 1941:54-5.
3 Annual Report of the Gold Coast Labour Department, 1947-8: 7.
4 Greenhalgh (1975:249) argues that the Consolidated African Selection Trust Ltd., which controlled the Gold Coast diamond mines, wanted stabilization from the 1920s, and began to provide free housing, churches, and non-profit-making stores within the mining compounds. Silver (1981: chapter 5) argues that the gold-mining companies adopted similar action only after the Second World War.
5 Major G. St. J. Orde-Browne, *Labour Conditions in West Africa*, Cmd. 6277, London 1941:58.
6 In 1921, when the Gold Coast mining companies asked permission to recruit

workers from Liberia, and bring the workers across the Sierra Leone-Liberia border, the Acting Governor reaffirmed in no uncertain terms the traditional opposition to private recruiting agencies recruiting within Sierra Leone itself. Acting Governor to Secretary of State, 15 December 1921, CO 267/593.

7   Enquiry into the wounding of 8 Africans at Prestea on 15 September 1930, *Gold Coast Sessional Paper XIX of 1930–31*. In a later incident at the same mine, forty-one miners were killed when a faulty mine lift collapsed. Papers relating to the Accident which occurred on the 5th June 1934 at the Prestea mine, in which forty-one persons were killed, *Gold Coast Sessional Paper 1 of 1935*.

8   Governor's Address to Nigerian Legislative Council, Lagos: Government Printer, 1925:98.

9   ibid., p. 94.

10 As Governor Bourdillon made clear in his scathing attack on colonial development funding in 1939, Governor to Secretary of State, 5 April 1939, CO 583/242/30415.

11 Also published in the same year was a report commissioned by the International Missionary Council, on the implications of wage labour in the copper mines of central Africa (Merle Davis, 1933). This report echoed many of Orde-Browne's concerns.

12 Report of the Committee appointed to enquire into the Question of Unemployment, *Nigeria Sessional Paper 46 of 1935*.

13 ibid., p. 3.

14 Annual Report of the Nigerian Colliery Department, 1938.

15 Annual Report of the Nigerian Colliery Department, 1939:4.

16 In the Gold Coast gold-mines, the new labour surplus allowed the companies to cut daily wage rates by one-third in the early 1930s (Silver, 1981:104).

17 Secretary of State to all Governors, 9 November 1935, CO 323/1429/1766.

18 The Gambia replied that there was no labour to inspect; Nigeria that it was not yet ready for a Labour Department; Sierra Leone again that a Labour Department was unnecessary. Only the Gold Coast Government admitted that there were some problems – mainly that political officers could not guarantee regular access to the mines. CO 323/1429/1766.

19 Secretary of State to all Governors, 24 August 1937, CO 323/1429/1766.

20 Flood of the C.O. objected to the use of 'workers' in the circular, since 'the so-called lowly paid "worker" doesn't work', and suggested the term 'employee' instead. His complaints were overruled.

21 Governor to Secretary of State, October 1937, CO 323/1430/1766/3B.

22 Governor to Secretary of State, November 1937, CO 323/1430/1766/3B.

23 Governor to Secretary of State, 10 June 1938, CO 323/1430/1766/3B.

24 Governor's Address to Gold Coast Legislative Council, Accra: Government Printer, 1938. For details of the resurgence of mineworker militancy in this period, see Silver, 1981:133–4.

25 Capt. J. R. Dickinson, *Report on Labour Conditions in the Gold Coast*, 1938 CO 96/760/31359/2.

26 The Governor discussed the reports from these committees in a meeting at the Colonial Office on 3 October 1938, a meeting which was called partly as a result of the unrest in the West Indies. CO 96/752/31347.

27 J. R. Dickinson, *Report on Labour Conditions in the Gold Coast*, 1938:38.

28 ibid., p. 104.

29 Major G. St. J. Orde-Browne, *Labour Conditions in West Africa*, Cmd. 6277,

London 1941. In 1940, Orde-Browne undertook a visit to all British Colonies, in his new role as Colonial Labour Advisor.

30 ibid., p. 9.
31 ibid., p. 12.
32 Annual Report of the Nigerian Labour Inspectorate, 1940:2.
33 Annual Report of the Nigerian Department of Labour, 1942:3.
34 Annual Report of the Gold Coast Labour Department, 1939–40:2.
35 Annual Report of the Gold Coast Labour Department, 1942–3. Plans were in fact made to assist repatriation of destitute workers.
36 ibid.
37 Annual Report of the Gold Coast Labour Department, 1939–40:2.
38 Annual Report of the Gold Coast Labour Department, 1943–4:4.
39 Annual Report of the Gold Coast Labour Department, 1944–5:1.
40 Annual Report of the Gold Coast Labour Department, 1949–50:7.
41 Annual Report of the Nigerian Department of Labour, 1942:1.
42 Annual Report of the Nigerian Department of Labour, 1943:10.
43 Annual Report of the Nigerian Department of Labour, 1944:5.
44 ibid.
45 Annual Report of the Gold Coast Labour Department, 1939–40:1.
46 Annual Report of the Gold Coast Labour Department, 1939–40; 1940–1; 1946–7.
47 Annual Report of the Nigerian Department of Labour, 1945:22.
48 Annual Report of the Gold Coast Labour Department, 1945–6:3.
49 The Tudor-Davies Commission of 1945; the Harragin Commission of 1946; and the Miller Committee of 1947.
50 Annual Report of the Nigerian Department of Labour, 1945.
51 Annual Report of the Gold Coast Labour Department, 1945–6.
52 Annual Report of the Nigerian Department of Labour, 1946:2.
53 Annual Report of the Nigerian Department of Labour, 1947:7.
54 Annual Report of the Gold Coast Labour Department, 1950–1:4.
55 Annual Report of the Nigerian Department of Labour, 1949–50.
56 A National Emergency Committee was formed, which at a meeting at Enugu in December 1949 declared the slogan: 'Self-government for Nigeria Now' (Ananaba, 1969:110).
57 Annual Report of the Nigerian Department of Labour, 1947.
58 Annual Report of the Nigerian Department of Labour, 1948:26.
59 Annual Report of the Nigerian Department of Labour, 1952–3.
60 Annual Report of the Gold Coast Labour Department, 1948–9:8.
61 Annual Report of the Gold Coast Labour Department, 1952–3. The Committee was set up in 1951, and included trade union representatives, government officials, and representatives from the employers.
62 Annual Report of the Nigerian Department of Labour, 1949–50:8–9.
63 ibid., p. 29.
64 Annual Report of the Nigerian Department of Labuor, 1950–1:26.
65 Quoted in Kilby, 1961:274–5.
66 Governor to Secretary of State, 5 April 1939, CO 583/243/30415.
67 ibid., p. 34.
68 Sir Alan Burns, General Plan for Development in the Gold Coast, *Gold Coast Sessional Paper II of 1944*.
69 Preliminary Statement on Development Planning in Nigeria. *Nigerian Sessional Paper 6 of 1945*.

70 A Ten Year Plan of Development and Welfare in Nigeria, *Nigerian Sessional Paper 24 of 1945.*

71 *Report of the Commission of enquiry into disturbances in the Gold Coast,* Colonial 231, London 1948:54.

72 ibid.

8

The Failures of Colonialism

What this study demonstrates is the essentially makeshift character of West African colonialism. As an agent for capital accumulation, it was severely limited. Constrained on the one side by existing capitals which demanded cheap labour, cheap transport and cheap land, but generally deprecated ambitious projects for change, and threatened on the other side by fears of political disorder, the colonial states could not formulate a satisfactory strategy for capitalist development. The first proposals for land reform suggested one possible direction, based on private property in land and investment by European capital. In the absence of an adequate labour policy, however, this strategy was incoherent. It assumed a dual economy, with the new capitalist sector superimposed on existing and expanding commodity production. As later became clear, the two sectors were potentially in conflict. As long as commodity production offered Africans a way to money earnings, labour would not come forward for the proposed capitalist enterprises. If colonial administrators used their powers to enforce wage labour, African farmers might simply uproot themselves and move off to more promising terrain, and in the process jeopardize the continuity of agricultural production. Without full-scale proletarianization – never a possibility for the colonial states – labour was necessarily the fly in the ointment. The various ad hoc proposals of the early years – redeployment of slaves as free labourers, recruitment from the urban centres of Freetown and Lagos, recruitment of indentured labour from India or Ceylon – all foundered, and capital remained understandably reluctant to invest directly in the West African colonies.

Failing a solution to the labour problem, the colonial states retreated to their West African Policy which affirmed the centrality of commodity production, and downgraded capitalist enterprise to a subsidiary role. The expansion of agriculture was to rely on the African peasantry, secured in its access to land by traditional property relations. Investment in plantation production was dismissed as inappropriate and unnecessary. Capital was welcome to continue in its merchant role, but beyond that, to invest directly only in mining and the processing of palm oil. This second strategy seemed to promise a happy unity of economic growth and political stability. The chiefs were confirmed in their position as political authorities with continuing powers over the regulation of communal land. Hopefully, they would employ this authority in the interests of the colonial states, providing the labour necessary for public works and maintaining political order throughout the colonies. Agricultural exports would increase – as the example of Gold Coast cocoa seemed to indicate – and the mines would mop up those few Africans who nevertheless desired waged work.

Though considerably more successful than the first projections, this policy was again marked by inconsistencies. Even the limited work-force required by private capital meant recourse to political persuasion, and the colonial states came under frequent pressure from the companies for freedom to operate different systems of labour supply. Moreover, the very success of African commodity production began to undermine the powers of the chiefs as farmers migrated to new areas, and bought or leased land. The colonial states threatened to lose out on all sides. The commitment to peasant production and communal tenure deprived them of control over the labour process, and hindered attempts to impose new techniques of production. At the same time, the peasantry challenged the constraints implied in the West African Policy, and demanded the right to buy land and raise mortgages without reference to their supposed traditional authorities. In the case of palm oil, it proved impossible to sustain the limited strategy for change involved in factory processing without plantation production. As became clear in this instance, it was a question of all or nothing. Processing factories could survive only in association with plantation estates, and since with few exceptions, the colonial states refused to condone the latter, the former inevitably failed.

When overall strategy lacked coherence, colonial practice was often one of cautious delay. Far-reaching proposals on land and labour matters were debated in official correspondence, but few of these reached the statute books. The history of the draft report of the West African Lands Committee was typical here. Its arguments were broadly accepted within the Colonial Office and by many local administrators; its assumptions entered into colonial practice, and acted as a deadweight on the ambitions of those like Rowe, who sought a more realistic land policy. But the report was never officially confirmed, and its detailed recommendations were dismissed out of hand. With the exception of Northern Nigeria, and later the Northern Territories of the Gold Coast, its principles were not carried through into administrative action. Even when there was a consensus on policy – and as has been shown, this was tenuous and short-lived – the colonial states lacked the political confidence to impose unpopular legislation.

Within this context, variations between individual administrators seemed to assume great significance. The history of colonialism sometimes reads as a history of eccentric individuals, each with his own preoccupations, rising to influence and falling again, in a process without much pattern: Chamberlain, Maxwell, Morel, Lugard, Temple,

Clifford, Rowe. How can strategic considerations be detected in a world where policies became so identified with particular individuals? I have argued that ideas took on strategic proportions when they were voiced sufficiently frequently to enter into the terms of debate, and that the occasional convergence of opinion makes it possible to define two major periods within British West Africa. But the periodic failures of legislative proposals meant that much of colonial practice appeared as day to day adjustment to changing conditions. The capacity to generate strategy, and subsequently to implement it, were both severely limited.

The subservience to African opinion, both in the retreat from the first strategy and in the incomplete implementation of the second, was remarkable. Time and again, proposals were shelved in the face of real or, more usually, anticipated opposition. The spectre of de-tribalization was invoked as an argument for cautious conservatism, but the strength of local attachment to the land was simultaneously used to deprecate excessive state intervention. This study has not documented the development of African opposition to colonialism, or the emergence of those political forces which gave weight to government fears. It has suggested only briefly the extent of African mobilization over land issues, and has merely hinted at the development of class consciousness among African workers (a study pioneered by Hopkins, 1966, and developed in Sandbrook and Cohen (eds.) 1975; and Gutkind, Cohen and Copans (eds.) 1978). This counts as a major absence, when so much of the argument rests on colonial fears of disorder. But it is partially justified by evidence that it was projected, rather than existing, opposition which so exercised colonial officials. For these officials, the de-tribalized African was more a theory than a reality, and, if anything, colonial reports denied indications that the phenomenon already existed. The fragility of colonial control was such that proposals were abandoned on the faintest suspicion of disaster. The experience of India or East Africa was cited as proof of the dangers attending rapid change; even the experience of Britain was brought to bear on the projected problem of unemployment. It was not only active opposition within West Africa which paralysed colonial action; the mere thought of possible tension was often enough to justify delay.

Fear of course was often turned into its opposite: the administrators of the makeshift settlement would never describe themselves as bowing to African strength but rather as defending African weakness. This ideology of protection was often deeply felt, but still it was ideology. The real task of the colonial states was to promote colonial interests, and if I have stressed how poorly they carried this out, this is not to deny their primary function. When firms engaged in the West African trade expressed their grievances or called for a change, their views were always considered, and even those officials most committed to African development would lend a sympathetic ear. When merchant companies pressed for better terms for buying land in the towns, the colonial service worked hard to find a solution. And despite the impatience with what were seen as the excessive demands of the mining companies, the state continued to accept responsibility for labour supplies to the mines. Relations even with Lever were ambiguous. Certainly he did not get the treatment he wanted, and fared much better in the Belgian Congo; his plans for the palm oil industry in British West Africa foundered on colonial resistance to plantation production. But he still succeeded in extracting considerable concessions in the form of monopoly privileges and financial subsidy, arousing much hostility from competing firms. The anti-capitalism of the West African Policy was not meant as a denial of existing interests, and colonial policy continually sought a compromise which would satisfy at least some of the requests of British firms. However much they might have prided themselves on their care for the 'natives', colonial administrators were not disinterested arbiters of competing interests. They acknowledged their duty towards British capital and they did what they could to satisfy demands.

The point then is not that officials refused to serve capital, nor that they pursued instead altruistic concerns. The point rather is that the strategies they adopted arose from the interplay between private pressures and public disorder. The acute sensitivity to potential unrest, often long before events would confirm the initial suspicions, indicates the weakness at the heart of the colonial service. Suspended as they were over societies in the throes of transition, lacking as they did even the partial legitimacy of elected governments, administrators took the line of least resistance. Where, for example, an alternative to proletarianization offered itself, they all too gratefully accepted. In British West Africa there were no powerful settlers pressing their case. The dominant firms were merchant companies, and even when these were joined at the beginning of the twentieth century by the chocolate and textile manufacturers, the picture hardly changed, for these representatives of industrial capital preferred to 'mimic' their mercantile allies and leave production in African hands. The mining companies were the major exception to this pattern, for they engaged in direct investment. But even here the predominance of alluvial rather than underground workings permitted for many years an alternative to settled wage labour. In other colonies, local interests often served as counters to official nervousness, and administrators had to swallow their fears. In British West Africa, by contrast, the reservations could be turned into matters of pride.

Yet this is not to say that British West Africa was untypical, for if the policies adopted were not universal, the tensions through which they were formulated had parallels elsewhere. In a challenging analysis of Kenya – a country they see as peculiarly representative of colonialism in Africa, for it was situated midway between peasant and settler production – John Lonsdale and Bruce Berman have drawn attention to similar contradictions of the colonial state. Muddling its way through the pressures upon it, the Kenyan state too found labour the 'fly in the ointment'.

In the years before the First World War, it had been able to sustain a partial compatibility between peasant and settler production, with the former accounting for the bulk of the trade. The expansion of African commodity production had secured for the British the support of the chiefs, for while the official salaries paid to them were derisory, they were able within this expansion to accumulate considerable wealth and power. Acting, as in West Africa, as the procurers of unpaid labour and guarantors of social control, these chiefs were not initially threatened by the creation of settler estates. Since the Africans who lost their land to Europeans were typically pastoralists, 'both settler and peasant production were able to expand before 1914, with their major contradiction raging half-hidden within the African labyrinths of lineage and clientage' (Lonsdale and Berman, 1979:502). The continued expansion of settler farming, however, began to impose strains on labour supply: the outflow of waged and 'squatter' labour began to undermine the authority of the chiefs, 'and so to threaten the shaky young framework of control' (ibid, 502). That there was competition between peasant and settler production is widely acknowledged in accounts of colonialism in Kenya; what marks the difference in this analysis is that Lonsdale and Berman do not see it as just an economic affair. It was not just that there was competition for labour and land; perhaps even more to the point, the fragile basis of colonial cohesion threatened to dissolve if the indigenous modes of production changed too rapidly. Again, as in the case of West Africa, an equilibrium had been possible, and from time to time it worked. But sustaining that precise balance between peasant and capitalist production, and maintaining the appropriate relationship between development and control, was not an easy matter. So if the presence of the settlers made for greater adventurism in both land and labour policies, and the state 'never ceased to try to provide the conditions for the reproduction of settler capitalism' (ibid., 504), it is nonetheless a half-truth to see Kenyan policies as simply shaped by settler demands. The strains showed through in a familiar disquiet with individualism, and complaints of the way tribal discipline had declined. The Kenyan state too had to 'cope with the contradictions', and like those in West Africa, it did not resolve the dilemmas it faced.

Colonialism everywhere was a precarious balancing act, though the pieces might be weighted differently and the scales could change. The 'accident' of white settlement, the incidence of mineral wealth, the pattern of pre-colonial land holdings, the extent of pre-colonial trade: all these and others could significantly alter the nature of colonial policies. The constant was that social control was always insecure, for the state was imposed externally and on to societies undergoing considerable change. Policy was formed out of a tension between the demands that were voiced and the fears of the future, and visions of political disruption were a continuing preoccupation. The result, as the example of British West Africa indicates, was hardly consistent and was makeshift in form.

The arguments of underdevelopment theory have tended to conceal this fundamental characteristic of colonialism. Implying as it does a capital which is both rational and omnipotent, and assuming a state that acts on this capital's behalf, underdevelopment theory has been unable to comprehend the very makeshift nature of colonialism. The debate has been set up between a colonialism that was largely benign and barely aware of capitalist concerns, and one which forcefully and consistently imposed capital's demands. Within the parameters of this debate, any suggestion that the colonial states faltered before African resistance, or even retreated in the face of local constraints, reads as proof for the more moderate view. In its determination to resist this conclusion, under-development theory has interpreted all colonial action, and indeed inaction, as inspired by the needs and structures of world capitalism. And what would otherwise be a surprising failure of capital accumulation simply proves once again what the theories try to show. To take the version associated with Samir Amin: accumulation on a world scale demands the blockage of capitalism in peripheral countries.

Capital however is not unitary. There are many capitals, with different and, in the short term, conflicting interests; the capacity of any state to promote a satisfactory strategy for capital depends on a combination of circumstances that was rarely present in colonial conditions. The state is not by definition at the service of capital. Far from assuming in advance that any state will generate and implement those policies appropriate to capital's long term needs, we have to treat the relationship between capital and the state as historically contingent. And if this is the case in advanced capitalist countries, how much more so is this true in the colonized world.

African societies were in a process of transition as the impact of more extended commodity production made its mark on indigenous social relations. The state which supervised this far-reaching process had little real power, a point that should not be lost in condemnation of the extensive use of force which characterized so much of colonialism's history. The reliance on direct coercion was in many ways the state's weakness rather than its strength, just as the freedom from the burdens of elected representation turned out to its disadvantage as often as not. In estimating the political consequences of proposed changes, administrators had to rely on guesswork rather than sound knowledge and they tended towards caution as a result. With little reason to presume substantial financial or military aid from Britain, they had every reason to fear a dissolution of the fragile colonial order. Their task was survival, and the measure of their success was the maintenance of control into the 1950s and 1960s. That they did not in the process ensure conditions for sustained capital accumulation is not surprising, and can be readily explained without recourse to the arguments of underdevelopment theory.

Yet as an analysis of the effects of colonialism, underdevelopment theory seems to retain considerable validity, for the peculiar combination of capitalist penetration without capitalist development is unquestionably the feature of the ex-colonized world. In the case of British West Africa, administrators discouraged (though without much success) the formation of an African capitalist class, only reluctantly conceding the right to accumulate property in land and raise business loans. Equally (though this is a point often obscured by underdevelopment theory's obsession with the presence or absence of indigenous capital) they discouraged the formation of an African working class, accepting wage labour as inevitable in the mines but pursuing alternatives elsewhere. When a reserve army of labour finally emerged in the 1930s, the colonial states responded not with enthusiasm but with vagrancy laws and proposals for repatriation. Uneven regional development, impoverished agriculture coexisting with high unemployment in African towns, a corrupt capitalist class that makes its living through the state: all these can be attributed to some extent to the effects of colonial rule, and all can be incorporated into the theses of underdevelopment theory, for they testify to what we could describe as a 'blockage' of capitalist development. My quarrel, it seems, is not so much with the question of what colonialism did but rather with the analysis of what brought it about. If this is indeed the case, then is the disagreement just academic?

Where I believe it matters is that my own account of colonialism forces us to demarcate more sharply the post-colonial world, to focus on subsequent change. Underdevelopment theory typically discourages periodization, for it notes that the achievement of independence was formal rather than real, and it subsumes all later modifications under the rubric of persistent underdevelopment. Not that its theories have ignored all the empirical evidence – many have noted that a number of third world countries (mostly outside Africa) have moved from being primarily exporters of primary products towards being manufacturing centres for exported goods. But within the evaluative framework of underdevelopment theory, the key question is whether such changes have promoted or distorted further development, and since the answer is usually in the negative, the changes are reduced to variations in form. The object of enquiry is not so much what capitalism is doing, but whether it can promote an idealized and autonomous form of development; any change which fails to satisfy the criteria (and most of them unquestionably fail) is then regarded as of minimal content (Phillips, 1977; Gülalp, 1986). World capitalism, according to underdevelopment theory, will modify its form but never its essence; underdevelopment is the name of the game.

For the mass of the population in underdeveloped countries, this has an important intuitive truth: the experiences of poverty, famine, repression and gross income inequalities hardly conduce to a confident note. But between the false continuities of underdevelopment theory and the naive complacencies of those who say things have now changed, there is a middle path. We have to direct our attention to understanding what is new, and this involves noting what was peculiar in the past. If colonial rule was, as I argue, so much hampered as an agent for change, then the achievement of independence marked for capital not so much a loss of empire as a chance to try again. The post-war proliferation of development initiatives appear not so much as a 'smokescreen' (Baran, 1957:11) for continuing underdevelopment, but as an ambitious (if so far largely unsuccessful) project to carry through the tasks that colonialism had failed to perform. And if Africa has remained largely peripheral in the subsequent flow of overseas investment or the relocation of manufacturing production, this should not blind us to the fact that the world economy has indeed entered a new phase.

References and Bibliography

Primary Sources

The main primary source is the unpublished correspondence between Colonial Office and colonial governors, held in the Public Record Office in London. This is supplemented by Colonial Office Confidential Print, and Sessional Papers of the West African Governments, also held in the Public Record Office.

1. Colonial Office Confidential Print

Correspondence Respecting the Engagement of Labourers in the West African Colonies for Service in the Congo Free State and their Alleged Ill-treatment, African West 432, 1893

Further Correspondence Respecting Engagement of Labourers in the West African Colonies for Service in the Congo Free State and their Alleged Ill-treatment, African West 473, 1896

Further Correspondence Relative to Affairs in Ashanti, African West 504, 1896

Correspondence Relating to Land Grants and Concessions in the Gold Coast Protectorate, African West 513, 1897

Further Correspondence (January 1897–December 1898) Relating to Land Concessions and Railways on the Gold Coast, African West 531, 1899

Memorandum on the British Possessions in West Africa, African West 534, 1897

Gold Coast: Further Correspondence (December 1898–December 1900) Relating to Land Concessions and Regulations, African West 578, 1900

Correspondence Relating to the Administration of Ashanti and the Northern Territories. African West 649, 1902

Further Correspondence Relating to Concessions and Railways, African West 652, 1902

Further Correspondence (November 1901–April 1905) Relating to Railway Construction in Lagos and Nigeria, African West 695, 1905

Correspondence (1902–1905) Relating to Cotton-Growing in West Africa, African West 745, 1906

Further Correspondence (January 1906–June 1907) relating to Cotton Growing in West Africa, African West 835, 1907

Further Correspondence (June 1906–July 1908) relating to Railway Construction in Nigeria, African West 845, 1908
Further Correspondence Relating to Botanical and Forestry Matters, African West 953, 1912
Correspondence (November 1909–September 1911) Relating to Concessions and the Alienation of Native Lands on the Gold Coast. African West 977, 1911
Correspondence (December 9, 1912–March 13, 1915) relating to Palm Oil Grants in West Africa, African West 1023, 1915
West African Lands Committee: Draft Report, African West 1046, 1916
West African Lands Committee: Minutes of Evidence, African West 1047, 1916
West African Lands Committee: Correspondence and Papers laid before the Committee, African West 1048, 1916
West Africa: Palm Oil and Palm Kernels: Report of a Committee appointed by the Secretary of State from the Colonies, September 1923, to consider the best means of securing improved and increased production. Colonial 10, 1925
Correspondence (September 20, 1924–April 16, 1932) Relating to the Palm Oil Industry in West Africa, African West 1113, 1932
Report of the Commission of enquiry into disturbances in the Gold Coast, Colonial 231, 1948

2. Gold Coast Sessional Papers and other Publications

Governor's Addresses to Gold Coast Legislative Council.
Annual Reports of the Lands Department, Labour Department
Papers relating to the Cocoa Industry, *Sessional paper II of 1916–17*
W. S. Tudhope: Enquiry into the Gold Coast Cocoa Industry: Final Report, *Sessional Paper IV of 1918–19*
Report of the Committee Appointed to Consider the Conditions of the Cocoa Industry, *Sessional Paper XVIII of 1918–19*
Correspondence Relating to the Scientific Investigation of the Oil Palm, *Sessional Paper III of 1920–21*
Correspondence Relating to the Development of the Oil Palm Industry, *Sessional Paper IV of 1924–25*
Proposed Reforms in Respect of the Land Legislation of the Gold Coast primarily in order to promote security of title, Accra: Government Printer, 1927
Report of the Committee on Agricultural Policy and Organisation, *Sessional Paper XVII of 1927–28*
Land Legislation of the Gold Coast, Vol. II, Accra: Government Printer, 1930
Despatches Relating to the Oil Palm Industry with particular reference to a subsidy scheme for Oil Palm Mills, *Sessional Paper III of 1930–31*
Memorandum on the Creation of a Fund for Improving the Quality and Marketing of Cacao, *Sessional Paper XVIII of 1930–31*
Enquiry into the wounding of 8 Africans at Prestea on 15 September 1930, *Sessional Paper XIX of 1930–31*
Papers relating to the Accident which occurred on the 5th June 1934 at

the Prestea mine, in which 41 persons were killed, *Sessional Paper I of 1935*
C. Y. Shephard: Report on the Economics of Peasant Agriculture on the
Gold Coast, *Sessional Paper I of 1936*
Report on Mr H. A. Dade's visit to the Gold Coast; Swollen Shoot of
Cacao, *Sessional Paper V of 1937*
Sir Alan Burns: General Plan for Development in the Gold Coast, *Sessional Paper II of 1944*

3. Nigeria Sessional Papers

Governor's Addresses to Nigerian Legislative Council.
Annual Reports of the Agricultural Department, Colliery Department,
Lands Department, Labour Department
Report of the Commission of Inquiry appointed to inquire into certain
incidents at Opobo, Abak and Utu-Etun-Ekpo, *Sessional Paper 12 of 1930*
Report on the Commercial Possibilities and Development of the Forests
of Nigeria, *Sessional Paper 7 of 1934*
The Nigerian Goldfield, *Sessional Paper 17 of 1935*
Report of the Committee appointed to enquire into the Question of
Unemployment, *Sessional Paper 46 of 1935*
Report on the Progress of Co-operation in Nigeria 1935–37, *Sessional Paper 2 of 1938*
Report on the Progress of Co-operation in Nigeria for the year 1937–38,
Sessional Paper 8 of 1939
Preliminary Statement on Development Planning in Nigeria, *Sessional Paper 6 of 1945*
A Ten Year Plan of Development and Welfare in Nigeria, *Sessional Paper 24 of 1945*

4. Sierra Leone Sessional Papers

Report on a Journey through the Colony of Sierra Leone by the Commissioner of Lands and Forests, *Sessional Paper 4 of 1923*
Despatches relating to the Sierra Leone Oil Palm Industry and the Establishment of Oil Palm Plantations, *Sessional Paper 12 of 1925*
Report by C. Y. Shephard on his visit to Sierra Leone in 1934, *Sessional Paper 4 of 1935*
Report by F. A. Stockdale, Agricultural Advisor to the Secretary of State
for the Colonies, on his visit to Sierra Leone in January 1936, *Sessional Paper 2 of 1936*
Correspondence relating to the Colonial Development Fund Assisted
Schemes, *Sessional Paper 6 of 1936*

5. Parliamentary Papers

Compulsory Native Labour, Parliamentary Paper 20, Vol. LXX, London
1908
Northern Nigeria Lands Committee: Minutes of Evidence and Appendices. Cd.
5103, London 1910

Report of the Committee on Emigration from India to the Crown Colonies and Protectorates: Part I: Report, Cd. 5192, London, 1910

Report of the Committee on Emigration from India to the Crown Colonies and Protectorates: Part II: Minutes of Evidence, Cd. 5193, London 1910

Report of the Committee on Emigration from India to the Crown Colonies and Protectorates: Part III: Papers laid before the Committee, Cd. 5194, London 1910

Memorandum on the Subject of Government Action in Encouragement of Cotton Growing in Crown Colonies, Cd. 5215, London 1910

Report on the Legislation Governing the Alienation of Native Lands in the Gold Coast Colony and Ashanti, Cd. 6278, London 1912

Palm Oil Ordinance, Cd. 6512, London 1912

Correspondence respecting the Grant of exclusive rights for the extraction of oil from palm fruits, Cd. 6561, London 1913

Report of Committee on edible and oil-producing nuts and seeds, Cd. 8247, London 1916

Report to the Board of Trade of the Empire Cotton Growing Committee, Cmd. 523, London 1920

Committee on Trade and Taxation for British West Africa1, Cmd. 1600, London 1922

Private Enterprise in British Tropical Africa, Cmd. 2016, London 1924

Report by the Honourable W. G. A. Ormsby-Gore on his visit to West Africa during the year 1926, Cmd. 2744, London 1926

Report of the Commission on the Marketing of West African Cocoa, Cmd. 5845, London 1938

Statement of Policy on Colonial Development and Welfare, Cmd. 6175, London 1940

Labour Conditions in Africa, Cmd. 6277, London 1941

6. Unpublished private documents

Papers of the British Cotton Growing Association
The Cadbury Papers
    (both in the University of Birmingham Library)

Secondary Sources

1. Books and Pamphlets

Abraham, A. (1978) *Mende Government and Politics under Colonial Rule: a historical study of political change in Sierra Leone 1890–1937* Sierra Leone: Sierra Leone University Press

Adeleye, R. A. (1971) *Power and Diplomacy in Northern Nigeria 1804–1906: the Sokoto Caliphate and its Enemies* London: Longman

Amin, S. (1973) *Neo-Colonialism in West Africa* London: Penguin

Amin, S. ed. (1974) *Modern Migrations in Western Africa* London: Oxford University Press

Amin, S. (1975) *Accumulation on a World Scale* New York: Monthly Review

Amin, S. (1976) *Unequal Development* Brighton: Harvester Press

Ananaba, W. (1969) *The Trade Union Movement in Nigeria* Nigeria: Ethiope Publishing Corporation

Auchinleck, C. G. (1927) *Notes on a Visit to the Netherlands, Indies and the Federated Malay States* Accra: Government Printer

Austin, D. (1964) *Politics in Ghana 1946-1960* London: Oxford University Press

Baran, P. A. (1957) *The Political Economy of Growth* New York: Monthly Review

Bauer, P. T. (1954) *West African Trade: A Study of Competition, Oligopoly and Monopoly in a Changing Economy* London: Cambridge University Press

Birtwhistle, C. A. (1908) *Cotton Growing and Nigeria* London: British Cotton Growing Association

Brewer, A. (1980) *Marxist Theories of Imperialism: a critical survey* London: Routledge and Kegan Paul

Buell, R. L. (1965; first edition 1928) *The Native Problem in Africa* London: Frank Cass

Busia, K. A. (1951) *The Position of the Chief in the Modern Political System of Ashanti* London: Oxford University Press

Cardinall, A. W. (1931) *The Gold Coast 1931* Accra: Government Printer

Clapham, C. (1985) *Third World Politics: An Introduction* London: Croom Helm

Cox-George, N. A. (1973) *Studies in Finance and Development: The Gold Coast (Ghana) Experience* London: Dennis Dobson

Crowder, M. (1962) *The Story of Nigeria* London: Faber

Crowder, M. (1968) *West Africa Under Colonial Rule* London: Hutchinson

Crowder, M. and Ikime, O. eds. (1970) *West African Chiefs: their changing status under colonial rule and independence* Nigeria: University of Ife Press

Curtin, P. D. (1969) *The Atlantic Slave Trade* Madison: University of Wisconsin Press

Curtin, P. D. (1975) *Economic Change in Precolonial Africa: Senegambia in the Era of the Slave Trade* Madison: University of Wisconsin Press

Davies, P. N. (1973) *The Trade Makers: Elder Dempster in West Africa, 1852-1972* London: Allen and Unwin

Dickson, K. B. (1969) *A Historical Geography of Ghana* London: Cambridge University Press

Dike, K. O. (1956) *Trade and Politics in the Niger Delta 1830-1885* London: Oxford University Press

Elias, T. O. (1951) *Nigerian Land Law and Custom* London: Routledge and Kegan Paul

Emmanual, A. (1972) *Unequal Exchange: A Study of the Imperialism of Trade* London: New Left Books

Fieldhouse, D. K. (1982) *The Colonial Empires: A Comparative Survey from the Eighteenth Century* London: Macmillan, 1982

Frank, A. G. (1969a) *Capitalism and Underdevelopment in Latin America* New York: Monthly Review Press

Frank, A. G. (1969b) *Latin America: Underdevelopment or Revolution* New York: Monthly Review Press

Frankel, S. H. (1938) *Capital Investment in Africa: Its Course and Effects* London: Oxford University Press

Froebel, F.; Heinrichs, J. and Kreye, O (1980: German edition 1977) *The New International Division of Labour* London: Cambridge University Press

Gann, L. H. and Duignan, P. (1968) *Burden of Empire: An Appraisal of Western Colonialism in Africa South of the Sahara* London: Pall Mall

George, H. (1881) *Progress and Poverty: An enquiry into the cause of industrial depression and of increase of want with increase of wealth. The Remedy.*

Gutkind, P. C. W. (1974) *The Emergent African Urban Proletariat* Montreal: Centre for Developing-Area Studies, McGill University

Gutkind, P. C. W., Cohen, R. and Copans, J. eds. (1978) *African Labour History* London: Sage

Gutkind, P. C. W. and Wallerstein, I. eds. (1976) *The Political Economy of Contemporary Africa* London: Sage

Hailey, Lord (1956) *An African Survey* London: Oxford University Press

Hancock, W. K. (1942) *Survey of British Commonwealth Affairs, Vol. 2: Problems of Economic Policy, 1918–1939* London: Oxford University Press

Hayford, J. E. Casely. (1971: first edition 1913) *The Truth About the West African Land Question* London: Frank Cass

Helleiner, G. K. (1966) *Peasant Agriculture, Government and Economic Growth in Nigeria* Homewood, Illinois: Richard D. Irwin

Hetherington, P. (1978) *British Paternalism and Africa 1920–1940* London: Frank Cass

Heussler, R. (1963) *Yesterday's Rulers* London: Oxford University Press

Hill, P. (1963) *The Migrant Cocoa-Farmers of Southern Ghana: A Study in Rural Capitalism* London: Cambridge University Press

Hill, P. (1970) *Studies in Rural Capitalism in West Africa* London: Cambridge University Press

Holloway, J. and Picciotto, S. eds. (1978) *State and Capital: A Marxist Debate* London: Edward Arnold

Hoogvelt, A. M. M. (1982) *The Third World in Global Development* London: Macmillan

Hopkins, A. G. (1973) *An Economic History of West Africa* London: Longman

Howard, R. (1978) *Colonialism and Underdevelopment in Ghana* London: Croom Helm

Hyden, G. (1980) *Beyond Ujamaa in Tanzania: Underdevelopment and an Uncaptured Peasantry* London: Heinemann

Jones, G. H. (1936) *The Earth Goddess: a study of native farming on the West African Coast* London: Longman

Kay, G. B. (1972) *The Political Economy of Colonialism in Ghana* London: Cambridge University Press

Kay, G. (1975) *Development and Underdevelopment: A Marxist Analysis* London: Macmillan

Kimble, D. (1963) *A Political History of Ghana: the rise of Gold Coast nationalism, 1850–1928* Oxford: Clarendon Press

Kirk-Greene, A. H. (1966) *Principles of Native Administration in Nigeria: Selected Documents 1900–1947* London: Oxford University Press

Kubicek, R. V. (1966) *Administration of Imperialism: Joseph Chamberlain at the Colonial Office* Durham, U.S.A.: Duke University Press

Langdon, S. (1981) *Multinational Corporations in the Political Economy of Kenya* New York: St. Martin's Press

Lever, W. H. (1927) *Viscount Leverhulme* London: Allen and Unwin

Leys, C. (1975) *Underdevelopment in Kenya: The Political Economy of Neo-Colonialism* London: Heinemann & James Currey

Locke, J. (1690) *Two Treatises of Civil Government*

Lugard, F. D. (1922) *The Dual Mandate in British Tropical Africa* London: Blackwood

Macmillan, W. H. (1938) *Africa Emergent* London: Faber

McPhee, A. (1971: first edition 1926) *The Economic Revolution in British West Africa* London: Frank Cass

Meek, C. K. (1968; first edition 1946) *Land Law and Custom in the Colonies* London: Frank Cass

Meillassoux, C. ed. (1971) *The Development of Indigenous Trade and Markets in West Africa* London: Oxford University Press

Merle Davis, J. (1933) *Modern Industry and the African* London: Macmillan

Metcalfe, G. E. (1964) *Great Britain and Ghana: Documents of Ghana History* London: Nelson

Miers, S. and Kopytoff, I. eds. (1977) *Slavery in Africa: Historical and Anthropological Perspectives* Madison: University of Wisconsin Press

Morel, E. D. (1968; first edition 1902) *Affairs of West Africa* London: Frank Cass

Morel, E. D. (1920) *The Black Man's Burden* London: The National Labour Press

Nicolson, I. F. (1969) *The Administration of Nigeria 1900–1960* Oxford: Clarendon Press

Nzula, A. T.; Potekhin, I. I. and Zusmanovitch, A. Z. (1979; first edition 1933) *Forced Labour in Colonial Africa* London: Zed Press

Oliver, R. and Atmore, A. (1967) *Africa since 1800* London: Cambridge University Press

Orde-Browne, Major G. St. J. (1933) *The African Labourer* London: Oxford University Press

Orr, C. W. J. (1965: first edition 1911) *The Making of Northern Nigeria* London: Frank Cass

Ottenberg, S. (1971) *Leadership and Authority in an African Society: The Afikpo Village Group* New York: University of Washington Press

Pedler, F. (1974) *The Lion and the Unicorn in Africa: United Africa Company, 1787–1931* London: Heinemann

Rattray, R. S. (1969: first edition 1923) *Ashanti* London: Oxford University Press

Rey, P. P. (1971) *Colonialisme, Neo-colonialisme et Transition au Capitalisme* Paris: Maspero

Rey, P. P. (1973) *Les Alliances de Classes* Paris: Maspero

Robinson, K. (1965) *The Dilemmas of Trusteeship: Aspects of British Colonial Policy Between the Wars* London: Oxford University Press

Roxborough, I. (1979) *Theories of Underdevelopment* London: Macmillan

Sandbrook, R. and Cohen, R. eds. (1975) *The Development of an African Working Class* London: Longman

Seddon, D. ed. (1978) *Relations of Production: Marxist approaches to economic anthropology* London: Frank Cass

Smith, R. (third edition 1988, first edition 1969) *Kingdoms of the Yoruba* London: James Currey

Strickland, C. F. (1933) *Co-operatives for Africa* London: Oxford University Press

Suret-Canale, J. (1971) *French Colonialism in Tropical Africa 1900–1945* London: C. Hurst and Co.

Swainson, N. (1980) *The Development of Corporate Capitalism in Kenya* London: Heinemann & James Currey

Szereszewski, R. (1965) *Structural Changes in the Economy of Ghana* London: Weidenfeld and Nicolson

Taylor, J. G. (1979) *From Modernization to Modes of Production* London: Macmillan

Temple, C. L. (1968; first edition 1918) *Native Races and Their Rulers* London: Frank Cass

Wallerstein, I. (1980) *The Capitalist World Economy* Cambridge: Cambridge University Press

Ward Price, H. L. (1933) *Land Tenure in the Yoruba Provinces* Lagos: Government Printer

Warren, B. (1980) *Imperialism: Pioneer of Capitalism* London: New Left Books

Watson, J. L. ed. (1980) *Asian and African Systems of Slavery* Oxford: Blackwell

Wedgwood, J. C. (1908) *Henry George for Socialists* London: I.L.P. Publications Department

Wilks, I. (1975) *Asante in the Nineteenth Century* London: Cambridge University Press

Williams, G. ed. (1976) *Nigeria: Economy and Society* London: Rex Collings

Wilson, C. H. (1954) *The History of Unilever, 2 vols* London: Cassell

Woddis, J. (1960) *Africa: the Roots of Revolt* London: Lawrence and Wishart

Woolf, L. (1920) *Empire and Commerce in Africa: A study in economic imperialism* London: Labour Research Department

2. Articles

Abbott, G. C. (1970) 'British Colonial Aid Policy' *Canadian Journal of History V*: 73–89

Alagoa, E. J. (1970) 'Long-distance trade and states in the Niger Delta' *Journal of African History XI* (3):319–29

Beckman, B. (1980) 'Imperialism and Capitalist Transformation: Critique of a Kenyan Debate' *Review of African Political Economy 19*:48–62

Berg, E. J. (1965) 'The development of a labour force in sub-saharan Africa' *Economic Development and Cultural Change XIII* (4):394–412

Bettelheim, C. (1972) Appendices I and III. *In: Unequal Exchange: A Study of the Imperialism of Trade* A. Emmanuel. London: New Left Books

Bradby, B. (1975) 'The Destruction of Natural Economy' *Economy and Society IV* (2):127–61

Brenner, R. (1977) 'The Origins of Capitalist Development: A Critique of Neo-Smithian Marxism' *New Left Review 104*:25–92

Clifford, Sir H. (1919) 'Recent Developments on the Gold Coast' *Journal of the African Society XVIII*: 241–53

Cocquery-Vidrovitch, C. (1976) 'The Political Economy of the African Peasantry and Modes of Production' *In: The Political Economy of Contemporary Africa* ed. by P. C. W. Gutkind and I. Wallerstein. London: Sage

Cooper, F. (1979) 'The problem of slavery in African studies' *Journal of African History 20* (1):103–25

Dupre, G. and Rey, P. P. (1973) 'Reflections on the pertinence of a theory of the history of exchange' *Economy and Society 2* (2):131–63

Fage, J. D. (1969) 'Slavery and the slave trade in the context of West African history' *Journal of African History X* (3):393–404

Foster-Carter, A. (1978) 'The Modes of Production Controversy' *New Left Review 107*:47–77

Goody, J. (1980) 'Slavery in Time and Space' *In: Asian and African Systems of Slavery* ed. by J. L. Watson Oxford: Blackwell

Green, R. H. and Hymer, S. H. (1966) 'Cocoa in the Gold Coast: A Study in the Relationship between African Farmers and Agricultural Experts' *Journal of Economic History XXVI* (3):299–319

Greenstreet, D. K. (1964) 'The Guggisberg Ten-Year Development Plan' *The Economic Bulletin of Ghana VIII* (1):18–26

Greenstreet, D. K. (1971) 'Public Administration: Development and Welfare Planning in the British Territories of West Africa During the Forties' *The Economic Bulletin of Ghana I* (2):3–23

Greenstreet, M. (1972a) 'Labour Conditions in the Gold Coast During the 1930s with Particular Reference to Migrant Labour and the Mines: Part I.' *The Economic Bulletin of Ghana 2* (2):32–46

Greenstreet, M. (1972b) 'Labour Conditions in the Gold Coast During the 1930s with Particular Reference to Migrant Labour and the Mines: Part II' *The Economic Bulletin of Ghana 2* (3):30–40

Gulalp, H. (1986) 'Debate on capitalism and development: the theories of Samir Amin and Bill Warren' *Capital and Class 28*: 139–59

Gutkind, P. (1967) 'The Energy of Despair: Social Organisation of the Unemployed in Two African Cities: Lagos and Nairobi' *Civilisations 17* (3):186–214 and *Civilisations 17* (4):380–405

Henley, J. S. (1980) 'Capitalist Accumulation in Kenya – Straw Men Rule OK?' *Review of African Political Economy 17*:105–8

Hill, P. (1968) 'The myth of the amorphous peasantry: A Northern Nigerian case study' *Nigerian Journal of Economic and Social Studies July*:239–60

Hogendorm, J. (1977) 'The economics of slave use on two "plantations" in the Zaria Emirate of the Sokoto Caliphate' *International Journal of African Historical Studies X* (3):369–83

Hopkins, A. G. (1966) 'The Lagos strike of 1897: an exploration in Nigerian Labour History' *Past and Present December*:133–55

Hughes, A. and Cohen, R. (1978) 'An Emerging Nigerian Working Class: The Lagos Experience 1897–1939 *In: African Labour History*, ed. by P. C. W. Gutkind, R. Cohen and J. Copans. London: Sage

Hymer, S. H. (1970) 'Economic Forms in Pre-Colonial Ghana' *Journal of Economic History XXV* (1):33–50

Igbafe, P. A. (1975) 'Slavery and emancipation in Benin, 1897–1945' *Journal of African History XVI* (3):409–29

Johnson, M. (1974) 'Cotton Imperialism in West Africa' *African Affairs 73* (291):178–87

Kaplinsky, R. (1980) 'Capitalist Accumulation in the Periphery – the Kenyan Case Re-examined' *Review of African Political Economy 17*: 83–105

Kilby, P. (1961) 'African labour productivity reconsidered' *The Economic Journal 71*:273–91

Klein, M. A. (1971) 'Slavery, the slave trade, and legitimate commerce in late nineteenth century Africa' *Etudes d'Histoire Africaine II*:5–28

Klein, M. A. (1978) 'The study of slavery in Africa' *Journal of African History XIX* (4):599–609

Laclau, E. (1971) 'Feudalism and Capitalism in Latin America' *New Left Review 67*:19–38

Leys, C. (1978) 'Capital Accumulation, Class Formation and Dependency – the Significance of the Kenyan Case' *In: Socialist Register*, ed. by R. Miliband and J. Saville. London: Merlin

Leys, C. (1980) 'Kenya – What Does "Dependency" Explain?' *Review of African Political Economy 17*:108–13

Lonsdale, J. and Berman, B. (1979) 'Coping with the contradictions: the development of the colonial state in Kenya, 1895–1914' *Journal of African History 20*:487–505

Lovejoy, P. E. (1973) 'Plantations in the economy of the Sokoto Caliphate' *Journal of African History XIX* (3):341–68

Manning, P. (1969) 'Slaves, Palm Oil, and Political Power on the West African Coast' *African Historical Studies II* (2):279–88

Mason, M. (1969) 'Population density and "slave-raiding" – the case of the middle belt of Nigeria' *Journal of African History X* (4):551–64

Mason, M. (1973) 'Captive and client labour in the economy of the Bida Emirate: 1857–1901' *Journal of African History XIV* (3):453–71

Mason, M. (1978) 'Working on the Railway: Forced Labour in Northern Nigeria, 1907–1912 *In: African Labour History*, ed. by P. C. W. Gutkind, R. Cohen and J. Copans London: Sage

Miliband, R. (1970) 'The Capitalist State – A Reply to Nicos Poulantzas' *New Left Review 59*:53–60

Nworah, K. D. (1971) 'The West African Operations of the British Cotton Growing Association, 1904–1914' *African Historical Studies IV* (2):315–30

Nworah, K. D. (1972) 'The Politics of Lever's West African Concessions, 1907–1913' *International Journal of African Historical Studies V* (2):248–64

Omosini, O. (1972) 'The Gold Coast Land Question, 1894–1900: Some Issues Raised on West Africa's Economic Development' *International Journal of African Historical Studies V* (3):453–69

Phillips, A. (1977) 'The Concept of "Development"' *Review of African Political Economy 8*:7–20

Plange, N-K. (1979) "Opportunity Cost" and Labour Migration: a Misinterpretation of Proletarianisation in Northern Ghana' *Journal of Modern African Studies 17* (4):655–76

Poulantzas, N. (1969) 'The Problem of the Capitalist State' *New Left Review 58*:67–78

Rodney, W. (1966) 'African slavery and other forms of social oppression on the upper Guinea coast in the context of the Atlantic slave-trade' *Journal of African History VII* (3):431–43

Smith, S. (1980) 'The ideas of Samir Amin: theory or tautology?' *Journal of Development Studies 17* (1)

Swainson, N. (1977) 'The Rise of a National Bourgeoisie in Kenya' *Review of African Political Economy 8*:39–55

Thomas, R. G. (1973) 'Forced labour in British West Africa: the case of the Northern Territories of the Gold Coast 1906–27' *Journal of African History XIV* (1):79–103

Warren, B. (1973) 'Imperialism and Capitalist Industrialisation' *New Left Review 81*:3–44

3. *Theses*

Bowden, J. H. (1980) *Development and Control in British Colonial Policy, with reference to Nigeria and the Gold Coast, 1935–1948* PhD thesis: University of Birmingham

Dumett, R. E. (1966) *British Official Attitudes in relation to Economic Development in the Gold Coast 1874–1905* PhD thesis: London University

Greenhalgh, P. (1975) *An Economic History of the Ghanaian Diamond Mining Industry 1919–1973* PhD thesis: University of Birmingham

Nworah, K. K. D. (1966) *Humanitarian pressure groups and British attitudes to West Africa 1895–1915* PhD thesis: London University

Pearce, R. D. (1978) *The Evolution of British Colonial Policy towards Tropical Africa, 1938–48* D Phil thesis: Oxford University

Silver, J. B. (1981) *Class Struggle and Class Consciousness: An Historical Analysis of Mineworkers in Ghana* PhD thesis: University of Sussex

Southall, R. J. (1975) *Cadbury on the Gold Coast: The Dilemma of the 'Model Firm' in a Colonial Economy* PhD thesis: University of Birmingham

Index

The Enigma of Colonialism

98–100, 102, 103–4, 105, 106, 157; vs. peasant production, 73–4, 77, 85–110, 115, 150; *see also* agriculture

poll tax, 43, 56n

Portuguese traders, 17

Poulantzas, N., 10

pre-capitalist modes of production, 2–3, 7, 9–10, 131

pre-colonial West Africa, 2, 3, 9–10, 16–25; chiefs' power, 23–4; conflicting notions of development, 22–3; land tenure, 22–4; legitimate trade, 21–2, 24; slavery, 16, 17–21, 22, 24

Prestea Mine, Gold Coast, 137, 153n

primitive accumulation, 7

Principe, 71

prision labour, 42, 103

private property (in land), 4, 59, 60–1, 62–6, 67–8, 69, 74–6, 77–8, 111, 112, 113, 116, 156; and peasants, 118–32; *see also* capital, private

Protectorate (Public Lands) Ordinance (1896), 62–3

public land (state ownership and control), 60–1, 62–6, 74, 77, 81n, 111, 112–13, 114; royalties, 64, 65

Public Lands Bill (1897), 62, 63–4, 65, 68, 69, 113

Public Lands Holding Ordinance (1897), 62–3

Public Works Department (PWD), labour recruitment by, 40, 41, 42

railway workers, 141

railways, railway construction, 27, 28, 33, 36, 37, 38, 39, 40, 41, 42, 44, 48, 51n, 66, 111, 113, 144

Rattray, R.S., 121–2, 123, 124

Registration of Titles Ordinance (1933), 130, 135n

A Report on Economic Agriculture on the Gold Coast (1889), 27

Report on Labour Conditions in the Gold Coast (1938), 143, 146

Rey, Pierre-Philippe, 9–10, 11, 15n

roads, 28, 36, 40–1, 43; Native, 40; 'political', 40, 41

Rodger, Governor of Gold Coast, 45

Rodney, W., 17, 25n

Rose's Lime Juice factory, Gold Coast, 136

Rowe, Lieutenant-Colonel R.H., 120–1, 122–3, 124, 125–6, 130,

133n, 157, 158; *Land, Planning and Development*, 126

Royal Colonial Institute, 71

Royal Niger Company, 26, 29

rubber industry, 95

runaway slaves, 30, 31, 32, 52n, 53n

Sandbrook, R. and Cohen, R., 158

São Tomé, 34, 71, 87

Sapele palm oil plantation, 98

Second World War, 132, 142, 144, 146, 148

Sekondi, 27, 121, 144

Sekondi-Kumasi railway, 42

sexual division of labour, 93–4, 104

Seysie palm oil mill, 100–2, 104, 109n

Shephard, C.Y., 110n; *Report on the Economics of Peasant Agriculture in Gold Coast*, 90

shifting cultivation, 72

Sierra Leone, 14, 26, 32, 82n; development plans, 151; Labour Department, 142; labour force/recruitment, 34–6, 37, 39, 40, 43, 44, 142, 146, 153n; palm oil industry, 92, 93–4, 96, 97, 103–4; slavery, 18, 21, 24, 28, 29, 30, 32, 33, 36; Trade Union Ordinance (1939), 146

Sierra Leone Company, 51n

Silver, J.B., 26, 44–5, 47, 56–7n, 140, 141, 152n

Slater, Governor A.R., 32, 114, 123, 124

Slave Dealing Proclamation (1901), 30

slave raiding, 29–30, 31, 32

slave villages or 'plantations', 18–20, 29

slavery, slave labour, slave trade, 5; abolition of, 19, 21, 28, 29, 32–3; Atlantic trade, 17, 19, 25n; canoe-slaves, 29, 32; domestic/household, 18, 30; and kinship, 18; legislation for the preservation of, 31–3; and pawning, 18; plantation or 'farm' slaves, 31–2; pre-colonial, 16, 17–21, 22, 23, 24, 28; redemption or ransoming of slaves, 33; runaway slaves, 30, 31, 32, 52n, 53n; transition to free labour from, 33–4; under colonialism, 28–34, 35, 36, 37, 46

Slavery Proclamation (1901), 30, 31

Smith, S., 8